Migration Patterns Across the Mediterranean

SOUTHERN EUROPEAN SOCIETIES

Series Editors: Manuel Fernández-Esquinas, *Institute of Advanced Social Studies (CISC)* and Laura Oso, *Faculty of Sociology, University of A Coruña, Spain*

Editorial Board: Luís Baptista, Daniel Bertaux, Paola Borgna, María Teresa Consoli, Consuelo Corradi, Márius Domínguez, Ana Ferreira, Lígia Ferro, Frédéric Lebaron, Eleni Nina-Pazarzi, Apostolos Papadopoulos, Manuel Pérez Yruela, Roland Pfefferkorn, Alejandro Portes, Benjamín Tejerina and Cristóbal Torres

This innovative series presents cutting edge research on society, institutions and governance in the South of Europe. Featuring state-of-the-art analyses and applied research into a diverse range of social concerns, this series tackles the complexities and trajectories of southern Europe at a crossroads in its history. These authoritative books address major social issues informing academic debate and public policies at both a European and national level.

Titles in the series include:

Children's Lives in Southern Europe
Contemporary Challenges and Risks
Edited by Lourdes Gaitán, Yannis Pechtelidis, Catarina Tomás and Natália Fernandes

Social Problems in Southern Europe
A Comparative Assessment
Edited by Francisco Entrena-Durán, Rosa M. Soriano-Miras and Ricardo Duque-Calvache

Contingent Workers' Voice in Southern Europe
Collective Experiences of Protection and Representation
Edited by Sofía Pérez de Guzmán, Marcela Iglesias-Onofrio and Ivana Pais

Migration Patterns Across the Mediterranean
Exchanges, Conflicts and Coexistence
Edited by Adelina Miranda and Antía Pérez-Caramés

Migration Patterns Across the Mediterranean

Exchanges, Conflicts and Coexistence

Edited by

Adelina Miranda

*Professor of Anthropology, University of Poitiers and
a member of the MIGRINTER Research Centre (Migrations
Internationales, Espaces et Sociétés), France*

Antía Pérez-Caramés

*Senior Lecturer of Sociology, Research Group Societies in
Motion (ESOMI), Department of Sociology and Communication
Sciences, University of A Coruña, Spain*

SOUTHERN EUROPEAN SOCIETIES

Cheltenham, UK • Northampton, MA, USA

Published by
Edward Elgar Publishing Limited
The Lypiatts
15 Lansdown Road
Cheltenham
Glos GL50 2JA
UK

Edward Elgar Publishing, Inc.
William Pratt House
9 Dewey Court
Northampton
Massachusetts 01060
USA

A catalogue record for this book
is available from the British Library

Library of Congress Control Number: 2023933742

This book is available electronically in the **Elgar**online
Sociology, Social Policy and Education subject collection
http://dx.doi.org/10.4337/9781800887350

ISBN 978 1 80088 734 3 (cased)
ISBN 978 1 80088 735 0 (eBook)

Printed and bound in Great Britain by TJ Books Limited, Padstow, Cornwall

Contents

Contributors

Fabio Amato is full Professor of Geography at University of Naples L'Orientale (Italy). He is president of the study centre MoMi (Mobility, International Migration). His research concentrates on urban and social geography. The theme of migration and the transformation of Italian urban space has been a leitmotif in his studies, and recently he conducted research in Niger. In more recent years he has focused on the questions on the evolution of social geography theory and on issues of cultural geography with reference to the issues of popular geopolitics.

Maurizio Ambrosini, PhD, is Professor of Sociology of Migration at the University of Milan, Department of Social and Political Sciences, Italy, and Chargé d'enseignement at the University of Nice-Sophia Antipolis (France). He is the author of more than 300 publications in the field of migration studies. His articles have been published in several leading international journals.

Imad Amer holds a Master of Architecture from the Lebanese University, and he is also trained in urban planning. He is part of the MAGYC (Migration Governance and asYlum Crises) team at the French Institute for the Near East (Beirut, Lebanon), funded by the European Union's Horizon 2020 (grant agreement 822806).

María-Jesús Cabezón-Fernández, PhD in Philosophy and Letters (University of Alicante, Spain, 2018). Associated researcher in the Center for the Study of Migrations and Intercultural Relations (CEMyRI) at the University of Almeria, Spain (since 2019). She has participated in several research projects funded by H2020, Erasmus+, AMIF and FEDER. She has collaborated with the University of Neuchâtel (Switzerland) and ESOMI (University of A Coruña, Spain).

Francesco Saverio Caruso is Lecturer of Economic Sociology at the Magna Graecia University of Catanzaro, Italy. His research interests include labour migrations, migrant labour in agriculture, social movements, and urban conflicts. Among his publications are *La politica dei subalterni* (2015, Derive Approdi) and *Sopravvivere a Rosarno* (2020, Rubbettino).

Francisco Checa y Olmos is Professor of Social Anthropology at the University of Almería (Spain). Her research interests include the social integration of migrants, political discourses on immigration, migrant labour in agriculture, and hijab on migrant Muslim women. He has conducted research in Spain, Belgium, Italy, Portugal, Chile, Mexico and Morocco. He has published 100 articles and chapters in Spain, France, Mexico, Italy and Ecuador.

Alessandra Corrado is Associate Professor of Sociology of Environment and Territory at the University of Calabria (Italy). Her research interests include migrant labour in agriculture, migration and development, migration and rural areas, agri-food systems, and ecological conflicts. She has been a visiting researcher in Spain, France, Italy, Mali, Ecuador, Argentina and Chile. She has published a number of peer-reviewed articles and chapters.

Kamel Doraï is researcher at the French National Centre for Scientific Research (CNRS) based at Migrinter, University of Poitiers (France) and was Director of the Department of Contemporary Studies at the French Institute for the Near East, Ifpo (Lebanon). His work focuses mainly on asylum and refugees in the Middle East. He has published several articles and chapters on Palestinian and Syrian refugee camps in Jordan and Lebanon, and urban refugees in Syria and Lebanon.

Mustapha El Miri is a Senior Lecturer in Sociology at Aix-Marseille University, France, and a researcher at the Institute of Labour Economics and Industrial Sociology (LEST-UMR7317). His research interests are sociology of migration, social policy, economic sociology, sociology of the state, sociology of globalisation and sociology of racism. In the last few years, his main research has focused on migrations between Morocco and Europe, racialisation of sub-Saharan migrants, and global racism. He currently leads an international research group, MIJMA, on 'International migration of young and of self-employed minors. Migration of young African minors to Europe: transnationalization and the process of early empowerment'.

Belén Fernández-Suárez is Senior Lecturer in Sociology at the University of A Coruña, Spain. She is member of the Societies in Motion Research Team (ESOMI). Her main lines of research are migration and local integration policies. She works in the H2020 project 'Welcoming Spaces in Europe: revitalizing shrinking areas by hosting non-EU migrants' and the research and development project 'Integration and return of the "new Spanish emigration": a comparative analysis of the Spanish communities in the UK and France'

Wolfgang Kaiser is Professor Emeritus of Early Modern History at the University Paris 1 (Panthéon Sorbonne) and Director of Studies at the School for Advanced Studies in Social Science (EHESS). Education, fellowships and teaching positions at Berlin, Aix-en-Provence, Florence, Paderborn, Konstanz and Paris. Fields of interest: urban history, history of the Mediterranean, *Ars Mercatoria*, mobility and control, cross-cultural trade.

Alberto Capote Lama has a PhD in Human Geography and is a Lecturer at the Department of Human Geography in the University of Granada, Spain. He did his postdoctorate at the University of Casablanca, Morocco. His main lines of research are emigration and immigration in their social space; Spain as an observatory; population geography; and interculturality in the school environment. He has also carried out research at universities in France, Tunisia and Morocco.

Alice Latouche is a PhD student in Sociology at the University of Poitiers, France, and at the University of Paris 8, France. She graduated in International Cooperation, Humanitarian Aid and Development Policies at the University of Paris 1 Panthéon-Sorbonne, and in Political Sciences at the School for Advanced Studies in Social Science (EHESS). Her work focuses on the impact of border policies on the socio-spatial vulnerabilities of migrant women in the Greek hotspots.

Jorge Malheiros is an Associate Professor of Human Geography at IGOT of the University of Lisbon (ULisboa), Portugal, co-coordinator of Research Group ZOE (Urban and Regional Change and Policies) at the Centre of Geographical Studies, and member of the directive Board of the interdisciplinary Colégio Tropical (ULisboa). He has published mostly in Portuguese and English about international migration, migrants' integration, and urban socio-spatial organisation and segregation. Is a member of the editorial board of the IMISCOE-Springer collection on migration, and Portuguese correspondent of SOPEMI–OECD (2001–2022).

Adelina Miranda is an anthropologist, Professor at the University of Poitiers, France, and a member of the MIGRINTER Research Centre. Her approach to migrations is based on a localised, historicised and relational perspective. She also uses a deconstruction of both an androcentric and an adult-centric vision as the core of her academic research. This academic posture is part of a movement of renewal in the field of migration, which is based on multidisciplinary and intersectional interpretative approaches.

Claudia Moatti, Emeritus Professor of Roman History in Paris 8, France, and Adjunct Professor of Classics and Law at the University of Southern California, USA, has studied the intellectual transformations of the Roman society under the Republic (*The Birth of Critical Thinking*, Cambridge University Press, 2010), and the conception of the political community (*Res publica. Histoire romaine de la chose publique*, Fayard, 2018). Her current project, 'Migration and law in the Ancient Mediterranean', has been developed within a broad international research program she has been heading from 2002 to 2009 with Wolfgang Kaiser, under the title 'Le contrôle de la mobilité des personnes en Méditerranée, de l'Antiquité à l'époque moderne', in collaboration, and since 2016 under the title 'The experience of mobility across time', and which has given birth to four edited books.

Michel Peraldi, anthropologist, Director of Research at the French National Centre for Scientific Research (CNRS). Director from 2005 to 2010 of the Jacques Berque Centre for the development of Social Sciences in Rabat (Morocco), researcher for IRIS at the School for Advanced Studies in Social Science (EHESS), Paris, since September 2010. He has worked for over 20 years on the migratory dynamics in the Mediterranean basin, informal trade circuits between Maghreb and Europe, the history of organised crime economies; articulating socio-economical methodology with urban anthropology of cities affected by these economies and hosting the social networks organising it: Marseille, Istanbul, Naples and Tangiers.

Antía Pérez-Caramés is sociologist and Senior Lecturer at the Department of Sociology and Communication Sciences at the University of A Coruña, Spain, where she is part of the Societies in Motion Research Team (ESOMI). Her lines of research have focused on the study of international migration, demographic ageing, and the analysis of gender relations and care. Within this framework, she has carried out research on recent migratory dynamics in Spain, with particular emphasis on the phenomena of the 'new Spanish emigration' and the return of immigrants. She is currently developing a research project on the impact of crises on migratory movements to and from Spain, and an applied research project with Cape Verdean migrant women in Galicia.

Natalia Ribas-Mateos is a Maria Zambrano Researcher at the Autonomous University of Barcelona, Spain (UAB, TRANSMENA Project) and MESOPOLHIS UMR 7064, Aix-Marseille University, France. She has taught in universities in Spain and elsewhere, and was twice a Marie Curie Fellow (UK–US and France) and also a Ramon y Cajal Fellow in Spain. She has published extensively in Spanish, French and Arabic.

Acknowledgments

The editors would like to thank their respective research groups, MIGRINTER (University of Poitiers, France) and the Societies in Movement Research Team (ESOMI, University of A Coruña), for their support in the publication of this book. Specifically, research funds have been provided from the aid for the consolidation and structuring of competitive research units of the Xunta de Galicia 2019–2021 (ED431C 2018/025). They would also like to acknowledge and give special thanks to Deborah Rolph for her translation and proofreading work.

Introduction to *Migration Patterns Across the Mediterranean*

Adelina Miranda and Antía Pérez-Caramés

In the early 1990s the theoretical construct of the Southern European Migration Model (SEMM) was created in order to better explain the characteristics of the migratory movements of Italy, Spain, Portugal and Greece, under the assumption that their shared recent history and socio-economic traits explained the similarities observed in their migratory patterns.

Three decades have passed since the original formulation of the SEMM, during which time it has continued to be employed empirically and developed by various authors, resulting in contributions to the debate that require critical analysis in order to formulate an updated version of the model. This book revisits the construct, providing an analysis that takes into consideration the challenges posed by the diverse temporal, spatial and political scales of the Mediterranean, as well as examining both the similarities, and the variability and heterogeneity of the migratory phenomenon in the region. Our approach adopts a scale large enough to embrace a multidisciplinary analysis of the interrelationships of migratory processes, and a perspective that is critical of Eurocentrism to critically review the interpretative categories applied to migratory phenomena, focusing particularly on the formulation of the SEMM.

The following two broad perspectives will serve to provide a critical account of the ruptures and continuities found in the SEMM. First, a connection between the observed current migratory trends and the extensive history of migrations in the Mediterranean is retraced. The book details the diverse nature of the history of migration in this area, organised around the concurrence of different migratory trends across a range of time periods and actors involved. From this perspective the colonialisms that have permeated and structured the relationships between the countries situated on both sides of the Mediterranean are considered. Second, the need for a change in the interpretative paradigm which takes the plurality of migratory patterns into consideration is highlighted. The book offers a contextualisation of the current political situation which deconstructs the categories applied to migrants and migration phenomena such as the exiled, the political refugees, the asylum seekers, the authorised and unauthorised migrants, the return migrants and their descendants, the traders, and the expelled migrants.

It is also important to address the changes in conditions for migration, mobility and exile in the Mediterranean stemming from the socio-economic transformations that accompanied the birth of modern nation-states. Indeed, the study of migration in the countries situated on the southern and eastern shores leads us to look at the Mediterranean not only from Europe, but also from Africa and the Middle East. This decentred perspective in relation to Europe shows that Mediterranean migratory processes are based on a plurality of poles, tensions, and confrontations in time and space.

THE SEMM AND THE MEDITERRANEAN

In order to explain the singularities of the group of countries comprising Italy, Spain, Portugal and Greece, which in the early 1990s were beginning to become places of immigration rather than emigration, migration processes in Southern Europe have traditionally been addressed through what has been called the 'paradigm of the Southern European Migration Model', a theoretical construct proposed by various scholars (see King and Rybaczuk, 1993; Arango and Baldwin-Edwards, 1999; Anthias and Lazaridis, 2000; King et al., 2000; King, 2001; Venturini, 2004; Enrico, 2012, among others).

The emergence of the SEMM as a paradigm and a theoretical construct for explaining international migration processes in this region since the end of the Second World War was first used in the analysis of *Gastarbeiter* migration that dates from the 1960s, when migrants from Southern European countries (Italy, Spain, Greece and Portugal) started travelling towards the north (France, the United Kingdom, Germany, Belgium and Switzerland). After the oil crisis of the 1970s this began to change, with those nations most accepting of immigration adopting more restrictive policies, resulting in part of the migration flow originating in countries south of the Mediterranean beginning to head towards Italy, Spain, Greece, and later Portugal. During the 1980s this flow became more substantial due to the modification of labour market conditions in Northern Europe and the arrival of immigrants in these countries as a 'temporary detour', linked to the absence of restrictive immigration regulations. During the 1990s, immigration became a structural element of Southern European countries. Despite their high unemployment rates and a long history of emigration, greater numbers of immigrants settled in Southern European countries, with the Mediterranean Sea being described as a kind of European Rio Grande (King, 1996).

Concepts and theoretical constructs such as the SEMM, Euro-Mediterranean migration, and the Mediterranean Migration Model directly question the 'Mediterranean' nature of migrations, requiring a perspective that does not essentialise these migratory processes. Circulations in the Mediterranean cannot be understood within the limits of each nation-state in the area which, for centuries, has been at the very heart of the processes of globalisation. The question is therefore asked as to whether an increased flow of people, goods and information is creating new forms of exchange. Are new borders being created and local socio-cultural stratifications redefined as a result of such migration?

Despite the variety of migratory flows in the Mediterranean region, immigration has long been perceived to be a consequence of the demands of industrial capitalism following the Second World War, with studies often focusing on the image of the male immigrant working in the industrial sector. However, a closer look at post-Second World War migration reveals that different kinds of immigration have consistently been significant, including during the 1960s and 1970s. The image of the proletarian immigrant does not adequately render the variability and diversity of the migration process, with colonial and post-colonial immigration overlapping in the Mediterranean context. Furthermore, in addition to the simultaneous presence of emigration and immigration, one must also consider the impact of transit migration. Historians have outlined the importance of transit as a component in all Mediterranean countries, with the Mediterranean migratory setting also being marked by political conflicts. The Palestinian, Kurdish and Armenian issues, the conflicts in the Balkans, and the tensions in the Middle East, all weigh heavily on Mediterranean migratory arrangements, as demonstrated most recently by the increase in the number of people arriving on the coasts of Italy, Spain and Greece.

Research that refers to the SEMM has allowed us to understand the dynamics of post-Ford era migration; however, it fails to address the following major issues. The first of these issues is related to the need to consider the Mediterranean setting as being linked to a larger scale, requiring a theoretical approach able to take into account the role of networks and diasporas (Paradiso, 2019; Lorcin, 2017). The phenomena of the interlocking (Bernes et al., 2017) and superposing of national, cultural and social borders produces particular patterns of alterity and identity (Mellino, 2005) that must also be taken into account.

The second of the issues that the model fails to consider is the relevance of economic and demographic conditions in Southern European countries (Ambrosetti et al., 2016; Ricucci, 2017). Migratory processes involving Southern European countries cannot be thoroughly understood without considering gender and generational dynamics. A third issue is the highly politicised nature of migration, and the fact that its management revolves around the production of irregularity (Ambrosini, 2018).

STRUCTURE OF THE BOOK

The Foreword, written by Natalia Ribas-Mateos and Jorge Malheiros, sets out the main arguments against a Eurocentric approach to migration in the Mediterranean. In their Conclusions, the final chapter in this book, the editors Adelina Miranda and Antía Pérez-Caramés gather and synthetise the critical points raised in each of the preceding chapters in order to propose an updated, denationalised and decolonised version of the SEMM.

The chapters of the book provide a comprehensive analysis of recent population movements in Southern European countries within the larger context and scope of the Mediterranean region as a whole, outlining changes in migration routes, the characteristics and profile of those who migrate, and the roles of the diverse countries involved (countries of origin, transit, first and subsequent destinations), taking into account how these affect migratory strategies and projects, the reasons behind and purposes of migration, policies implemented, and recent political, social and economic changes in Mediterranean societies.

First, in 'An extended foreword to a critique on Mediterranean Europe as a place of migration', Natalia Ribas-Mateos and Jorge Malheiros select two fundamental topics as the basis for a meaningful analysis of Mediterranean Europe: place and contemporary mobilities. The authors recall the importance of the dynamics linking the rural and urban worlds. The connections between rural and urban should be seen in the perspective of a continuum rather than that of two opposite types of places. Therefore, while cities have historically formed the core of the Mediterranean, the place of rural societies should not be forgotten. This dynamic vision alters an essentialist view of borders. It also serves to demonstrate the contemporary relevance of mobility, of the mobility of people both inside and outside the Mediterranean region, in connecting with borders.

Since colonial times, migrations have contributed to creating a caravanserai (Ribas-Mateos, 2017) with cosmopolitanism traits, and a model of Mediterranean Europe must therefore hold both the longitudinal and latitudinal links (and their construction) in greater consideration than the breaks. It should explore the dynamics and the diversity of the region, and combine processes and perspectives departing from various places: some in North Africa, and others in Europe.

This book explores these questions in two broad parts. Part I, entitled 'Mobilities and Colonialisms' proposes a perspective that traverses past and present, thus questioning the continuities and ruptures that exist in different historic moments.

Colonisation and decolonisation have influenced and continue to influence the migratory events of the Mediterranean shores, where forms of colonialism occupy a specific place within the construction of continuities and disconti-nuities. Migratory phenomena in the Mediterranean region originated in part from the political financial and cultural continuities which still shape relations between colonising and colonised countries today (Liauzu, 2009), and as such transcend differences, continuing to fuel the mechanisms for building alterity. Part I provides the reader with an understanding of the porosity that exists between the scientific and socio-political categories of migration, as well as the process of the stratification of individual and collective memory over time on both sides of the Mediterranean. Current migration dynamics are marked by the construction of a European geopolitical context that has created a gap between the countries around the Mediterranean, which is unprecedented in certain respects. The representation of migratory phenomenon participates in the construction of a supranational identity through a supposed opposition between a 'Christian West' and an 'Islamic East', now fixed around the figure of the 'Islamic' migrant. The colonial imaginary has accompanied and continues to accompany this political construction at the basis of the collec-tive perception and symbolic elaboration of current mobilities. Therefore, Mediterranean migrations are 'postcolonial' since they refer to the political, economic and cultural continuities and ruptures that still shape the relation-ships between countries that were colonisers and countries that were colonised.

The analysis proposed by Wolfgang Kaiser and Claudia Moatti in Chapter 1, entitled 'Human mobility in the pre-modern Mediterranean', provides the basis for a revision of migration paradigms from a historical perspective. This contribution allows us to return to the roots of the development of migration paradigms. By underlining the multitude of causes of mobility, the authors demonstrate the futility of systematically positioning it in opposition to sed-entariness, thus underlining the need to review the freedom/force duality, and that of keeping the tensions between migratory flows and the existence of structural xenophobia in societies ever present.

The analysis of the pathways of people in mobility and of reception policies highlights status gradations, which make any unitary definition of the term 'foreigner' futile. Freedom of movement must be considered to be a negotiated privilege that falls within the sphere of positive law. The authors recall that freedom of movement was most often experienced not as a characteristic of free people, even less as a subjective right, but as a positive right, regulated by a set of institutions. The recognition of this was in no way based on a natural principle, nor on simple norms, but on negotiation. It is the analysis of this mode of interaction and its transformations over the centuries that allows us to understand the evolution of societal practices and the phenomenon of migra-tion, their historicity, that is to say their discontinuity.

In Chapter 2, 'Migration and otherness in the Mediterranean region: colonial past and postcolonial continuities through the envision of the "Other Moor"',

María-Jesús Cabezón-Fernández demonstrates that the current processes of otherness are based on the historical sedimentation of representations of the other. In order to understand the way in which migrant otherness is constructed, the author outlines the continuities that refer to the articulation of the collective imagination of the 'Other Moor', and to a lesser extent the 'Other Spanish'. Each period of Hispanic-Muslim history corresponds to an evolution of stereotypes associated with the Moors. This chapter confirms that identity (Hispanicity in this case) around the Mediterranean has always been constructed from historical exchanges. As the analysis of the Algerian case study demonstrates, it is important to take into account the Mediterranean migratory system.

Chapter 3 by Mustapha El Miri, 'The weight of colonial cultural legacy in scholarly and political discourses on migration: for a denationalisation of the migration issue', offers a critical and original reading of the complex relation-ship between colonialism and immigration in France. This link suggests that the manner in which colonial memory is treated conditions the place given to migrants and, in turn, conditions the institutional, legal, intellectual and social accommodations that this entails for 'native' French society. The author recalls the violence of the debates and controversies around the question of colonial memory, and that in France, migration only became an object of study at a late stage. The chapter examines the links between colonial memory and migra-tion and the history of the French colonial period, which is also the result of a long-standing and porous relationship between science and politics on these issues, and analyses its effects on the place of 'immigrants'.

Part II, titled 'Beyond National Migratory Dynamics', provides an analysis of the plural forms of migration. From the 1970s onwards, as previously mentioned, the entry of new emigration, immigration, settlement and transit countries on the migration scene was witnessed. This variability of population movements was first apparent in the countries of Southern Europe.

As Fabio Amato demonstrates, in Chapter 4, 'Migration in Italy: a mul-tiscalar analysis', case studies of the countries of Southern Europe allow us to focus on the arrangement of different migratory scales. Italy stands out as a country of immigration, but continues to be a country of emigration, and has also become a transit stop on the way to other European countries. A long history of emigration is an element that conditions the interpretation of a place of immigration especially since, following the 2008 crisis, a resumption of departures abroad and/or to the north of the country have been noted. As the author points out, in order to study Italian migration, one must take into account the processes of territorialisation in response to increased pressure from global migration. The place that migrants occupy in the spheres of work, housing and education confirms that a multiscalar approach (from local to regional, national to international) is required to restore the complex articulation between these different phenomena, generating localised migratory morphologies that change over time.

Italian migration needs to be placed in a wider context of reflection. Indeed, if migration phenomena are considered from the different spatial and temporal scales of the Mediterranean, it appears that the emergence of new migration dynamics requires a rethinking of the interpretative models that present Mediterranean migrations as a unilinear movement linking the 'South' to the 'North'.

In Chapter 5, 'The Maghreb of transit, new laboratory of postcolonial migrations', Michel Peraldi demonstrates the importance of this phenomenon at the level of the Maghreb countries. According to the author, we are in the presence of a complex mutation in migration in the Maghreb, rather than a simple change, with migration being primarily a matter of autonomy, either individual or diasporic. In contrast to the era of Fordist migration, we are currently seeing a clear fragmentation of migrant categories and reasons for migration, regardless of destination. The author concludes that if we accept that a transformation of the mechanics and dynamics of migration from the colonial to the transnational is taking place here, it is not only migratory modalities that are changing and new figures that are appearing, but a more fundamental change in the relationship to the world is occurring, marked by the privatisation and feminisation of flows, and increased autonomy in journeys. This process determines transformations at different migratory scales as well as on the European level. Looking at the contemporary migratory map of the Mediterranean, the boundaries between categories of migrants appear blurred and reversible, and the distinctions between 'new' and 'old' migration, irregular and political migration, pendular, stabilisation and return migration, are constantly being questioned. In countries of recent immigration such as Italy, Portugal and Spain, the phenomenon of emigration abroad continues to be fuelled by young graduates and skilled workers, bringing intra-European migration to the forefront.

In Chapter 6, 'Gender and emigration: labour market integration and work–life balance strategies of young Spanish female migrants to France and Germany', Belén Fernández-Suárez and Alberto Capote Lama study the recovery of migration flows from Spain to France and Germany after the 2008 economic crisis. The authors highlight the socio-structural elements in the societies of Southern Europe that might have encouraged these intra-European migrations, and also how educational profile and gender are explanatory elements in the establishment of these new migrations. They note a predominance of young people with a university degree among migrants, and the increase in female migration. The authors underline in an original manner how these migrations should be understood in the light of other social relations such as gender and class. They analyse the integration processes of these young migrants and how, when they become mothers, they try to balance what it means to be a mother in the country of origin as well as in the host country.

Mediterranean Migration Model researchers have stressed that foreign migrants have arrived in response to a demand generated by the informal economy, and in particular the unskilled sectors. These post-Fordist immigrant flows are part of the tertiarisation process of the economy, and respond to the needs of the primary and service sectors. Thus, the comparative analysis between Italy and Spain carried out by Francisco Checa y Olmos, Francesco Saverio Caruso and Alessandra Corrado in Chapter 7, 'A Southern European model of migrant agricultural labour: two case studies in Andalusia (Spain) and Calabria (Italy)', demonstrates the existing correlations between the Southern model for agricultural labour exploitation, and the Mediterranean model of migration. The development of agricultural industrialisation and the transformation of the rural world were supported by migrant labour. The chapter focuses on these processes of agrarian change in two areas in Southern Europe: the province of Almería in Andalusia (Spain) and the Sybaris plain in the province of Cosenza, in Calabria (Italy). The case studies demonstrate that in the countries of Southern Europe, which include Italy, Spain, Greece and Portugal, the processes of informalisation and segmentation of the labour market increase demand for local labour supply especially in low-skilled, poorly paid, dirty, demanding, highly precarious and even dangerous sectors, such as agriculture, construction, care, service, home delivery, cleaning, and irregular self-employment. This situation produces the social conditions for exploitation and segregation that in turn produce a climate of social tension that cyclically results in racist policies, and uncontrolled and xenophobic events. However, the rural–urban dimension of the two contexts of reference seems, in fact, to favour the passage from an informal and circular migration to a more stable family migration.

Maurizio Ambrosini's analysis in Chapter 8, 'The care shortage and social acceptance: why the welfare needs of native families subvert immigration policies', confirms that the 'familist' welfare state in Southern European countries does not respond adequately to changes in society, and that the work of immigrant women is used to compensate for the dysfunctions and shortcomings of an inadequate social policy. This has often occurred outside the legal framework, through the informal hiring of immigrants without a legal status. Tolerance is the general rule in regard to immigrant women working in the service of Italian families and taking care of their frail seniors. An analysis of Italy's 'triangle of care' involving frail old people, relatives as 'care managers', and immigrant 'care workers', confirmed that the domestic care worker can be seen as a way to save the social order, resulting in Italian families playing a crucial role in migrant irregularity and campaigns for the regularisation of unauthorised immigrants.

The management of the agricultural and care sectors in Southern European countries raises the issue of the articulation between globalised capitalism and the implementation of specific migration policies. The contributions of Kamel Doraï and Imad Amer, as well as that of Alice Latouche, allow us to look at this articulation from two angles: that of conflicts and that of the category of vulnerability.

In Chapter 9, 'Lebanese migration policy since 2011 and its role in the Syrian refugee movement', Kamel Doraï and Imad Amer recall how the Mediterranean migratory context is marked by political conflicts. The Kurdish and Armenian issues, the conflicts in the former Yugoslavia, and the tensions in Lebanon, have a strong impact on Mediterranean migration patterns. The historical scale of the phenomenon of forced migration in the Middle East is a constituent element of analysis of changes in the regional socio-political context. In the Middle East, where conflicts have generated large refugee groups, the existence of structured and ancient diasporas is key to the understanding of current refugee mobility. An analysis of the case of Syrian reveals two essential conditions. The first is that the management of displaced persons and refugees includes regulation concerning Syria migrants and their access to residency and the labour market. The policies implemented by the Lebanese government have placed Syrians on the margins of society, despite the fundamental role they have played in the reconstruction of the country, and in the agricultural region of the Bekaa. The second of the features marking migration in the region is the blurring of categories, and the coexistence within the same population of people with different legal statuses.

Alice Latouche takes a gendered perspective in Chapter 10, 'Repoliticising gendered vulnerability: the blind spots of vulnerability-focused humanitarian programmes in Greece', to highlight the dual consequence of the implementation of specific policies aimed at women asylum seekers. The first of these consequences is that this 'vulnerability' relies heavily on stereotypes of gender that exclude men, and force women to 'perform' their vulnerability according to the implicit expectations of the evaluators. The second is that the experiences of 'vulnerable' migrant women demonstrate how the accommodation policies actually reinforce their precariousness, by forcing women to accept undeclared jobs within the same gendered and racialised sectors of employment. The only options available for them are often undeclared, in the gendered sectors of care, the sex trade or the tourist industry, a dynamic previously analysed by the Southern European Migration Model in the 1990s. The author shows that beyond a humanitarian category of 'vulnerable women', the migration policies create long-term precariousness. This Southern region will also be analysed from a family, cross-generational and gender dynamics perspective, permitting us to set aside the unstable borders that are characteristic of the geopolitical definition of this region, as well as to deconstruct an essentialist vision based on a reductionist interpretation of the phenomenon of migration.

REFERENCES

Ambrosetti, E., Strangio, D. and Wihtol de Wenden, C. (2016). *Migration in the Mediterranean: Socio-economic Perspectives*. London and New York: Routledge

Ambrosini, M. (2018). *Irregular Immigration in Southern Europe: Actors, Dynamics and Governance*. London and New York: Springer.

Anthias, F. and Lazaridis, G. (2000). *Gender and Migration in Southern Europe: Women on the Move*. New York: Routledge.

Arango, J. and Baldwin-Edwards, M. (1999). *Immigrants and the Informal Economy in Southern Europe*. London: Routledge.

Bernes, L.-A., Bousetta, H. and Zickgraf, C. (2017). *Migration in the Western Mediterranean: Space, Mobility and Borders*. London: Routledge.

Enrico, P. (2012). Il modello migratorio mediterraneo dell'immigrazione. In Miranda, A. and Signorelli, A. (eds), *Pensare e ripensare le migrazioni*. Milano: Sellerio, pp. 48–60.

King, R. (1996). Migration and development in the Mediterranean region. *Geography*, 81 (1): 3–14.

King, R. (ed.) (2001). *The Mediterranean Passage: Migration and New Cultural Encounters in Southern Europe*. Liverpool: Liverpool University Press.

King, R., Lazaridis, G. and Tsardanidis, C. (eds) (2000). *Eldorado or Fortress? Migration in Southern Europe*. London: Palgrave Macmillan.

King, R. and Rybaczuk, K. (1993). Southern Europe and the international division of labour: From mass emigration to mass immigration. In King, R. (ed.), *The New Geography of European Migrations*. London: Belhaven, pp. 175–206.

Liauzu, C. (2009). *Colonisations, migrations, racismes. Histoires d'un passeur de civilisation*. Paris: Syllepse.

Lorcin, P. (ed.) (2017). *The Southern Shores of the Mediterranean and Its Networks: Knowledge, Trade, Culture and People*. London: Routledge.

Mellino, M. (2005). *La critica postcoloniale Decolonizzazione, capitalismo e cosmopolitismo nei postcolonial studies*. Milano: Meltemi.

Paradiso, M. (2019). *Mediterranean Mobilities and Europe's Changing Relationships*. New York: Springer.

Ribas-Mateos, N. (2017). *The Mediterranean in the Age of Globalization: Migration, Welfare, and Borders*. New York: Routledge.

Ricucci, R. (2017). *The New Southern European Diaspora: Youth, Unemployment, and Migration*. London: Lexington Books.

Venturini, A. (2004). *Postwar Migration in Southern Europe 1950–2000: An Economic Analysis*. Cambridge: Cambridge University Press.

Foreword: a critique of Mediterranean Europe as a "migration place"

Natalia Ribas-Mateos and Jorge Malheiros

Critical thinking is a broad classification for a diverse array of reasoning. In this Foreword we will underline different topics by breaking down arguments and claims, to see how these apply to a supposed model of Mediterranean Europe, in order to advance a critical understanding of the Introduction and the following chapters, identify significant commonalities, enhance connections and facilitate dialogue with the authors and their ideas. This Foreword will outline the broad contours of such critical thinking through the discussion of two topics that we have selected as the basis for a meaningful analysis in Mediterranean Europe: (1) the topic of place (which includes Mediterranean borders, an exploration of cities and the changing rural world); and (2) the topic of contemporary mobilities.

FRAMING THE TOPIC OF PLACE

The 7 Climates are traversed by 7 Seas of which we speak following, if it pleases God. The 7 Seas are called also Gulfs. Six are contiguous; one only is separated without communication with the others.
They are; 1) the China and Indian Seas at 13 degrees latitude and to their south is the Equator; 2) the Gulf of Persia, 440 parasanges in length; 3) the Gulf of the Red Sea, 1400 miles long; 4) the Mediterranean Sea, 18 miles wide at the Detroit; 5) the Gulf of Venice, 1100 miles long; 6) the Pontus Euxine, 1300 miles from the Detroit; 7) the Caspian Sea, 1000 miles x 650 miles.

(Preface to Al-Idrisi World Map, 12th Century)

The idea of place corresponds to a notion inspired by cultural geography. A place is not a simple location in abstract space (Holzer, 2003), but a spatial entity with a meaning and a value that is lived, conceived and appropriated by social communities (Tuan, 1977). Places have a memory and an identity, and result from the consequential transformation and appropriation of a physical space by a community. In this sense, places have not only a socio-cultural value but also a political one.

Using this notion of place as a point of departure, the first problem we face is identifying a reference point for the discussion. The debate can be launched by asking: Is it really meaningful to consider the Mediterranean or even Southern Europe as places where 'common' geopolitical features and socio-cultural processes are strong enough to justify unified approaches? Obviously, there is no single answer to this question. From a historical perspective, the geopolitical unity of the Mediterranean region was much stronger in the past, when this sea was conceived as the Mare Nostrum, the space around which the Roman Empire was structured and the ancient Greek *thalassocracies* established their navigation routes.

Moreover, to the set of common natural features that justify the classification of the Mediterranean as one of the world's biomes and climate zones[1] corresponded the construction of a connected socio-political space, the division of which only became clear after the 15th and 16th centuries (Lois-Gonzaléz, 2021). After the 7th century, the vital dynamics of the region were marked by the diverging geosocial paths of Christianity, Catholicism in particular, organised in medieval times around the central power of Rome; and Islam, with a less centralised structure but oriented towards the East having places such as Mecca and Baghdad as references. In fact, if religion played an important role in the division between the North and South (and East) Mediterranean, the deepening of the division that transformed the Mediterranean Sea from being a place of connection to one of cultural, socio-economic and political hard borders lay in the geopolitical changes that marked the trajectory of the European continent after the 15th century.

The beginning of Portuguese and Spanish expansion in the 15th century opened the route for European colonialism and expanded the worldview of Europeans. Geographically, this meant that the Mediterranean progressively lost centrality to the Atlantic, the navigation route to Asia and the connection to the Americas. The arrival of the Spanish vessels led by Columbus to the Americas in 1492, and the fall of the Kingdom of Granada in the same year (the last area ruled by Islamic leaders in the Western part of the North Mediterranean), had a determining symbolic impact, on both the deepening of the Mediterranean divide (between the expansionist Christian North and the Islamic-dominated South and East) and its geopolitical peripheralisation. In addition, the political transformation of Europe in the second half of the 17th century with the Peace of Westphalia, which opened the path to the principles and characteristics of the modern nation-state geopolitical format that European domination later 'exported' to the entire world, turned European nations inward-looking and pushed them further from the African and Middle Eastern nations that shared the Mediterranean space.

The Reformation and Counter-Reformation processes of the first half of the 16th century contributed to the socio-cultural and political break between Northern and Southern Europe (especially in the west of the continent), a division that has progressively deepened as a result of capitalist development supported by industrialisation and modern imperialism in the 19th century. The political and economic centre of Europe was relocated to the northwest of the continent after the 17th century, when the hegemonic empires of the Netherlands, followed by the United Kingdom and fiercely challenged by France (Modelski, 1978), became the dominant countries, thus relegating the Iberian powers to a secondary position, making the internal divisions of Europe clearer (Lois-González, 2021), and creating a new system of domination. The domination of the world system (Wallerstein, 1984) by the Central and Northern European powers in the 19th century that resulted in vast colonial empires extending over the Caribbean, the Pacific islands and the Asian (including the Middle East) and African continents is crucial in understanding the contemporary construction of the geopolitical zoning of the world, and had a fundamental impact on European societies.

As a result, going back to our region of interest, the impact was also fundamental to such societies. Not only are the macro-regional spaces of Europe and the Mediterranean viewed as separated places, but they are also structured by a hierarchy that still influences both commonsense and geoeconomic approaches. The division still prevails between the enhanced stereotypical images of the developed and disciplined countries of Northern Europe, and the undisciplined, unindustrious people of the less developed Southern European nation-states. These stereotypes have their roots in the transfer of the geopolitical and economic centre of the world to Northwest Europe after the 16th century, and were strengthened by the disciplinary culture of the industrial capitalism of the 19th century. Southern European nation-states that declined after the 16th century would become dominated formally, for example as was the case with Greece in relation to the Ottoman Empire, or informally, as with Portugal in relation to the United Kingdom (Lenine, 1916/1984). In the colonial partition a direct colonisation came into force; the colonised South and East Mediterranean mostly fell under the colonial rule of the British and French, with fragments ruled by Spain, and was exploited for the benefit of their metropolitan industrialisation processes.

The post-World War geopolitical order was marked by South and East Mediterranean countries achieving independence, and by the emergence of dictatorships in several Southern European countries that only ended in the 1970s, and so did not affect the historical process of division. Having become democratic states, Greece, Spain and Portugal joined the European Union (EU) in the 1980s. As the financial crisis of 2008 has recently revealed, despite being economically, politically and even symbolically 'more European', Northern Mediterranean countries remained distinctly peripheral places, with politicians and even citizens of Northern and Central Europe continuing to hold a prejudiced view of the region which is reflected in their discourse.

Therefore, an approach that might be derived from the analysis of the Mediterranean Sea as a barrier, with Southern (and Eastern) countries on one side and Northern countries on the other, constituting two distinct macro-places, would be an oversimplification. Relations between peripheral countries on the shores of the Mediterranean tend to be weaker than those between central countries and those on the peripheries (Fernandes et al., 2021). The latter relations were enhanced by specific connections (migration, trade, culture, and so on) between the shores of the Mediterranean supported by specific colonial and postcolonial ties, examples being the connection between Northern Morocco and Andalucía, the 'proximity' between Marseille (the colonial harbour *par excellence*) and the coast of Algeria, and the flows between Sicily (and other Italian islands) and the Libyan shore. Despite these existing connections, the role of the longitudinal barrier to South–North migration, attributed in political and securitarian terms to the Mediterranean Sea, cannot be overlooked. However, and in spite of the deadly consequences of dramatic crossings that receive daily media exposure, migration flows continue, and the Mediterranean remains porous. Thus, we once more face the inescapable image of a dangerous but still permeable sea. Additionally, as mentioned by Fernandes et al. (2021), there are other processes that simultaneously affect various Mediterranean countries, sometimes generating interpretations whose impact spreads beyond specific borders. The concept of the 'Third Italy', developed in the 1980s and 1990s by Italian authors such as Bagnasco (1977) and Garofoli (1992), aimed to capture the dynamics of 'semi-peripheral' regions characterised by diffuse industrialisation and made waves in Southern Europe[2] and even in North Africa (Fernandes et al., 2021). The 'Arab Spring', that spread from Tunisia to several other North African countries in 2011, has also contributed to bringing together the two shores of the Mediterranean with regard to contemporary mobilities (Beaugrand and Geisser, 2016).

The Mediterranean has long been conceived of as the heart of civilisation, the *plaque tournant* of migration, the meeting place between East and West. Despite the significant socio-cultural and geopolitical divide that marks the European and the African and Asian shores of the Mediterranean, according to Brenner's (2000) classification system the Mediterranean can be characterised as a contemporary region, on a macro-regional scale, where multiple scales converge and interact. Such a space can be viewed from the perspective of many time periods, creating continuous forms of movements (Ribas-Mateos and Sempere Souvannavong, 2006), and multidimensional networks between different Mediterranean spaces. This concept is sometimes referred to as 'caravansar', in reference to its circular nature. The ability to take advantage of the space in terms of mobility varies by social class, gender, age and ethnicity, and by regional area. A critical perspective of the geography and geopolitics of the Mediterranean should nonetheless not be limited by the relevance of the

'Mediterranean Rio Grande' and the loss of unity, in a Braudelian sense, but should instead focus more on its connections (and their construction), both longitudinal and latitudinal, than on its barriers. It should explore the dynamics and the diversity, and combine processes and perspectives departing from various places, some in North Africa, and others in Southern Europe.

The Legacy of the City as the Core Mediterranean Place

The dynamic understanding of the long historic and socio-economic perspective of the Mediterranean world requires a reading of its cities. They represent the effective pillars of the spatial structure of the Mediterranean and were constituted as 'world-cities' or *villes monde* (as per Fernand Braudel, where the city is the main nexus of an *économie-monde*), which forms a meeting place for people coming from very diverse geographical and cultural backgrounds. In the 15th and 16th centuries the urban system of the Mediterranean was the most compact and integrated in the world, from Istanbul to Lisbon, and incorporating big cities such as Venice, Naples, Genova and Barcelona (Braudel, 1966). Profoundly open to the exterior, this system of powerful cities with large commercial hinterlands has led to the development of cultures of migration and circulations involving both local populations and foreigners settling in these places. A culture of contact developed within the Mediterranean space, with an internal dimension corresponding to the cities and their hinterlands, and an external one that led to contacts with the cities of Northern Europe and the Near East and Middle East.

The beginning of the construction of the world system as described by Wallerstein (1984) with Iberian navigation and the conquests of the 15th and 16th centuries increased contacts and led to the articulation of the urban system of the Mediterranean with cities in South Asia and the Far East. As previously mentioned, the centrality of the Mediterranean gave way to the centrality of the Atlantic, a process that became more pronounced when the leadership of the European expansion – that would turn into European imperialism – moved towards the emerging powers of Central and Northern Europe and their main cities: Amsterdam, London, Paris or Liverpool.

Though the early stages of industrial capitalism emphasised the logic of spatial concentration in the Northern European capitals to which other urban centres have progressively joined, metropolises on both sides of the Mediterranean have also acknowledged significant processes of change and growth, especially after the second half of the 20th century. Significant change in several Mediterranean cities had already occurred during the second half of the 19th century, framed by the impulse of modern urban planning with its principles of sanitation and embellishment. Early examples of this process of urban reform that are still visible in the centres of several metropolises include the reconstruction of central Lisbon after the 1755 earthquake, Haussman's comprehensive urban reform of Paris from 1852, and the 1860 expansion of Barcelona drawn up by Ildefons Cerdà. Istanbul and Cairo underwent significant modernisation dating back to the Ottoman Empire of the 19th century and to the reigns of Muhammad Ali Pasha and Isma'il Pasha in Egypt. The establishment of European imperialism in North Africa during the 19th and early 20th centuries led to more urban reforms in cities such as Algiers, Oran, Cairo, Casablanca and Tangiers (see Ribas-Mateos, 2015, for more examples), that contributed to restructuring the urban space with the repositioning of city centres, the introduction of European-style constructions, and the segregation between the new 'European' quarters and the pre-colonial spaces. Despite the commonality in the principles and timing of the structural and physical changes in urban space, the advent of European imperialism in the Southern Mediterranean has contributed both to deepening the divide between the two shores, and to promoting specific connections between the metropolises and their colonies.

The notion of place involves the relationship between physical space and its population, which justifies an analysis of the demographic dynamics at the centre of which we find migration. If relevant cultural diversity was already present in the urban system of the Mediterranean of the late 15th century in the two cities of Istanbul and Lisbon, that bookmark East and West, we should investigate the urban population growth and urbanisation of the 20th century, in particular that of the post-Second World War period, to understand the current nature of Mediterranean metropolises. Globally, between the 1950s and the 1980s, the spatial concentration of manufacturing and services led to an intense rural–urban migration of people attracted by the possibility of work. The population of Istanbul increased tenfold between the 1950s and the end of the century; the population of Tunis tripled between 1956 and 1984; and Algiers experienced an increment of approximately 50 per cent between 1966 and 1977 (Turan, 2010; Stambouli, 1996; Hadjri and Osmani, 2004). Today, the conurbation of Cairo–Giza is the largest metropolis in Africa, with a population just over 20 million. Northern Mediterranean cities also experienced a rural exodus in the same period, resulting in significant urban population increases as well as informal suburban expansion promoted by a lack of building regulations. At the same time as the rural exodus, Southern European countries exported thousands of migrant workers to Central and Northern European countries between the 1950s and the early 1970s. Southern Mediterranean countries did the same about a decade later, during the Fordist virtuous cycle of capitalism (Ribas-Mateos and Malheiros, 2002). The process that contributed to reducing the population of the rural areas of Northern Mediterranean countries did not prevent the continuous growth of their metropolitan areas,[3] even if current growth is much slower. Urbanisation in Eastern and Southern Mediterranean regions is even greater.[4]

Although contemporary cosmopolitanism arrived later to the metropolises of the Mediterranean than it did to their counterparts in Central and Northern Europe, it is now a relevant phenomenon, especially in the case of Southern European cities, with thousands of migrant workers and their families settling in these cities following the increase in international migration of the 1980s (King, 2000). The migration turn has been explained by the expansion in public works and construction that followed the entry of Greece (in 1980), Portugal and Spain (in 1996) into the European Community that enabled their access to extensive development funds. In addition to the recruitment of foreign workers to this activity branch, also the progress of intensive market agriculture in several regions of Italy, Spain and Greece, and the development of the service sector that followed the expansion of consumption, have been responsible for this increase in the demand for non-EU workers. Also, the limited level of institutionalisation experienced by Southern European countries in certain areas of public policy, that authors such as Ferrera (2010) have sought to explain in the light of three variables (the role of the family and especially the role of women in taking care of the family, the extension of the informal economy, and low administrative capacities) contributes to explain the recruitment of migrant workers, namely women. In such a welfare frame, the family finds it increasingly difficult to assume the tasks and responsibilities that ensure care in the countries of the Mediterranean regime, strongly based on 'familism'. It is in this context, aggravated by the very high ageing level of these societies, where we see the connection between the crisis of welfare seen as a crisis of care, and the commodification of care through migration chains that mainly target women's immigrant labour. This largely informal solution seems to contribute to resolving the care crisis in the short term, but it can call into question the medium- to long-term sustainability of the welfare regime, the integration of immigrants, and the need to ensure social justice (Moreno et al., 2014).

Having taken into consideration the population and economic activities in the main urban spaces and their consequences for the dynamics and diversity of the urban labour markets, it is not a surprise that the proportion of immigrants in these Mediterranean metropolises is always higher than in the respective countries, and that diversity is now a hallmark of these spaces. With the exception of Paris, Madrid and Barcelona are the EU cities with the highest absolute foreign population numbers. Athens and Lisbon also rank in the top ten cities in terms of foreign-born inhabitants.[5] The percentages of the foreign-born population tend to be smaller in the cities of the Southern Mediterranean, but their role as places of refuge and/or transit spaces to Europe where migrants tend to accumulate are transforming the panorama.

Crossings to Europe are hindered by the control of the Mediterranean by EU authorities in partnership with the police and armed forces of the North African countries, as the result of cooperation agreements signed with the purpose of preventing migration and returning migrants. Many migrants are currently taken by Moroccan, Algerian and Libyan authorities to their southern borders and left there without humanitarian support. Despite the expulsions and the rotation of the migrants, their regular presence is now a fact in many North African metropolises. Mediterranean cities have historically been the core of Mediterranean spaces. These cities are restless places that structure regions and act as nodules of intra-regional and international connections. Despite historical ups and downs, these urban places are marked by cultural and social diversity, and interact with each other but often establish stronger links with places beyond the Mediterranean region, reproducing on an urban level what previously formed the discussion in terms of regions and countries.

The Changing Nature of Mediterranean Rural Societies: Non-Urban Places

We have assumed that metropolises form the core of the Mediterranean world, and mentioned the depopulation process experienced by rural areas (rural exodus). Despite the concentration of economic activities, wealth and population in urban spaces, it is necessary to refer to rural places in the Foreword to this book. The definitions of the 'Mediterranean world' by the geographers and historians of the late 19th century and the first half of the 20th century, such as Vidal de la Blache, Fernand Braudel, Pierre Birot and Orlando Ribeiro, included key aspects such as the rural landscape, often being portrayed romantically, and supporting socio-cultural elements. Rather than perceiving of rural and urban spaces as opposite types of places, the connections between them should be viewed from the perspective of a continuum.

With regard to Mediterranean landscapes, degradation of some traditional sensitive ecosystems such as several wetlands has occurred (Sivgnon, 2007), along with the expansion of monoculture (for example, of olives) with consequences in terms of excessive homogeneity, biodiversity loss and soil erosion (Paniza Cabrera et al., 2007). Long summer droughts and the concentration of rain in the winter months are climatic traits that influence both the type of vegetation and the various land systems that, despite local specificities, share common natural and agricultural traits (Ribeiro, 1945/2021; Claval, 2007). The two dominant modes of land use in rural Mediterranean spaces were intensive polyculture of vineyards, olive trees, cereals (namely wheat and rye), together with legumes and some fruits (figs, almonds, carob, citrus fruits), and extensive cereal monoculture combined with raising cattle (Ribeiro, 1945/2021; Birot and Dresch, 1953). Claval (2007) recalls a system, based on the Vidalian perspective, in which the local land systems provided the basic resources for the survival of their populations, but these were not sufficient to support wealthier and more complex civilisations. This required the settlement of trading structures supported by a network of cities, essential for the organisation of the socio-political and economic systems. In different historical cycles, rural–urban interaction took different forms, from the exchange food and raw materials to migration, financial capital, ideas and, more recently, mass tourism. The contemporary rural world is experiencing significant economic and social changes that are associated with the presence of immigrants: men, women and entire families.

Since the 1980s, major reforms in the agriculture sector have taken place in the Mediterranean, particularly in Southern European countries, as the result of the European Union Common Agricultural Policy (CAP) and the progressive intensification of foreign investment (Paniza Cabrera et al., 2007; Pereira et al., 2016). Although this financing process has taken place at a different pace in various countries, it generally features the intensification of agricultural activity in terms of capital and labour, an orientation towards global markets, and an expansion of agro-industry (see the case of the Spanish province of Huelva), and frequently a regional or local specialisation in certain products. Within this process, food chains become consumer-driven and dominated by transnational food suppliers and big international supermarkets, resulting in significant changes in the Mediterranean ecological and agro-food systems (Pereira et al., 2016). Social systems have also undergone profound change, with the replacement of family agriculture by external investment, and the expansion of the hallmarks of ageing and depopulation. The intensification of global market-oriented agriculture has led enterprises to extensively recruit foreign workers as a way of ensuring labour needs are met (especially in the seasonal peaks) at reduced costs (Escrivà, 2022; Gimenez Romero, 1992; Kasimis, 2008; Pereira et al., 2016). The presence of migrant workers coming from distant geographical origins marked by socio-cultural features very different from those of local populations represents a huge potential (in terms of innovation, and demographic and economic sustainability) but is also a challenge due to the emergence of forms of employment exploitation, housing exclusion, cultural clashes and racism.

The Border as a Place of Nuance

The Mediterranean setting is key for observing cross-border mobility in historical terms. It also serves to demonstrate the contemporary relevance of mobility – of people both inside and outside the Mediterranean region – in connecting with borders. The Euro-Mediterranean context can be described in diffuse and general ways, in relation to the presence of border restrictions in mobility filters, proliferation of the *maquila* export-assembly industry, the existence of a binational community, and humanitarian action.

Most border regions currently feature militarised border enforcement as well as similar (non-)humanitarian policies, directed at asylum seekers and irregular migration (see Ribas-Mateos and Dunn, 2021 for a consideration of the humanitarian/non-humanitarian focus from different angles). State policies are generally becoming increasingly inhumane, and humanitarianism goals are, in principle, provided by advocates and activists, in addition to the welfare state and international institutions. Year on year, militarised barriers (combined natural and human-made) that prevent the entry of migrant labourers and the working classes from the Global South are strengthened against both the uninspected entry of unauthorised workers and entry attempts by asylum seekers. But in current policies we can also witness the official rejection of humanitarianism of various kinds, both in the state management of migrant bodies to avoid bad political publicity, as well as resistant humanitarianism from below by activists and organisations.

The Mediterranean setting – beset by conditions of socio-economic crisis, weak social policies, restricted borders, and multiple forms of mobility – exceeds rigid, established fields of investigation and spills over into the relationships between the EU, Southern Europe, North Africa, the Arab/Berber North Africa, the Middle East (including Iran, Turkey and Kurdistan) and the Balkans. Its borders are intertwined with mobility filters that differentiate people according to social categories in what is one of the most militarised and heavily patrolled areas in the world, and which has become, over the last decade, the most lethal border region in the world. Despite the quantity of research carried out in recent years (compared to the 1990s) and frequent exposure in the media, the Mediterranean world needs to be understood from a *longue durée* perspective of policies in the changing construction of 'Fortress Europe'. Thus, we would like to consider how the transformation of borders in the Mediterranean (also including the Middle East here) is accompanied by severe social inequalities expressed in different ways: increasing limitations on the mobility of refugees and migrants, yet decreasing limitations on the cross-border flow of goods; the proliferation of refugee encampments and settlements (formal and informal); human vulnerability and rights violations; and expanded border securitisation (Mezzadra and Neilson, 2013).

Due to the context of mixed migration flows,[6] camps of all sorts are becoming a central step in migrants' and especially refugees' journeys, as they constrain their mobility and drastically limit their access to human and social rights; as a result, many contemporary authors are considering the importance of humanitarian work during their border fieldwork research. One classic example from the Middle East is the humanitarian images that politically position the concepts of 'refugee' and 'camp' as moral indictments of the states and agencies that impact upon refugees' lives. In the case of the Palestinian camps, the idea of not settling into new countries has come to be seen as a form of agency, with the refugees focused instead on their economic survival and return. The refugees are viewed as revolutionaries rather than recipients of international aid or subjects of humanitarian crises (Marron, 2016). A current case in point is the situation of the 'migrants trapped in Libya' where United Nations institutions, European actors, national actors, multiple militias, non-governmental organisations (NGOs), a hegemonic media and an independent media all play an important role in creating and revealing a complex situation of multiple forms and sources of violence – particularly sexual and gender-based – and eliciting a politics of compassion and mobility in the Mediterranean (for the Libyan case, and the Lebanese case regarding Syrian refugees, see Ribas-Mateos, 2020).

In this humanitarian border setting, the politics of compassion is illustrated by the following two examples. The first example is Morocco, with Jiménez's (2019) illustration of the politics of compassion in the processes of European externalisation of borders in the Western Mediterranean region. By means of migration control policies, a process of victimisation occurs when counting, investigating and assisting the migrants. According to Jiménez, these humanitarian practices position the migrants as passive 'objects in receipt of compassion', while mediators such as aid workers, doctors and translators are considered as active subjects, and are recipients of funds dedicated to implementing migration policies. The second example is provided by Poguisch's (2018) theoretical–empirical work on the Central Mediterranean route, in which she analyses post-2013 migration policies, including Operation Mare Nostrum, where 'saving lives was put on the European Agenda', and later treaties between Italy and Libya. The treaties were an attempt to integrate humanitarian rhetoric into governmental migration management policies. However, Poguisch points out multiple ambiguities in the humanising policies: for example, the contradiction between border control and humanitarian rescue preventing many migrants from reaching Europe. NGOs currently working in the Mediterranean do so from a humanitarian perspective that is both rational and emotional, with a fraternal spirit and a concern for the situation of other human beings, by expressing compassion and solidarity. This has arisen along with the displacement of millions of additional people in a brief period, resulting from multiple conflicts, many of which are tied to disastrous foreign policy and coercive interventions in the Middle East and North Africa by the United States and major European powers.

The construction of the Mediterranean setting has involved socio-economic changes in Southern European countries, the impact of the Arab Spring on mobility, the capsizing of boats of migrants in the Mediterranean, EU emergency policies, and the proliferation of push-backs. All of this has resulted in borders being pushed South, towards sub-Saharan Africa, especially between 2011 (with the beginning of the Arab Spring) and 2015, and from 2015 onwards, creating a crisis of border externalisation paired with a new phase of turbulence at the maritime frontier.

MIGRATION AND MOBILITIES

Traditional migration studies assumed that migrants brought with them a strong sense of place of their country of origin as well as a unidirectional return project. Reterritorialisation is characterised by the reconstruction of daily routines and insertion into a new socio-spatial fabric at destination (Haesbaert, 2007). This implies an adaptation to the local and national features and norms, but in many cases is embedded in co-ethnic relations and support. More recently, the centrality of this territorialised 'society' has shifted as networks and mobility intersect across the globe, drawing a profiled place according to Lefebvre's (1991) classification, articulated by a confluence of networks and paths, in a continuous interrelationship of mobility and societies, resulting in multiterritoriality (Haesbaert, 2007). Globalisation has resulted in one of the most significant transformations in the spatial organisation of power, and economic and political activity. It is our belief that theories of globalisation synthesise all these elements, distorting the classical notion of territoriality and the binary connection to countries of origin, driving the articulation of new concepts. In this scenario, globalisation and mobility find a way to break with the traditional binary perspectives (immigrant–emigrant; origin–destination; departure and return) in transnationality, allowing for a reconstruction of the connections between spaces at various scales and pointing to new perspectives on migrant families and recipients of remittances, capital and information flows.

Challenges to the concept of conventional mobility behaviours and patterns of seasonal or circular mobility, and the consequences of (im)mobility in times of global pandemic, call for further research. While transnationalism is not entirely novel, it did reach a particularly high degree of intensity on a global scale at the end of the 20th century, the reasons for which correspond to the processes associated with increasing global economic interaction, a reduction in transport costs, progress in the new technologies of information, and decolonisation (seen from a current controversial context of decolonisation and post-colonisation). If increased circularity, clear in the design of human corridors and the feminisation of international mobility (especially since the beginning of the 1990s), is to be considered decisive in current global migration, it is an additional significant element in terms of covering new paradigmatic regions and migration poles (for example, West Africa, Southern Europe, the Persian Gulf). In addition to this, it is now possible to observe the configuration of new countries of emigration, immigration or transit, which involve the Maghreb or Turkey. Studies into circularity, inspired by the work of authors such as Alain Tarrius, have presented mobility as a resource, with its origins in the analysis of migration complexities in the Mediterranean region. Tarrius's work affirms that migrant identities are not reaffirmed through permanence in place, but are marked by movement, understood as something that combines geographical mobility and connection with the territory. He coined the term 'circular territories' to refer to certain population groups characterised by 'movements, comings and goings, by constant ins and outs in worlds designated as different' (Tarrius, 2000: 8). Such perspectives allow us to address issues arising from the study of social structure in migration, in connection with analytical time–space re-readings, which go beyond the polygonal space delimited by national sovereignty, and point to the relevance of network space. Along similar lines, Peraldi et al. (2001) propose that contemporary migration flows can no longer be conceived of in the same way as Fordist and controlled migration (in Sayad's terms; Sayad, 2004). According to Peraldi et al., the novel forms of mobility associated with economic adaptation, demonstrated by his empirical studies carried out in Marseille in the 1990s, demonstrate a variety of movements (including commuting), built on functional routes such as pilgrimage, commerce or diaspora (family celebrations, care arrangements, and so on) (Ribas-Mateos, 2017).

Undoubtedly, the mobility paradigm that appears to have wobbled during the global COVID-19 epidemic is a clear starting point. The theoretical proposal of the mobility turn forms part of a critique of the social sciences, in which theories were derived from the assumption that migration phenomena begin from a static position. In contrast to this, researchers such as Sheller and Urry (2006) point out that the 'mobility turn' aims to study strategies motivated by 'family projects, for leisure and enjoyment, by politics or protest' (Sheller and Urry, 2006: 208). This paradigm does pay close attention to the concept of 'space', rather than the controversial new role of the state, and includes the study of movements that take place 'in the de-territorialised and de-centralised world, without a centre of power and without fixed barriers' (Sheller and Urry, 2006: 209). As Sassen (2013) points out, when we stop in this space, the focus is on the gap between the territory and the legal construction of the sovereign territorial authority of the state, that is, territoriality.

Temporality creates temporary chains, flows, interactions, negotiations, crossings and meetings, producing a social situation that differs from sedentary societies with their own specific rules and norms (Tarrius, 2009). And in this sense, temporality is connected to the idea of circularity, creating a new supra-level space of migration networks called migration camps, in which migration and social networks are reproduced by migrants. The conception of circular migration thus represents a range of movements of subjects that repeat on a regular basis for certain periods of time, creating continuous forms of movement between different spaces, and for varying periods of time in the Mediterranean space (sometimes also referred to as 'caravansar' in reference to such circularity). Clearly, the ability to utilise this mobility space varies by regional area and by social class, gender, age and ethnicity.

Mobility in the Mediterranean can be examined on the basis of key axes of analysis (global care chains and relocation of care services, technological changes, marriage strategies, circularity and transnational practices). Mobility is intrinsically a resource (access to social economic or even cultural capital in other national spaces, for example), but also works as an engine generating a kaleidoscope of social inequalities that traverse the spheres of gender, generations, ethnicity and race. Such inequalities require a reflection on direct or indirect aspects of mobility such as asylum laws, or the segmented structures that characterise the organisation of the labour markets.

In his latest publication, *Memory and the Mediterranean*, Fernand Braudel retraces the Mediterranean in pre-historical times, as a long-standing scar on the earth: 'if the Mediterranean seems so alive, so eternally young in our eyes ... what point is there in recalling this sea's great age? What can it possibly matter, that the Mediterranean, an insignificant breach in the earth's crust ... is an ancient feature of the geology of the globe?' (Braudel, 2001, 3).

NOTES

1. The Mediterranean is one of the zones of the widely used Köppen climate classification. Because climate zones have a longitudinal nature, the Mediterranean zone also includes California in the Northern Hemisphere, and has expression in Western and South Australia, south-western South Africa and Chile (Southern Hemisphere). The Mediterranean climate zone is not solely comprised of the region around the Mediterranean Sea, but the designation arose there along with various studies about its communalities in terms of climate and vegetation. See, for instance, Ribeiro (1968), who outlines the idea of a unified space – *strictu sensu* – in bioclimatic terms.
2. For Moreno et al. (2014: 100) the Mediterranean Southern European (MSE) model would appear as an articulated political project around the values of equality and solidarity with the most vulnerable groups (particularly the elderly). However, the 2008 financial crisis shook up this framework and opened up spaces in which specific political and economic interests are attracted by the possibility of increasing economic benefits (for example, private provision of health and education services for the most solvent sectors, strong liberalisation in the housing market, criticism of the role of the state, overvaluation of markets).
3. Madrid, Milan, Barcelona, Naples, Athens, Rome and Lisbon are ranked among the 12 largest urban metropolises of the European Union. The urbanisation indexes of Spain, Greece, Italy and Portugal are all over 66 per cent (CIA, 2020).
4. Libya, Turkey, Algeria and Tunisia have urbanisation rates over 70 per cent. Even in the cases of Egypt and Morocco, which display lower values, we

find some of the largest cities in Africa such as the Cairo–Giza conurbation. Alexandria and Casablanca are also placed in the top ten ranking of the most populated metropolises of Africa.

5. Because this dataset is not complete and several cities lack information, the ranking must be taken in relative terms (Eurostat, 2016. Archive: Urban Europe – statistics on cities, towns and suburbs – foreign-born persons living in cities, https://ec.europa.eu/eurostat/statistics-explained/index.php?title=Archive:Urban _Europe_%E2%80%94_statistics_on_cities,_towns_and_suburbs_%E2%80 %94_foreign-born_persons_living_in_cities&direction=next&oldid=294560).

6. Mixed migration flows correspond to:

    A movement in which a number of people are travelling together, generally in an irreg-ular manner, using the same routes and means of transport, but for different reasons. People travelling as part of mixed movements have varying needs and profiles and may include asylum seekers, refugees, trafficked persons, unaccompanied/separated children, and migrants in an irregular situation. (IOM, 2019: 141–142).

REFERENCES

Bagnasco, A. (1977). *Tre Italie: la problematica territoriale dello sviluppo italiano*. Bologna: Il Mulino.

Beaugrand, C. and Geisser, V. (2016). The role of diasporas, migrants and exiles in the Arab revolutions and political transitions. In Ribas-Mateos, N. (ed.), *Migration, Mobilities and the Arab Spring. Spaces of Refugee Flight in the Eastern Mediterranean*. Cheltenham, UK and Northampton, MA, USA: Edward Elgar Publishing, pp. 34–49.

Birot, P. and Dresch, J. (1953). *La Méditerranée et le Moyen-Orient, Tome 1: La Méditerranée Occidentale*. Paris: PUF.

Braudel, F. (1966). *La Méditerranée et le monde méditerranéen à l'époque de Philippe II*. Paris: A. Colin.

Braudel, Fernand (2001). *Memory and the Mediterranean*. Translated by Siân Reynolds. New York: Random House.

Brenner, N. (2000). The urban question as a scale question: reflections on Henri Lefebvre, urban theory and the politics of scale. *International Journal of Urban and Regional Research*, 24 (2): 361–378, doi: https://doi.org/10.1111/1468-2427 .00234.

CIA (2020). *CIA World Fact Book*. https://www.cia.gov/the-world-factbook/

Claval, P. (2007). About rural landscapes: the invention of the Mediterranean and the French school of geography. *Erde*, 138 (1): 7–24.

Escrivà, A. (2022). Globalization and health: gender issues in temporary agricultural work (Huelva). In Ribas-Mateos, N. and Sassen, S. (eds), *The Elgar Companion to Gender and Global Migration*. Cheltenham, UK and Northampton, MA, USA: Edward Elgar Publishing, pp. 324–333.

Fernandes, J.A., Ferrão, J., Malheiros, J. and Chamusca, P. (2021). Geography as a social science in Portugal. In Lois-González, R.C. (ed.), *Geographies of Mediterranean Europe*. Cham: Springer, pp. 15–38.

Ferrera, M. (2010). The South European countries. In Castles, F.G., Leibfried, S., Lewis, J., Obinger, H. and Pierson, C. (eds), *The Oxford Handbook of the Welfare State*. Oxford and New York: Oxford University Press, pp. 616–629.

Garofoli, G. (1992). *Economia del territorio: trasformazioni economiche e sviluppo regionale*. Milano: Etaslibri.

Gimenez Romero, C. (1992). Trabajadores Extrangeros en la Agricultura Española: Enclaves e Implicaciones. *Estudios Regionales*, 141: 127–147.

Hadjri, K. and Osmani, M. (2004). The spatial development and urban transformation of colonial and post-colonial Algiers. In Elsheshtaw, Y. (ed.), *Planning Middle Eastern Cities: An Urban Kaleidoscope*. London: Routledge, pp. 29–55.

Haesbaert, R. (2007). Território e multiterritorialidade: um debate. *GEOgraphia*, 9 (17): 19–45.

Holzer, W. (2003). O conceito de lugar na Geografia Cultural-Humanista: uma contribuição para a geografia contemporânea. *GEOgraphia*, 5 (10): 113–123.

IOM (2019). *International Migration Law – Glossary of Migration*. Geneva: International Organization for Migration.

Jiménez, M. (2019). Externalización fronteriza en el Mediterráneo Occidental: movilidades, violencias y políticas de compasión. https://www.researchgate .net/publication/290212829_Externalizacion_fronteriza_en_el_Mediterraneo _Occidental_movilidades_violencias_y_politicas_de_compasion (retrieved on 2 March 2019).

Kasimis, C. (2008). Survival and expansion: migrants in Greek rural regions. *Population Space and Place*, 14 (6): 511–524, doi: https://doi.org/10.1002/psp .513.

King, R. (2000). Southern Europe in the changing global map of migration. In King, R. and Charalambos Tsardanidis, G. (eds), *Eldorado or Fortress? Migration in Southern Europe*. London: Palgrave Macmillan, pp. 3–26.

Lefebvre, H. (1991). *The Production of Space*. Oxford: Blackwell Publishing.

Lenine, V.I. (1916/1984). *O Imperialismo, Fase Superior do Capitalismo* (tomo 2 das Obras Escolhidas). Lisboa: Edições Avante

Lois-González, R.C. (2021), The current legacy of geographies in Mediterranean Europe. In Lois-González, R.C. (ed.), *Geographies of Mediterranean Europe*. Cham: Springer, pp. 1–14.

Marron, R. (2016). Introduction: on the humanitarian cause. In Marron, R. (ed.), *Humanitarian Rackets and their Moral Hazards: The Case of the Palestinian Refugee Camps in Lebanon*. Abingdon, UK and New York, USA: Routledge, pp. 1–29.

Mezzadra, S. and Neilson, B. (2013). Fabrica mundi: producing the world by drawing borders. In Blackwell A. and Lee, C. (eds), *Scapegoat: Architecture, Landscape, Political Economy, Currency*, 4: 3–19.

Modelski, G. (1978). The long cycle of global politics and the nation-state. *Comparative Studies in Society and History*, 20 (2): 214–235.

Moreno, L., del Pino, E., Mari-Klose, P. and Moreno-Fuentes, F.J. (2014). Los sistemas de bienestar europeos tras la crisis económica. Colección Estudios no. 3 Serie Análisis Área Políticas Sociales. Madrid.

Paniza Cabrera, A., Cancer Pomar, L., Garcia Martinez, P. and Cuesta Aguilar, M.J. (2007). The Common Agricultural Policy and rural landscape changes: the example of Carcheles, Jaen, Spain. In Roca, Z., Spek, T., Terkenil, T., Pleininger, T. and Hochtl, F. (eds), *European Landscapes and Lifestyles: The Mediterranean and Beyond*. Lisbon: Edições Universitárias Lusófonas, pp. 277–282.

Peraldi, M., Bettaieb, A. and Manry, V. (2001). L'esprit de bazar. En Mobilités transnationales maghrébines et sociétés métropolitaines: Les routes d'Istambul. In Péraldi, M. (ed.), *Cabas et containers. Activités marchandes informelles et réseaux migrants transfrontaliers*. Paris: Maisonneuve et Larose, pp. 329–381.

Pereira, S., Moreno, L., Estevens, A., Esteves, A. and Malheiros, J. (2016). Reconfiguración de áreas rurales y explotación de mano de obra inmigrante: el caso de Odemira, Portugal. *Estudios Migratorios Latinoamericanos*, 81 (July–Dec): 227–250.

Poguisch, T. (2018). Confini Fantasma dell'Europa. In Bellinvia, T. and Poguisch, T. (eds), *Razzismo, confini, marginalità. Decolonizzare le migrazioni.* Milano-Udine: Mimesis/CartografieSociale, pp. 41–60.

Ribas-Mateos, N. (2015). *Tanger, Maroc: La sociologe d'une ville-frontière (A Sociological Study of Tangiers, Morocco).* London and New York: Mellen Press.

Ribas-Mateos, N. (2017). *The Mediterranean in the Age of Globalization: Migration, Welfare and Borders.* New Brunswick, NJ: Transaction Publishers.

Ribas-Mateos, N. (2020). Borders and mobilities in the Middle East: emerging challenges for Syrian refugees in 'Bilad Al-Sham. In Babar, Z. (ed.), *Mobility and Forced Displacement in the Middle East.* London: Hurst, pp. 19–32.

Ribas-Mateos, N. and Dunn, T. (eds) (2021). *Handbook on Human Security, Borders and Migration.* Cheltenham, UK and Northampton, MA, USA: Edward Elgar Publishing.

Ribas-Mateos, N. and Malheiros, J. (2002). Immigration and place in northern Mediterranean cities: issues for debate. In Fonseca, M.L., Malheiros, J., Ribas-Mateos, N., White, P. and Esteves, A. (eds), *Immigration and Place in Mediterranean Metropolises.* Lisbon: Luso-American, pp. 293–308.

Ribas-Mateos, N. and Sempere Souvannavong, J.D. (2006). El negocio de la maleta en Alicante y Tánger: descifrando el circuito mediterráneo. In Beltrán, J., Oso, L. and Ribas-Mateos, N. (eds), *Empresariado étnico en España.* Madrid: Ministerio de Trabajo y Asuntos Sociales y Fundación CIDOB, pp. 289–310.

Ribeiro, O. (1945/2021). *Portugal, o Mediterrâneo e o Atlântico.* Lisboa: Letra Livre.

Ribeiro, O. (1968). *Mediterrâneo – Ambiente e Tradição.* Lisbon: Fundação Calouste Gulbenkian.

Sassen, S. (2013). When territory deborders territoriality. *Territory, Politics, Governance*, 1 (1): 21–45, doi: https://doi.org/10.1080/21622671.2013.769895.

Sayad, A. (2004). *The Suffering of the Immigrant.* Cambridge: Polity.

Sheller, M.Y. and Urry, J. (2006). The new mobilities paradigm. *Environment and Planning A*, 38 (2): 207–226, doi: https://doi.org/10.1068%2Fa37268.

Sivgnon, M. (2007). The Greel wetlands: from degradation to rehabilitation. In Roca, Z., Spek, T., Terkenil, T., Pleininger, T. and Hochtl, F. (eds), *European Landscapes and Lifestyles: The Mediterranean and Beyond.* Lisbon: Edições Universitárias Lusófonas, pp. 243–246.

Stambouli, F. (1996). Tunis city in transition. *Environment and Urbanization*, 8 (1): 51–63, doi: https://doi.org/10.1177%2F095624789600800117.

Tarrius, A. (2000). *Les nouveaux cosmopolitismes. Mobilités, identités, territoires.* La Tour d'Aigues: Editions de l'Aube.

Tarrius, A. (2009). Intérêt et faisabilité de l'approche des territoires des circulations transnationales. In Cortès, G. and Faret, L. (eds), *Les circulations transnationales: lire les turbulences migratoires contemporaines.* Paris: Armand Colin, pp. 43–51.

Tuan, Y-F. (1977). *Space and Place: The Perspective of Experience.* Minneapolis, MN: University of Minnesota Press.

Turan, N. (2010). Towards an ecological urbanism for Istanbul. In Sorensen, A. and Junichiro, O. (eds), *Megacities: Urban Form, Governance, and Sustainability.*

Library for Sustainable Urban Regeneration. London and New York: Springer, pp. 223–242.

Wallerstein, I.M. (1984). *The Modern World System*. New York: Academic Press.

PART I

MOBILITIES AND COLONIALISMS

1. Human mobility in the pre-modern Mediterranean

Wolfgang Kaiser and Claudia Moatti

The importance of mobility in pre-contemporary societies is no longer in question. The image of a largely immobile population proposed by historical demography has been rendered obsolete by the research carried out in recent decades (Canny, 1994; Lucassen, 1999; Bade, 2002; Balard, 2006), due mainly to a revision and broadening of what is meant by 'mobility', 'migration' and 'diaspora' (Moatti, 2018). From the concept of migration, defined as a radical change of residence and social environment, and for a long time considered to be an exceptional phenomenon up until the Industrial Revolution (Zelinsky, 1971), has emerged the broader concept of mobility, understood as a social process, and thus socially decisive in addition to being inseparable from other social phenomena. It is important to consider the importance, in the structuring of social life, of regional micro-mobilities and seasonal mobilities, of the phases of mobility in individual lives, of the sharing of roles within families, over several generations, in chains of migrations, and of the close links between geographical and social mobility. The notion of diaspora has also evolved, moving away from the victim model. According to the English sociologists Robin Cohen (2008) and William Safran (1991, 1999), it is defined by three criteria: initial dispersion, absence of assimilation into the host society, and maintenance of the link with the origin. What differentiates diaspora from migration is therefore the role played by the country of origin across borders, in terms of identity and memory. Understood in such terms, the notion has been applied to situations never before considered to be diasporas, such as work, trade, knowledge and administration.[1] The principle of these diasporas is that they allow the constitution of vast networks of exchanges (Delgado, 2017), while also favouring, through the diffusion of information and the constitution of reception structures, the dispersion of migrants towards ever more distant regions (Monge and Muchnik, 2019); and that they disappear when the members of the diaspora are integrated in the place of reception or return to their country. This broad use of the notion of diaspora has had several effects. In particular, it has made it possible to 'decolonise' the first Phoenician or

Greek migrations to the far West, while recognising their organised character, far from the chaotic images that the ideas of migration and mobility arouse.

By emphasising the importance for the structuring of social life of all these mobilities, these approaches have broadened the spectrum of human movement, taking into account local as well as distant mobility. Distance is always relative to the means of communication, and what we call local migration might in ancient times have been an uprooting phenomenon, such as migration flows in antiquity to and within the Italian peninsula and the rural exodus (Ducellier, 1992; Erdkamp, 2016; Zeller, 2003), or the exchanges in early modern times between supply areas and the demographic basins of cities. In contrast to the historians of demography, who thought in terms of concentric micro-spaces around a given place, historians of migratory flows have shown, despite the difficulties in quantifying their results, that in pre-modern periods, mobility, whether temporary or definitive, was indispensable to the life of rural villages because of the insufficiency of local resources; that cities were real hubs, which could compensate for the structural over-mortality of their population only through significant immigration (Hin, 2013; Pizzorusso, 2009).

Given the observation that Europe is a 'peninsula made of peninsulas' (Darwin, 2008: 95), it also seems to apply to the Mediterranean (Lestringant, 2002). In this space, which was rarely unified, and even often fragmented to the extreme, the circulation of people constituted, in the words of Fernand Braudel, a structural and structuring fact, which formed the very basis of the Mediterranean reticular system. A vision that the Ancients would not have denied, if we judge by the memory of archaic migrations in the ancient historiography, and by the omnipresence of travel in the first great texts: the account of the Egyptian Ounamon in the 11th century BCE, the saga of Ulysses, that of Aeneas, up to the experience of St Paul who hypostasises the figure of the stranger. To analyse this pre-modern mobility, it is necessary to distinguish three spatial scales – the Mediterranean scale, to highlight networks and migrations, while taking into account the importance of certain historical ruptures; the urban scale, to underline both the role of cities and towns in the history of mobilities, and the influence of these mobilities on urban development and on the formation of identities; and finally, the political scale, that of the states – to ask which policies have favoured or opposed the freedom of movement, a notion on which a more general reflection will be offered in the Conclusion to this chapter.

THE MEDITERRANEAN AS A RETICULAR SPACE

Fernand Braudel's theory postulating cultural unity made this space a historical actor in a global history, dominated in early modern times by Europeans and obeying a historical process of communicating vessels – Mediterranean decline and rise of the Atlantic world – where Venice and Genoa were to be replaced by Antwerp and Amsterdam. The rhetoric of personalisation that characterises this master narrative, according to which the 'inland sea' was a 'world economy' later relayed by other spaces, has not been taken up by the most recent works of synthesis. But the matrix of unity remains present, for example in interpretations of the Mediterranean as an ecosystem of great stability, where the natural connectivity of the sea constitutes essential risk management in the face of fragmentation and ecological uncertainties (Horden and Purcell, 2000; Tabak, 2008; contra Gambash, 2016; Moatti, 2021). Approaching the question from the angle of mobilities, their logic and their constraints permit an escape from this project: it opens up the possibility of thinking differently about discontinuity and transition, about transformations and innovations in this culturally saturated Mediterranean space endowed with an extraordinary historical breadth. In fact, the Mediterranean space has only gradually become a multipolar world, while the various mobilities that this space has experienced have not always structured it in a continuous manner: their history is also made up of reconfigurations and ruptures.

A Multipolar World

From the second millennium, Mycenaean trade in the south of Italy, Sicily and Sardinia, contact between Cyprus and Sardinia and the trade routes opened by the Iberian Peninsula, which the Greeks and Phoenicians developed in the following millennium (Broodbank, 2013), linked the different regions of the Mediterranean East together, as well as the West and the East, according to very extensive and progressively constituted networks. The Levantine groups, for example, did not move *en masse* in the 9th century BC towards a *terra incognita* to appropriate it, but did so in several waves as a result of established contacts and multiple partnerships of exchanges. Once there, they formed 'economic enclaves' (Portes, 1987), sites of settlement or centres of production. In all three cases, these mobile groups, heterogeneous in terms of sex, age, social class, occupation and ethnic origin, maintained a link with their place of origin. The dispersion of these peoples continued from the West for a long period subsequently, examples of which include Carthage to Sardinia, Sicily and the Iberian Peninsula (Mastino, 1985).

The intensity of the interactions and their reticular structure favoured an accumulation of benefits, progress in the technology of transport by sea (Arnaud, 2005), and urban development, whether cosmopolitan places of trade (*emporia*), such as Pithekoussai or Gravisca in Archaic Italy, or colonies (Riva, 2010; Malkin, 2011; Broodbank, 2013). They also brought about a certain commercial unification of the Mediterranean basin (Guarracino, 2007), and perhaps even the formation of a sort of *ius mercatorum* (Nörr,

2009)[2]. From this perspective, the Roman Republic (509–527 BCE) did not immediately cause a fundamental rupture: it created new networks, negotiating first with Carthage, then with the rest of the Mediterranean basin from the 3rd century onwards by means of bilateral agreements and alliances. It also gradually tried to control maritime circuits, to the detriment of Syria, Rhodes, the Greek cities and Carthage, destroyed in 146. It was with the Roman expansion in the Mediterranean, in the 2nd century BCE, that both forced and free mobility towards Italy developed on a large scale (Tagliafico, 1995): Carthaginian, Illyrian and Greek slaves arrived *en masse*; commercial, artisanal, artistic and intellectual migrations from the eastern basin multiplied. At the same time, many Italian businessmen emigrated to the Greek cities of the continent, the Aegean islands or the micro-Asiatic regions, and also to the Iberian Peninsula, the south of Gaul, or to the allied kingdoms (Numidia and Mauritania, for example). With Caesar, and especially Augustus, the foundation of colonies in extra-Italian territories increased the diaspora of Roman citizens, mainly the poor and former soldiers. Under the Empire, commercial connections developed thanks to the creation of secure land and sea routes, or artificial ports, as was the case in Africa and the Near East (Hitchner, 2012; Stone, 2014; De Souza, 2000), accompanying the movement of goods (African or Spanish oil, wine from Gaul and Spain) (Morley, 2007). Movements multiplied within provinces (Haley, 1991) and between different regions (Lassère, 2006; Lefebvre, 2006); in Mauritania Tingitana (modern Morocco), constituted as a province under Claudius between 42 and 45 CE, migrants were career soldiers, and merchants of Spanish, Italian, Syrian, Arab, Greek, Dacian and Macedonian origin. Conversely, a large number of people from this province (and all African provinces) moved to the Mediterranean (Lassère, 1977; Handley, 2011).

The empire did not, however, form a globalised world (Morley, 2007): connectivity was not the same everywhere, and mobility was not limited to commercial movements. But unification had made the Mediterranean basin a secure space. And even the changes that occurred at the end of the 3rd century with the revival of piracy, and from the 5th century onwards with the decline of the Empire, invasions and crises, did not bring mobility to a halt; inscriptions even demonstrate a peak in the number of travellers in the 5th century (Handley, 2011).

During the entire imperial period, relations with neighbouring and even very distant regions (the Great North, the Red Sea, India, Ceylon, China) also developed rapidly. The Mediterranean had long been open to other seas and other spaces, notably the Black Sea and the Red Sea, but from then on it was the *mare nostrum* as a whole that opened up to the most distant worlds, for several centuries under the control and protection of the Roman state (Wilson, 2015). Provided that historians employ varied scales and multiple angles of observation, what is visible in the imperial framework remains so following the political and religious fragmentation. Thus, seen from Cairo in the 9th century (on the basis of the Genizah documents; Goitein, 1967; Goldberg, 2012; Valérian, 2019), or from Cairo and Istanbul around 1600 (Hanna, 1998; Faroqhi et al., 1994), the Eastern Mediterranean appears to be a prosperous world; whereas the European perspective gives a darker picture. The Levant trade of Europeans in early modern times constitutes only a small part of the volume of the Ottoman Empire's internal trade, and it does not sound the death knell of the intense caravan trade via the Arabian Peninsula and Persia with the Indian world (Kaiser, 2008a). The discovery of the Cape route, which constitutes a symbolic key event in the master narrative of the Mediterranean decline, in fact only acquired major importance in the 18th century (De Vries, 2003).

The Nature of Migration

Numerous works have focused on the reality of human mobility and have attempted to establish its causes. The political origins of migration flows have been highlighted: exiles and outcasts were thrown out of ancient or medieval cities as the result of internal political struggles, the annexation of territories by the Romans led to the emigration of administrators and colons, the Christian crusades were accompanied by permanent settlements in the Near East. Migration also has military origins: conquest opened markets and agricultural opportunities; it increased the quantity of servile labour, both male and female (Woolf, 2013), also leading to the displacement of populations. Finally, there are cultural origins, such as the attraction of philosophical schools in the classical world and of universities in the medieval period, or of pilgrimages in all eras. Migration was due as much to rational choices as to relationships of domination (Gastaut, 2016).

To explain mobility, much emphasis has also recently been placed on the unequal distribution of material and human resources (Horden and Purcell, 2000). It is said that it was the scarcity of resources that led to the expulsion of people, the search for new lands, and the increase in trade, and it was the scarcity of people and labour that led to the acceptance of, and even the granting of citizenship to, foreigners. It has long been argued that unequal distribution of wealth stimulates interaction (De Charruca, 2001). In the Middle Ages, this argument included a theological dimension that continues in early modern times to underlie pleas for free trade and free movement: the inequality of wealth was willed by God to encourage men to engage in gentle civilising trade (Perrot, 1992).

Mobility and Sedentariness

At a more modest and concrete level, a multitude of other causes of mobility can be identified, demonstrating that systematically positioning it in opposition to sedentariness is futile. Conceiving of these two categories together, instead of opposing them as norm and exception, is one of the achievements of recent work on human movement (Cavaciocchi, 1994; Hoerder, 2002; Morris, 2005). The complementarity between sedentary life and mobility is evident in, for example, the organisation of seasonal work or itinerant trade in the Mediterranean. In early modern Western Europe, the peddlers of Northern Italy who supplied Northern Europe with citrus fruits, or the booksellers and pastry cooks in Mediterranean cities who originated in Alpine villages, were examples of trade that linked very large and distant spaces (Fontaine, 1993). This temporary mobility, which follows the rhythm of the seasons or certain cycles of life, requires a very complex organisation, to replace the men who leave with other migrants,[3] in addition to (well attested in early modern times) extensive credit networks for the transfer of benefits, inheritance systems and flexible family forms. Transhumance, too, has been the object of precise regulations and bitter conflicts since antiquity (see, e.g., Brun, 1996; Russo and Salvemini, 2007; Cardete, 2019; Costello and Svensson, 2018). Life on the move thus has nothing to do with the images of chaos that social fantasies portray. This is also true for those who made the frontier their resource, such as the nomads who freely crossed the territory of the Roman Empire, or the barbarian tribes who, sedentary on its margins, lived between the two spaces. In early modern times, real relays with distant worlds (Heather, 2017) occurred, including the rural clans in the margins of the Republic of Genoa who engaged in the arms trade with Milan (Raggio, 1990), the smugglers of the Iberian Peninsula (Aparicio, 2006), and the actors of the ransom economy who ensured the transfer of funds between the two shores of the Mediterranean (Kaiser, 2008b). Cabotage, the dominant ancient practice of maritime navigation and trade, also combined elements of sedentary life (possession of land) and phases of mobility (journeys in caravans, or from port to port) that could last several years (Horden and Purcell, 2000), and required largely implicit knowledge of the rhythms of production and markets (Buti, 2005; Salvemini, 2007).

Ruptures and Continuities

The existence, at different times, of the regular structures discussed in previous sections does not exclude the fact that reconfigurations caused by ruptures have occurred. The establishment of the Assyrian Empire in the first millennium BC, for example, led to a reconfiguration of the eastern basin of the

Mediterranean and to large-scale forced population movements (Broodbank, 2013); the Roman hegemony imposed on the whole of the Mediterranean area from the 2nd century BC provoked, as we have said, a dual movement of immigration of foreigners towards Italy, and emigration of Roman citizens towards the provinces. The economic needs of the Empire, peace and security then increased geographical and social mobility, which benefited North Africa in particular (Stone, 2014), while Roman military victories were followed by a new form of migration: the settlement of defeated barbarians on Roman territory or on its borders (Modéran, 2004).

As connectivity is not constant or identical everywhere (Bresc, 2004), many other events have modified the migratory paradigms, in the sense of increasing or reducing the phenomenon. Ruptures can be analysed not only on a local scale, with the abandonment of certain sites (for example, Carthage in favour of Tunis in the 7th century CE), or the development of others (Cyprus, which became a refuge for Near Eastern populations between 1260 and 1330, threatened by Mamluk raids and Mongol incursions into Syria–Palestine) (Balard and Picard, 2014); but also on a global scale, for example when the 7th-century Arab conquest, or the later Reconquista, forced a large number of exiles onto the roads. The early modern era also saw new configurations: the displacement of the Mediterranean slave trade towards the Atlantic coast (De Almeida Mendes, 2008) as a result of the drying up of ancient sources of slaves due to the Ottoman advance and, simultaneously upstream, to the European Atlantic expansion. In the 16th century, about 10 per cent of the population of Lisbon were black slaves and/or freedmen (Lahon, 2005). Other major causes of a reconfiguration of Mediterranean networks were the Ottoman penetration into the Balkans, which caused the flight of many people to the West, and the waves of expulsions of Jews and Muslims, new Christians or *conversos* and *Moriscos* from the Iberian Peninsula in the 16th and 17th centuries. The expulsion of more than 200 000 *Moriscos* strengthened the groups of 'Andalusians' in Morocco and in the Ottoman regencies in the Maghreb that were formed during the Reconquista. The expulsion of Iberian Jews increased the Jewish population of Istanbul and contributed to the development of intercultural trade hubs such as Livorno, where the Jewish 'nation' constituted 10 per cent of the population in the 18th century, and Salonika, where Jews made up more than half of the population in 1529 and nearly two-thirds in 1613 (Mazower, 2007). These reconfigurations in the wake of the expulsions had not been foreseen by the Catholic kings; on the other hand, they were clearly intended by the Grand Duke of Tuscany, who tried to attract the Jews by granting them privileges in the *Livornina* of 1593, even though he had created a ghetto in Florence shortly before. He understood that these migrants arrived not only with goods but also with skills and, above all, with contacts, including with their country of origin; this is attested by the winding paths of the people who crossed the shores, such as Samuel Pallache, a Spanish Jew from Fez, in the service of the Moroccan sultan, agent of the King of Spain, trader, diplomat and privateer between Fez, Madrid, Amsterdam and London at the beginning of the 17th century (Garcia Arenal and Wiegers, 2003). Mobilities weave innumerable links that go far beyond contacts between states, sometimes creating 'multi-territorialities' (Badie, 1995). Their forms reflect the state of the Mediterranean world; the state of knowledge concerning the land and sea routes, ports, islands and cities; and also the inns, post offices and customs posts, which were staging posts for the travellers as well as sometimes control points.

CIRCULATION, PASSAGE AND RECEPTION STRUCTURES

Cities, hubs for the circulation of people and goods, are characterised in the long term by the tension between large migratory flows on which urban growth and prosperity depend, and a structural xenophobia whose institutional matrix is the sedentary nature and availability of the leading groups. The movement of people made it necessary to create reception structures, such as colleges, associations, *stationes* and *xenodochia* in ancient cities (see, e.g., Moatti, 2013; Fauchon-Claudon and Le Guennec, 2021), and hospitals which in medieval times welcomed the poor, pilgrims, merchants and soldiers. The intensification of exchanges is thus accompanied by a differentiation of places and institutions, and sometimes by their specialisation, which testifies to the development of asymmetries in intercultural relations. Thus, the ancient model of the *Khân* or *funduq*, established in the Middle East for the reception of merchants and goods, first spread widely in the medieval period (Concina, 1997). But, in early modern times, the enclosure and transformation of *funduqs* into storage depots in European ports of the Mediterranean was a clear sign of their inhospitality to Muslim merchants (Constable, 2004). The creation of a *Fondaco dei Turchi* in Venice at the beginning of the 17th century was clearly designed to reduce the visibility of 'Turkish' merchants (in reality often Ottoman subject Greeks) to a minimum, and to closely control their presence (Concina, 1997). Similarly, the French, English and Dutch *funduqs* built in Tunis in the mid-17th century served as a dual enclosure: that of the privileges granted and the regulations imposed which channelled contacts and made passage through intermediaries compulsory. The wall both protected and enclosed (Revault, 1984). In general, the mistrust or, at least, the ambivalent attitude of the authorities towards those who move is reflected in a whole set of practices whose modifications are indications of societal evolution.

Thresholds

Entering a city is a real initiation rite, through which the recognition of differ-ences takes place. It is the moment of a double identification: of the place by the traveller, and of the traveller by the others. In some societies, the arrival of the foreigner even gives rise to certain rituals: duels, purifications, inter-rogations and the production of documents. Does this mean that the stranger is always viewed with suspicion, and that by entering the city, they would do it violence? Obviously, the arrival creates a world order with definition of boundaries, categorisation of people, and even new identities (Leed, 1991). Whether passing through the gates of ancient Rome, asking for a welcome at the *funduq* of the French in Aleppo in the 16th century, or that of the Turks in Venice in the 17th century, or arriving in the port of early modern Marseille, the moment of entry has a magnifying glass effect that highlights the variety of movements of populations and the welcomes reserved for them (Moatti, 2013). Depending on the time and place, the threshold to be crossed may be either at the gate or inside the city, or it may be organised in a succession of checkpoints. In early modern times, the presentation before an innkeeper was one of these thresholds, because the urban authorities required, in French cities and other European countries, that he declare the people he was lodging. In fact, if the authorities aspired to a quadrillage of the city, or aspired to, in 18th-century Europe, a police utopia of public order and happiness, realistically they had to rely on social practices and knowledge (Houte and Blanchard, 2019). The urban magistrates could only hope that the landlords would faith-fully observe the norms established by them. The concrete application of their orders depended, however, on the reliability of these intermediaries, on their experienced eye and on their relevant judgement. Not only could controls be carried out in different places, but they sometimes involved real information networks and a multitude of actions. In Greek or Roman ports, the recognition of a fiscal or economic privilege generated a whole series of verifications that attest to the existence of a port bureaucracy, but also of real 'logbooks' (Bresson, 2000). In medieval, early and modern times, in order to protect the inhabitants from 'plagues', contagions and epidemics, the authorities demanded 'health bulletins' and 'quarantine certificates', set up lazarets and quarantine stations outside the cities and ports, created screening procedures and institutions such as health offices, a protective 'cordon' which was also used by the military (Hildesheimer, 1980; Cipolla, 1986; Chase-Levensone, 2021). All this required a great deal of information, which would help to iden-tify people, but also to authenticate their documents. This information, which came from the political authorities, from corporations (leave documents for journeymen or soldiers) or from communities (certificates of Catholicity or Sephardic membership), helped to create a space for communication between the political establishment, police and social controls. According to Georg Simmel's formula the status of the 'guest who stays', that is, the resident 'foreigner', was characterised by plurality (Simmel, 1908; see also Schütz, 1944, 1945). A complex relationship of proximity and distance was established with the receiving society, which was built through successive passages and routes in the urban space, understood at the same time as social fabric, physical space and an institutional framework (Kaiser, 1999; Cerutti, 2012; Moatti, 2014).

Foreignness

An analysis of these routes and policies of reception highlights the gradations of status, which render futile any attempt to provide a unitary definition of the term 'foreigner'. The effectiveness of the word lies in its formal character, which erases the multiplicity of situations of foreignness in Mediterranean cities (metics, peregrines, *incola*, host, *aubain*, *manant*, inhabitant, bourgeois, and so on) and thus reduces the complexity of experiences and relationships. This classificatory power to include and exclude is only fully deployed in pre-modern times when the term takes on the univocal meaning of 'non-national'. The procedures of control and identification of people on the move were themselves subject to multiple logics (fiscal, demographic, political, sanitary and sometimes police) which, far from being mutually exclusive, were more often than not cumulative, creating a saturated social and cultural space. The control itself was not always the work of state authorities but also emanated from local initiatives: from antiquity to early modern times, Jewish communities constantly played this role; similarly, seasonal migration was regulated by village corporals, who made deals with large landowners and supervised movements from the mountains to the plains. The same characteristics are found in all pre-modern periods, but there is no problematic unity, nor is there a linear development until the constitution (and stabilisation) of the territorialised nation-state. In these periods, it was indeed plurality that characterised the attitude of the authorities and the populations towards the newcomer. The forms of reception varied according to political structures, and to events as well – famine, religious or political crises, and war – so that within each period several models could exist. However, in general, control was most often exercised not over the territory, but over certain categories of populations, in order to regulate trade, to protect those who held a privilege, or to maintain public order or peace.[4]

Mixed Identities and In-between

One of the essential questions raised by the study of the circulation of people is that of their integration into the host society. For a long time this question has been thought of in terms of acculturation or cultural transfers, a concept which, assuming a reciprocal relationship between two identifiable poles, does not take into account the full complexity of the subject. It is more fruitful to question the forms of cultural circulation and to identify the strategies of actors in different contexts. One of the consequences of migration has indeed been the circulation of knowledge and cultural traditions, as well as of skills. This is true of forced migration: Portuguese Sephardic Jews entered thus into contact with Romaniote (that is, Hellenised) Jews in Istanbul, and Spanish *conversos* and *Moriscos* strengthened communities of 'Andalusians' in the Maghreb who maintained their links with their countries of origin and preserved cultural traits that are found in religious and culinary practices, in music as well as in poetry. Such cultural circulation also concerned those who converted to another religion, such as the European 'renegades' in the Maghrebian ports, who maintained relationships with their relatives in Christendom, and their massive presence in the ports at the end of the 16th and the beginning of the 17th centuries favoured the practice of the lingua franca made up of Arabic, Spanish, Italian and Greek words and expressions, a mixture that changed according to place and context. Of course, speaking the same language is not speaking with the same voice, but this language, which belonged to no one, created an intercultural space of interlocution that testified to a history woven in common (Dakhlia, 2008). Cosmopolitanisation is another form of cultural mixing. The multilingual inscriptions of ancient Rome reveal how immigrants, while maintaining a link with their homeland, accumulated different identities without trying to unify them. This phenomenon, which reflects their 'imaginary ubiquity', their feeling of being part of a network that they themselves had created through their mobility, is attested to throughout the Roman Mediterranean world; this is how the Empire was able to be thought of and constructed as a global world and as a reticular system (Moatti, 2013).

CONTROLS AND MANAGEMENT OF FLOWS

Many studies have focused on the free choice of migrants or on the environmental causes of mobility, sometimes forgetting the role of political power. In fact, the migration phenomenon involves a great diversity of actors with multiple forms of negotiation between them.

A Multitude of Actors

With the case of a group expulsion, it was necessary to count and to identify, that is, to have good demographic information, which sometimes led the administrations to stagger the measures taken. This is the case with the expulsion of the *Moriscos* from 1609 to 1614 (Benitez, 2009). The organisation of the departure requires a whole range of logistics: sending commissioners, requisitioning means of transport, negotiations with foreign powers that became transit lands and host lands. Finally, even representatives of the expelled participated in the series of diplomatic negotiations necessary to settle the fate of the expelled or exiled outside the place of origin, either in another domestic territory or outside the borders. For a large-scale movement to be effective, institutional support is needed, which can be both normative and symbolic in relation to the rituals of expulsion. But the part played by social negotiation in the mechanism (the self-identification of the populations concerned, as well as their capacity for resistance or semi-clandestine organisation) is just as important. It is in the articulation between these three dimensions – technological, institutional and social – that the nature of power, and also historical ruptures, become apparent. In the Roman world, for example, although legal provisions concerning mobility multiplied during the Empire, the role of institutions was undoubtedly much weaker than social pressure. By contrast, the arsenal of norms and institutions of the early modern Spanish monarchy was pioneering, even if here again social negotiation played a role, as shown by the tolerance of the authorities with regard to fraud or even the granting of exemptions. Negotiation is also a question of relations between political communities, as such relations are not only of predation or domination, but also of reciprocity. In Hellenistic times, for example, the recruitment of mercenaries by a city gave rise to an agreement with their metropolis, which maintained links with them during their service, even to the point of controlling their return or the movement of their families (Chaniotis, 2004). In ancient republican Italy, despite a certain fluidity in terms of mobility, the cities sometimes tried to define the conditions of legal emigration (Broadhead, 2004). Negotiation could also concern the status of the displaced population. In the Middle Ages, mercenaries in Islamic countries, sent to the Maghreb as a result of unequal agreements between the Spanish and Muslim powers, were partly under the authority of the sultan, but partly under that of their king (Lopez-Perez, 2014).

Freedom of Movement: A Negotiated Privilege?

Trade regulations were another area of negotiation, especially since trade or work demands were one of the main causes of mobility (MacMullen, 1974). They could take the form of peace treaties with economic clauses or bilateral trade agreements, which aimed to establish the security of trade or offered relief from taxes on goods; this took place between Greek cities and between Carthage and Rome, which, as early as the 6th century BCE, provided their respective nationals with a public guarantee on their goods and transactions (Bresson, 2005). They could also be unilateral agreements, such as the 'Capitulations' of the early modern era, which the Ottomans conceived as a *firmân*, a revocable grace granted by the sultan to Europeans. Thus, in the Mediterranean, the control of goods implied the control of men. These examples reveal the very subtle link between freedom and control. Granting merchants the freedom to trade was a way of providing them with a certain guarantee, but also of monitoring them. Thus, in order to sell their goods freely in Muslim countries, Westerners in medieval times first had to unload them in ports with customs, pay taxes and obtain a receipt, a veritable safe-conduct (Valérian, 2004), a procedure reminiscent of the clauses of the Romano–Carthaginian treaties. However, 'international' negotiation was not only an instrument of external regulation: it could also have an internal impact, depending on the period, favouring the control by a state of its own nationals. In the 16th century, in order to trade with the Maghreb, Spanish merchants had to apply for royal permission: this trade functioned as a permanent exception and the fee to be paid to obtain permission can be interpreted as a tax on a specific sector of trade. Thus, the economic privilege was a source of profit, while being a form of both surveillance and protection (Corrales, 2001).

CONCLUSION: THE MEDITERRANEAN AS A SPACE OF FREEDOM?

It is necessary to imagine what it meant, in these Mediterranean societies, to leave one's homeland and incur risks on the roads and in the cities. The 'right of seizure' or 'right of reprisal' on a foreigner, for example, was exercised from antiquity to early modern times, either in a private context, when a creditor obtained the right to seize the goods of a foreigner, because the latter belonged to the same homeland as the debtor who had fled; or in a public context, when a state made the nationals of another state pay for the injustices committed by their sovereign – what Jaucourt calls in the *Great Encyclopedia* an 'imperfect war' (Timbal, 1958; Bravo, 1980). Hence the need for the foreigner to be protected by privileges. Whether a question of the aftermath of war, the right to migrate, the establishment of commercial relations or embassies, a secure space was opened up by negotiations. This partially explains why the right of seizure disappeared under the Roman Empire. The Roman territory had indeed been constituted following victories and agreements, most often unilateral, under the terms of which conquered countries became provinces and their free inhabitants have become peregrines, that is to say submitted and identified foreigners. In this space based on different forms of negotiation, human circulation could seem fluid. In pre-contemporary Mediterranean societies, fluidity was always linked to the existence of regulations. For goods, freedom of movement meant immunity, but sometimes also constraints: the medieval *Stapelrecht* (right of storage), for example, obliged the passing merchant to offer his goods to the urban market; for people, it was most often synonymous with control and guarantees. Thus, freedom of movement was most often experienced in the Mediterranean not as a characteristic of free men, even less as a subjective right, but as a positive right, regulated by a set of institutions and whose recognition was in no way based on a natural principle, nor on simple norms, but on negotiation. It is the analysis of this mode of interaction and its transformation over the centuries that allows us to understand the evolution of societal practices and the phenomenon of migration, their historicity, that is to say their discontinuity.

ACKNOWLEDGEMENT

This chapter is a modified and expanded version of a previous article: "Mobilità umana e circolazione culturale nel Mediterraneo dall'età classica all'età moderna", In Corti P and Sanfilippo M. ed. *Migrazioni*. Storia d'Italia. Annali 24. Torino, Einaudi. (2009:5–20).

NOTES

1. Philip Curtin (1984), for example, a specialist in the slave trade in the early modern Atlantic space, used the concept of trade diasporas to trace the history of these communities of merchants who, although spatially dispersed, formed a nation distinct from both the society of origin and the host societies where they were settled and where they played the role of 'cultural mediators'.
2. In the various treaties known in the Mediterranean of the first millennium, three common features can be found: the limitation of foreign trade to specific zones, which also corresponds to the practice of the Greek emporia; the control of trade by the local authorities, and the public guarantee given to this trade; the protection of foreigners, especially shipwrecked people. These measures were intended to remedy all forms of violence: piracy, kidnapping or land grabbing, but also the despoiling of the shipwrecked. Negotiations thus created a Mediterranean order that made it possible to secure trade.
3. An African inscription from the 3rd century CE (CIL VIII 11824), recalls in the first person the social promotion of a peasant who, born poor and of low status, was a seasonal worker in Numidia for 12 years, then a hirer of men ('for eleven years I commanded teams of harvesters'), then a landowner and a notable. See also Tacoma (2016: Ch. 6).
4. Such are some of the conclusions of the programme '*La mobilité des personnes en Méditerranée. Procédures de contrôle et documents d'identification*', directed by Claudia Moatti and Wolfgang Kaiser.

REFERENCES

Aparicio, Á. (2006). *Europa en el mercado español. Mercaderes, represalias y contrabando en el siglo XVII*. Junta de Castilla y León: Consejería de Cultura y Turismo.
Arnaud, P. (2005). *Les routes de la navigation antique – Itinéraires en Méditerranée et Mer Noire*. Paris: Editions Errance.

Bade, K.J. (2002). Europa in Bewegung: Migration vom späten 18. Jahrhundert bis zur Gegenwart (München). *International Review of Social History*, 47 (1): 115–116.

Badie, B. (1995). *La fin des territoires. Essai sur le désordre international et sur l'utilité sociale du respect*. Paris: Fayard.

Balard, M. (2006). *La Méditerranée médiévale. Espaces, itinéraires, comptoirs*. Paris: Picard.

Balard, M. and Picard, C. (2014). *La Méditerranée au Moyen Âge, les hommes et la mer*. Paris: Hachette supérieur.

Benitez, R. (2009). La monarquía hispánica y el control de los moriscos expulsados (1609–1614). In Moatti, C., Kaiser, W. and Pébarthe, C. (eds), *Le monde de l'itinérance en Méditerranée, de l'Antiquité à l'époque moderne. Procédures de contrôle et d'identification*. Bordeaux: Ausonius Éditions, pp. 497–514.

Bravo, B. (1980). Sylan. Représailles et justice privée contre des étrangers dans les cités grecques. Étude du vocabulaire et des institutions. *ASNP*, 10: 675–987.

Bresc, H. (2004). Iles et tissu connectif de la Méditerranée médiévale. *Médiévales*, 47: 123–138.

Bresson, A. (2000). *La cité marchande*. Bordeaux: Ausonius Publications.

Bresson, A. (2005). Les accords romano-carthaginois. In Moatti, C. and Kaiser, W. (eds), *Gens de passage en Méditerranée, de l'Antiquité à l'époque moderne*. Aix-en-Provence: Maisonneuve & Laros, pp. 649–676.

Broadhead, W. (2004). Rome and the mobility of the Latins. In Moatti, C. (ed.), *La mobilité des personnes de l'Antiquité à l'époque moderne. Procédures de contrôle et documents d'identification*. Rome: Ecole Française, pp. 315–335.

Broodbank, C. (2013). *The Making of the Middle Sea: A History of the Mediterranean from the Beginning to the Emergence of the Classical World*. London: Thames & Hudson.

Brun, J.-P. (1996). La grande transhumance à l'époque romaine. *Anthropozoologica*, 24: 31–44.

Buti, G. (2005). Entre échanges de proximité et trafics lointains: le cabotage en Méditerranée aux XVIIe et XVIIIe siècles. In Cavaciocchi, S. (ed.), *Ricchezza del Mare, Ricchezza dal Mare, secc. XIII–XVIII*, vol. 1. Firenze: Le Monnier, pp. 287–316.

Canny, N. (ed.) (1994). *Europeans on the Move: Studies on European Migration, 1500–1800*. Oxford: Oxford University Press.

Cardete, M.C. (2019). Long and short distance transhumance in Ancient Greece: the case of Arcadia. *Oxford Journal of Archaeology*, 38 (1): 105–121, doi: https://doi.org/10.1111/ojoa.12162.

Cavaciocchi, S. (ed.) (1994). *Le migrazioni in Europa, secc. XIII–XVIII. Atti de la Venticinquesima settimana di studi, 3–8 maggio 1993*. Firenze: Mondadori Education.

Cerutti, S. (2012). *Etrangers. Étude d'une condition d'incertitude dans une société d'Ancien Régime*. Paris: Bayard.

Chaniotis, A. (2004). Mobility of persons during the Hellenic Wars: state control and personal relations. In Moatti, C. (ed.), *La mobilité des personnes de l'Antiquité à l'époque moderne. Procédures de contrôle et documents d'identification*. Rome: Ecole Française, pp. 481–500.

Chase-Levensone, A. (2021). Sanitary cordons, national borders, and continental frontiers in the early nineteenth century Mediterranean. In Moatti, C. and Chevreau, E. (eds), *L'expérience de la mobilité, de l'antiquité nos jours, entre précarité et confiance*. Bordeaux: Ausonius, pp. 265–280.

Cipolla, C.M. (1986). *Contro un nemico invisibile: epidemie e strutture sanitarie nell'Italia del Rinascimento*. Bologna: Il Mulino.

Cohen, R. (2008). *Global Diasporas: An Introduction*. New York and London: Routledge.

Concina, E. (1997). *Fondaci. Architettura, arte e mercatura tra Levante, Venezia e Alemagna*. New York: Universe Publishing.

Constable, O.R. (2004). *Housing the Stranger in the Mediterranean World: Lodging, Trade, and Travel in Late Antiquity and the Middle Ages*. Cambridge: Cambridge University Press.

Corrales, M.E. (2001). *Comercio de Cataluña con el Mediterráneo musulmán (siglos XVI–XVIII). El comercio con los enemigos de la fe*. Barcelona: Edicions Bellaterra.

Costello, E. and Svensson, Eva (eds) (2018). *Historical Archaeologies of Transhumance across Europe*. New York and London: Routledge.

Curtin, P.D. (1984). *Cross-Cultural Trade in World History*. Cambridge: Cambridge University Press.

Dakhlia, J. (2008). *Lingua franca. Histoire d'une langue métisse en Méditerranée*. Arles: Actes Sud.

Darwin, J. (2008). *After Tamerlane: The Global History of Empire Since 1405*. New York: Bloomsbury Publishing.

De Almeida Mendes, A. (2008), Les réseaux de la traite ibérique dans l'Atlantique nord (1440–1640). *Annales. Histoire, sciences sociales*, 63 (4): 737–768.

De Charruca, J. (2001). Le commerce comme élément de civilisation chez Strabon. *Revue internationale des droits de l'Antiquité*, 48: 41–56.

Delgado, A. (2017). Migrations phéniciennes vers l'Extrême-Occident: communautés de diasporas et groupes familiaux. In Garcia, D. and Le Bras, H. (eds), *Archéologie des migrations*. Paris: La Découverte, pp. 183–197.

De Souza, P. (2000). Western Mediterranean ports in the Roman Empire. *Journal of Mediterranean Studies*, 10: 229–254.

De Vries, J. (2003). Connecting Europe and Asia: a quantitive analysis of the Cape-route trade, 1497–1795. In de Vries, J., Flynn, D.O., Giráldez, A. and von Glahn, R. (eds), *Global Connections and Monetary History, 1470–1800*. Aldershot: Ashgate, pp. 35–106.

Ducellier, A. et al. (eds.) (1992) *Les chemins de l'exil. Bouleversements de l'est européen et migrations vers l'ouest à la fin du Moyen âge*. Paris: Armand Colin.

Erdkamp, P. (2016). Seasonal labour and rural–urban migration in Roman Italy. In de Ligt, L. and Tacoma, L.A. (eds), *Migration and Mobility in the Early Roman Empire*. Leiden: Brill, pp. 33–49.

Faroqhi, S., McGowan, B. and Pamuk, S. (eds) (1994). *An Economic and Social History of the Ottoman Empire, 1300–1914*. Cambridge: Cambridge University Press.

Fauchon-Claudon, C. and Le Guennec, M. A. (2021). Mobilités, accueil et hiérarchies sociales dans l'Occident romain tardo-antique (IVe–VIe siècles). *Revue Historique*, 697(1): 159–183, doi: https://doi.org/10.3917/rhis.211.0159#xd_co_f=NTc2MGY0 NTUtNWM0ZS00MGIyLThkNDktZDM5ZThjNTE1YTJi~.

Fontaine, L. (1993). *Histoire du colportage en Europe, XVe–XIXe siècle*. Paris: Albin Michel.

Fontaine, L. (2008). L'économie morale. Pauvreté, crédit et confiance et l'Europe pré-industrielle. Paris: Gallimard.

Gambash, G. (2016). Between mobility and connectivity in the Ancient Mediterranean: coast-skirting travelers in the Southern Levant. In Lo Cascio, E. and Tacoma, L.E.

(eds), *The Impact of Mobility and Migration in the Roman Empire*. Leiden and Boston: Brill, pp. 155–172.

Garcia Arenal, M. and Wiegers, G. (2003). *A Man of Three Worlds: Samuel Pallache, a Moroccan Jew in Catholic and Protestant Europe*. Baltimore, MD, USA and London, UK: JHU Press.

Gastaut, Y. (2016). Migration. In Albera, D., Crivello, M. and Tozy M. (eds), *Dictionnaire de la Méditerranée*. Arles: Actes Sud, pp. 934–938.

Goitein, S.D. (1967). *A Mediterranean Society. 1 Economic Foundation*. Berkeley, CA: University of California Press.

Goldberg, J. (ed.) (2012). *Trade and Institution in the Medieval Mediterranean. The Geniza Merchants and their Business World*. Cambridge: Cambridge University Press.

Guarracino, S. (2007). *Mediterraneo: immagini, storie e teorie da Omero a Braudel*. Milano: Bruno Mondadori.

Haley, Evan W. (1991). *Migration and Economy in Roman Imperial Spain*. Barcelona: Edicions Universitat Barcelona.

Handley, M. (2011). *Dying on foreign shores. Travel and Mobility in the Late-Antique West*, JRA Supplementary Series, 86: 75–78.

Hanna, N. (1998). *Making Big Money in 1600. The Life and Times of Isma,il Abu Taqiyya, Egyptian Merchant*. Syracuse: Syracuse University Press.

Heather, P. (2017). Refugees and the Roman Empire. *Journal of Refugee Studies*, 30 (2): 220-242, doi: https://doi.org/10.1093/jrs/few020.

Hildesheimer, F. (1980). *Le Bureau de la santé de Marseille sous l'Ancien régime*. Marseille: Fédération historique de Provence.

Hin, S. (2013). *The Demography of Roman Italy: Population Dynamics in an Ancient Conquest Society (201 BCE - 14 CE)*. Cambridge, UK and New York, USA: Cambridge University Press.

Hitchner, B.V. (2012). Roads, integration, connectivity and ecoperformance in the Roman Empire. In Alcock, S., Bodel, J. and Talbert, R. (eds), *Highways, Byways, and Road System in the Pre-modern World*. Chichester: John Wiley & Sons, pp. 222–234.

Hoerder, D. (2002). *Cultures in Contact: World Migrations in the Second Millennium*. Durham, NC, USA and London, UK: Duke University Press.

Horden, P. and Purcell, N. (2000). *The Corrupting Sea: A Study of Mediterranean History, A Corrupted Sea*. Oxford: Oxford University Press.

Houte, A.-D. and Blanchard, E. (2019). *Histoire des polices en France*. Paris: Belin.

Kaiser, W. (1999). Récits d'espace. Présence et parcours d'étrangers à Marseille au XVIème siècle. In Bottin, J. and Calabi, D. (eds), *Les étrangers dans la ville. Minorités et espace urbain du bas Moyen Âge à l'époque moderne*. Paris: Les Editions de la MSH, pp. 209–312.

Kaiser, W. (2008a). Mediterrane Welt. In Jaeger, F. (ed.), *Enzyklopädie der Neuzeit*. Stuttgart: Springer-Verlag, pp. 249–60.

Kaiser, W. (ed). (2008b). *Le commerce des captifs. Les intermédiaires dans l'échange et le rachat des prisonniers en Méditerranée, XVe–XVIIe siècles*. Roma: Ecole Française de Rome.

Lahon, D. (2005). Black African slaves and freedmen in Portugal during the Renaissance: creating a new pattern of reality. In Earle, T.F. and Lowe, K.J.P. (eds), *Black Africans in Renaissance Europe*. Cambridge: Cambridge University Press, pp. 261–279.

Lassère, J.M. (1977). Vbique Populus. *Peuplement et mouvements de population dans l'Afrique romaine de la chute de Carthage à la fin de la dynastie des Sévères (146 av. J.-C.–235 ap. J.-C.)* (Vol. 1, No. 1). Paris: Éditions du CNRS, pp. 626–643.

Lassère, J.-M. (2006). La mobilité de la population. Migrations individuelles et collectives dans les provinces occidentales du monde romain. In Akerraz, A., Ruggeri, P., Siraj, A. and Vismara, C. (eds), *L'Africa Romana. Mobilità delle persone e dei popoli, dinamiche migratorie, emigrazioni ed immigrazioni nelle province occidentali dell'Impero romano*. Roma: Carocci, pp. 57–92.

Leed, E.J. (1991). *The Mind of the Traveler: From Gilgamesh to Global Tourism*. New York: Basic Books.

Lefebvre, S. (2006). Les migrations des *Africani* en péninsule ibérique: quelle vérité? In Demougin, S. and Caballos Rufino, A. (eds), *Migrare: la formation des élites dans l'Hispanie romaine*. Bordeaux: Diffusion de Boccard, pp. 101–150.

Lestringant, F. (2002). *Le Livres des Îles. Atlas et récits insulaires de la Genèse à Jules Verne*. Genève: Librairie Droz.

Lopez-Perez, M.D. (2014). La movilidad de la guerra: mercenarios cataloaragoneses en las luchas maghrebíes (ss. XIII–XIV). In Moatti, C. (ed.), *La mobilité des personnes en Méditerranée de l'Antiquité à l'époque moderne: procédures de contrôle et documents d'identification*. Roma: École française de Rome, pp. 399–423.

Lucassen, J. (1999). *Migration, Migration History, History: Old Paradigms and New Perspectives*. Bern: P. Lang.

MacMullen, R. (1974). *Roman Social Relations, 50 BC to AD 284*. London: Yale University Press.

Malkin, I. (2011). *A Small Greek World: Networks in the Ancient Mediterranean*. Oxford: Oxford University Press.

Mastino, A. (1985). Le relazioni tra Africa e Sardegna in età romana: inventario preliminare. *L'Africa romana*, II: 27–89.

Mazower, M. (2007). *Salonica, City of Ghosts. Christians, Muslims and Jews 1430–1950*. London: Vintage.

Moatti, C. (2013). Immigration to Rome. In Erdkamp, P. (ed.), *The Cambridge Companion to Ancient Rome*. Cambridge: Cambridge University Press, pp. 77–92.

Moatti, C. (2014). Mobility and Identity between the second and the fourth centuries: the cosmopolitization of the identities in the Roman Empire. In Rapp, C. and Drake, Harold A. (eds), *The City in the Classical and post-Classical World: Changing Contexts of Power and Identity*. Cambridge: Cambridge University Press, pp. 130–152.

Moatti, C. (2018). Migration and mobility in the Roman world: new concepts and new catégorie. In Yoo, J., Zerbini, A. and Barron, C. (eds), *Migration and Migrant Identities in the Near East from Antiquity to the Middle Ages*. London: Routledge, pp. 12–28.

Moatti, C. (ed.) (2021). *La Méditerranée introuvable*. Paris: Karthala.

Modéran, Y. (2004). L'établissement des barbares sur le territoire romain à l'époque impériale. In Moatti, Claudia (ed.), *La mobilité des personnes en Méditerranée, de l'Antiquité à l'époque moderne. Procédures de contrôle et documents d'identification*. Roma: Ecode française de Rome, pp. 337–397.

Monge, M. and Muchnik, N. (2019). *L'Europe des diasporas (XVIe–XVIIIe siècles)*. Paris: PUF.

Morley, N. (2007). *Trade in Classical Antiquity*. Cambridge: Cambridge University Press.

Morris, I. (2005). Mediterraneanization. In Malkin, I. (ed.), *Mediterranean Paradigms and Classical Antiquity*. London and New York: Routledge, pp. 30–55.

Nörr, D. (2009). Terminologia giuridica predecemvirale e ius mercatorum mediterraneo. In Humbert, M. (ed.), *Le dodici tavole. Dai decemviri agli umanisti*. Pavia: IUSS Press, pp. 138–189.

Perrot, J.C. (1992). *Une histoire intellectuelle de l'économie politique (XVIIe–XVIIIe siècle)*. Paris: Éditions de l'École des hautes études en sciences sociales.

Pizzorusso, G. (2009). I movimenti migratori in Italia in antico regime. In Bevilacqua, P., De Clementi, A. and Franzina, E. (eds), *Storia delle emigrazione italiana*. Partenze. Roma-Bari: Dedalo, pp. 3–16.

Portes, A. (1987). The social origins of the Cuban enclave economy of Miami. *Sociological Perspectives*, 30 (4): 340–372, doi: https://doi.org/10.2307/1389209.

Raggio, O. (1990). *Faide e parentele: lo stato genovese visto dalla Fontanabuona*. Torino: Einaudi.

Revault, J. (1984). *Le Fondouk des Français et les consuls de France à Tunis (1660–1860)*. Paris: Editions Recherches sur les civilisations.

Riva, C. (2010). Trading settlements and the materiality of wine consumption in the North Tyrrhenian Sea region. In Knapp, A.B. and Van Dommelen, P. (eds), *Material Connections: Mobility, Materiality and Mediterranean Identities*. London: Routledge, pp. 210–232.

Russo, S. and Salvemini, B. (2007). *Ragion pastorale, ragion di Stato. Spazi dell'allevamento e spazi dei poteri nell'Italia di età moderna*. Roma: Viella Libreria Editrice.

Safran, W. (1991). Diasporas in modern societies: myth of homeland and return. *Diasporas*, 1 (1): 83–99, doi: https://doi.org/10.3138/diaspora.1.1.83.

Safran, W. (1999). Comparing diasporas: a review essay. *Diasporas*, 9 (3): 255–291, doi: https://doi.org/10.3138/diaspora.8.3.255.

Salvemini, B. (2007). Far negozio senza informazioni. 'Marinai' pugliesi nell'Adriatico settecentesco. In Kaiser, W. and Salvemini, B. (eds), *Informazioni e scelte economiche. Quaderni storici*, 124 (1): 155–203.

Schütz, A. (1944). The stranger: an essay in social psychology. *American Journal of Sociology*, 49 (6): 499–507.

Schütz, A. (1945). The homecomer. *American Journal of Sociology*, 50 (5): 369–376.

Simmel, G. (1908). Exkurs über den Fremden. In Simmel, G., *Soziologie: Untersuchungen Uber Die Formen Der Vergesellschaftung*. Leipzig: Duncker & Humblot, pp. 256–304.

Stone, D. (2014). Africa in the Roman Empire. *American Journal of Archaeology*, 118 (4): 565–600, doi: https://doi.org/10.3764/aja.118.4.0565.

Tabak, F. (2008). *The Waning of the Mediterranean, 1550–1870: A Geohistorical Approach*. Baltimore, MD: JHU Press.

Tacoma, L.E. (2016). *Moving Romans: Migration to Rome in the Principate*. Oxford: Oxford University Press.

Tagliafico, M. (1995). La deportazione degli Achei a Roma nel 167 a.C. In Sordi, M. (ed.), *Coercizione e mobilità umana nel mondo antico. Vita e pensiero*, 61, pp. 215–223.

Timbal, P.C. (1958). *Les lettres de marque dans le droit de la France médiévale*. Bruxelles: Université libre de Bruxelles.

Valérian, D. (2004). Le fondouk, instrument du contrôle sultanien sur les marchands étrangers dans les ports musulmans (XIIe–XIVe siècles). In Moatti, C. (ed.), *La mobilité des personnes de l'Antiquité à l'époque moderne. Procédures de contrôle et documents d'identification*. Rome: Ecole Française, pp. 677–698.

Valérian, D. (2019). *Ports et réseaux d'échanges dans le Maghreb medieval*. Madrid: EAN.

Wilson, A. (2015). Red-sea trade and the State. In de Romanis, F. and Maiuro, M. (eds), *Across the Ocean: Nine Essays on Indo-Mediterranean Trade*. Leiden, Netherlands and Boston, MA, USA: Brill, pp. 13–32.

Woolf, G. (2013). Female mobility in the Latin West. In Hemelrijk, E. and Woolf, G. (eds), *Women and the Roman City in the Latin West*. Boston and Leiden: MA, pp. 351–368.

Zeller, O. (2003). La ville moderne, in Pinol, J.L (ed) *Histoire de l'Europe urbaine*, vol. 1: De l'Antiquité au XVIIIe siècle (Paris 2003), pp. 593-858.

Zelinsky, W. (1971). The hypothesis of the mobility transition. *Geographical Review*, 61 (2): 219–249.

2. Migration and otherness in the Mediterranean region: colonial past and postcolonial continuities through the conception of the 'Other Moor'

María-Jesús Cabezón-Fernández

INTRODUCTION

The Mediterranean region is a complex web of cultures that have to some extent been in contact, dialogue and conflict for centuries. Since colonial times, migration flows have contributed to creating this cosmopolitan cara-vanserai (Ribas-Mateos, 2016), where processes of othering have taken place throughout this period in which cultural differences have been used as a marker to articulate the identity of the 'Other' in contrast to the 'Us', Occident and Orient. The West's collective imagination regarding the 'Other' Muslim, Arab or Maghrebi, can be analysed through the lens of postcolonial studies and Orientalism, for which a large body of academic literature exists in English and French due to the colonial past of these countries in Africa. Nevertheless, this theoretical approach was received in Spain 'more as a way of dealing with new "English" literature than as a critical tool' in the 'Anglo(Euro)centric' view (Fernández Parrila, 2018: 229–230). The historical relationships developed between Spain, Morocco and Algeria have led to a 'domestic' vision of the Orient. Is a specifically Spanish form of Orientalism, but above all, a particular conception of the 'Other Moor' ('Moor' being a term commonly used in Spain for Muslims, and individuals who come from an Arab country or from North Africa).

The focus of academic study, both in Spain and internationally, concerns the historical relations between Spain and Morocco, and to a lesser extent, those between Spain and Equatorial Guinea. Less research has focused on the historical exchange between Spain and Algeria. Scholars are currently revisiting these colonial exchanges and their imprint on processes of the hybridisation of identity (Aixelà-Cabré, 2019, 2020), otherness (Mateo Dieste, 2017), and on cultural legacy and its recreation. It can be seen from research into migration in Spain that the concept of the 'Moor' as an artificial category to homogenise the Maghrebi population, its culture and religion, still operates as part of a colonial discourse designed to reproduce social inequalities due to supposed cultural differences. For instance, such supposed differences are evident when analysing media discourse on Maghrebi migrants (women, unaccompanied minors, and so on), in terms of adaptation to the Spanish education system by adolescent migrants and hate speech discourse.

The aim of this chapter is to highlight the power of the postcolonial theoretical approach as a critical tool in analysing the social inequalities that are present on both shores of the Mediterranean and in processes of othering regarding the articulation of the cultural identity of the 'Other Moor'. The chapter begins with a reflection on the postcolonial approach and its usefulness in analysing migration flows in the Mediterranean region, through the analysis of Spanish Orientalism. In particular, I focus on the line of research from postcolonial scholars that understands postcolonial continuities operating not only in regions with a colonial past, but also in those without processes of colonisation or shorter periods, as happened between Spain and Algeria. Next, I analyse the articulation of the collective imagination of the 'Other Moor', and to a lesser extent the 'Other Spaniard', through historical exchanges. Finally, the chapter offers some reflections on postcolonial continuities based on the prevalence of the cultural stereotypes that exist of the Maghrebi population in Spain.

A BRIEF INTRODUCTION TO THE POSTCOLONIAL APPROACH IN MIGRATION STUDIES

Over the past few decades, critical scholars from various fields have recovered Colonialism as a fundamental theoretical framework with which to analyse the social inequalities operating in the world-system. Colonialism and postcolonialism (from Anglo-Saxon and French academia), and the decolonial turn (its variant in Latin America, and to a lesser extent in Spain) state that the intertwining of colonies, caused by their colonial past, continues to promote colonial continuities to this day. In other words, postcolonial continuities, which form the basis of neo-colonialism, are derived from the neoliberal economic system implemented across most regions of the world.

At the end of the 1970s and the beginning of the 1980s, when anti-discrimination movements addressing race and/or gender inequalities flourished, postcolonial studies started to offer an approach that was more representative. The term 'postcolonial' itself has weathered many changes, primarily due to the debate around what is understood by the term, with much focus given to definitions of the suffix 'post' (Omar, 2008). The difficulties in labelling the discipline, which focuses on the impact, transformation and reshaping of colonialism in the current context, has given rise to other terms such as 'neo-colonialism', or even the use of 'colonialism' instead of 'postcoloni-alism', to maintain the idea that the colonial processes which began in the past have never ended and still remain intact today. In the same vein, Coles and Walsh, quoting Said (1978), state that the representations of nations and social traits are built upon 'collective imaginations about cultural identity and difference' through 'binary and hierarchical oppositions' (Coles and Walsh, 2010: 1318).

One interesting contribution to postcolonial studies which addresses the continuities of colonial powers currently operating in the global context is the 'colonial matrix of power' formulated by Tlostanova and Mignolo (2009). These scholars argue that since 1492, colonial power has been developed around four key elements which remain present in the era of 'global coloni-ality' (Mignolo, 2000). They identify four categories that operate in all inter-connected spheres of daily life, stating that 'in each sphere there are struggles'. These consist of:

> 1) The control of the economy; 2) The control of authority; 3) The control of the public sphere – among other ways, through the nuclear family (Christian or bour-geois), and the enforcing of normative sexuality and the naturalization of gender roles in relation to the system of authority and principles regulating economic practices; [and] 4) The control of knowledge and subjectivity through education and colonizing the existing knowledges, which is the key and fundamental sphere of control that makes domination possible. (Tlostanova and Mignolo, 2009: 135).

Postcolonial continuities have also been analysed at the local level, as a way of considering the role of the dominated in the process of domination through their daily practices in the public and private spheres. Such issues are addressed by means of the study of postcolonial discourses (Bhabha, 1994; Said, 1978; Young, 2003), in which scholars maintain that colonialism structured societies and implemented hierarchies within them based not only on economic and political power struggles, but also on a discourse of domination. This discourse 'was legitimised by anthropological theories which increasingly portrayed the peoples of the colonised world as inferior, childlike, or feminine, incapable of looking after themselves' (Young, 2003: 2). Referring to the colonised pop-ulations in such terms was the basis for shaping an imaginary of the 'Other' at which colonisers looked in order to create a superior self-identification. In a similar vein, following on from Foucault's theories about the term 'dis-course', Said (1978) developed the idea of the 'colonial discourse', referring to statements created to enhance colonial legitimacy, and which transform ways of thinking into social practices that perpetuate the hierarchies of power.

Orientalism (Said, 1978) is a key work on the study of the construction of Europe in a dualistic relationship with the Orient, affirming that the Europe of today is a result of the tensions between the East and the West, and not exclusively a product of Western Enlightenment. Said's definition understands Orientalism to be the corpus of knowledge articulated by the imperial Europe of the 19th century to justify the processes of the colonisation of territories in Africa, Asia, the Arab World and Latin America. In this line of reasoning, Orientalism is a discourse which is designed to reproduce the dominant culture and to construct the identity of the 'Other' from the outside, based on the link between knowledge and power. Furthermore, the Orient is vast, and the imaginary created by Europeans is determined by their own relationships with the other 'Orient', their shared past and distinct regionalities. The discourse has a tendency towards axiomatic statements, and the creation of generalisations about Orientals and their characteristics arise from the partial vision and needs of the colonisers to formulate their own identity as colonisers. Bill Ashcroft and Pal Ahluwalia summarise this by saying that 'such objectification entails the assumption that the Orient is essentially monolithic, with an unchanging history, while the Occident is dynamic, with an active history. In addition, the Orient and the Orientals are seen to be passive, non-participatory subjects of study' (Ashcroft and Ahluwalia, 2001: 64).

When analysing postcolonial continuities from the social production of groups located in different positions in a social hierarchy, from those exerting symbolic power to those without the required capital to do so, migration flows and mobilities emerge as a key marker in transnationalising social inequalities (Ribas-Mateos and Cabezón-Fernández, 2021). This approach to the analysis of the social production of different groups at a local level is highly relevant when analysing regions that in the past formed part of a metropolis. In the Mediterranean region, the shared history and different forms of colonialism between the East and the West has configured the urban space that we know today and its social production, constructing a Mediterranean caravanserai (Ribas-Mateos, 2016).

There is a small branch of research in the Anglo-Saxon literature viewed through the postcolonial lens, that is dedicated to the postcolonial continuities and discontinuities of contemporary expatriates in the Global South. Coles and Walsh's (2010) research is an example of this, in which they summarise their findings related to cultural discourse on difference and the processes of self-identification in comparison to the (subordinated) 'other' of British expatriates in Dubai. These findings explain the deconstruction and reconstruction of hierarchies and frameworks of power between societies which are positioned respectively at the centre and the periphery of a world-system, with mainly imperial countries and colonies or ex-colonies serving to reinforce a structural inferiority based on race, gender (Fechter and Walsh, 2010: 1204), or even culture, history or religion. Korpela (2010) defines the 'colonial imagination' as 'how those involved in the colonial project defined the colonised lands and people, and such an imaginary was a very ethnocentric project' (ibid.: 1299). Korpela analyses the encounter of the 'Indian Other' in Varanasi by Westerners, who reduce their interaction with local people to the sole achievement of their goals, needs or search for 'Indian authenticity'. The term 'everyday racism', coined in 1991 by Essed, provides another way to express the result of the dichotomisation of the world and the reproduction of colonial behaviours, and was recovered by Leonard (2010) to express 'the ways in which macro-structural properties of racism intersect with, and are often produced through, the micro-inequities of daily life' (Leonard, 2010: 1250). Walsh's (2006, 2014) focus on the expatriate sense of belonging through everyday practices reflects the aims of these and other authors; a goal that arose in response to a lack of interest in expatriates and labour mobility that was manifest in early studies: to analyse the local and daily life of expatriates in their host country.

Recently, these ideas have been developed further by means of case studies carried out in other previously unresearched destinations such as Algeria and Morocco in Africa, and Mexico in Latin America. Fabbiano's (2016) research focuses on the current French trend of expatriation of individuals who have roots in Algeria and move there, motivated by a desire to deepen their knowledge of their genealogy. However, curiosity about the past does not eliminate the discourse and practices of segregation, which exist in the form of an 'us' versus 'them' mentality, reinforced by the geographical proximity of France that promotes this form of 'ephemeral settlement' (Fabbiano, 2016: 24). Similarly, in a case study carried out in Morocco, Peraldi and Terrazzoni (2016) analyse various transnational practices and the differences between French expatriates and 'settled' individuals. The profile of 'adventurers or pioneers' differs to that of the expatriated group. However, this postcolonial approach to analysing migration flows and mobilities is not common in Spain. This lack of research can be explained, to some extent, by the fact that Spain has developed its particular version of Orientalism based on the differences between the strength and administrative nature of its historical exchange with Morocco primarily, but also with Algeria, and those between Algeria and France, and the United Kingdom and India.

POSTCOLONIALISM AND THE PARADOX OF SPANISH ORIENTALISM

Spain has developed its own approach to Orientalism in relation to its long-shared history with countries in North Africa. Fernández Parrilla (2018) states that, for Spain, Said's (1978) Orientalism is not a useful category of analysis, as the norm of a 'dominant metropolitan centre ruling a distant territory' was not the case in relation to Spanish colonialism in North Africa, due to their geographical proximity. Furthermore, he states that 'this unique position of Spain, as a place that was orientalising and colonising (at the same time it was orientalised) is a complex and ambivalent situation that created (and still creates) many disorientations' or in other terms, 'disoriented postcolonialities' (Fernández Parrilla, 2018: 229) comprising what have come to be known as the 'paradoxes of Spanish Orientalism' (Hopkins and McSweeney, 2017). While this assertion was made in response to criticism of Said's *Orientalism* by Spanish academics, Said had previously addressed the issue himself, expressing this same idea in the Spanish second edition of *Orientalism* in which he highlights the relationship between Spain and Islam. López García (1990) mentions that Spanish Orientalism remained apart from European Orientalism due to its 'ethnocentric' position and sole focus on 'domestic Orientalism', being open only to those European Orientalists researching issues related to the Hispanic-Oriental past (ibid.: 24), with academics belonging to this branch declining to attend the international conferences organised across Europe, from 1873 to that held in New Delhi in 1963.

In his summary of the evolution of Spanish Orientalism, López García (2016) sets out two schools of thinking – Arabism and African studies – stating that whereas Orientalism is defined as the 'knowledge of Oriental cultures, Arabism is defined as the 'school made up of those who cultivate the Arab language and civilisation' (ibid.: 108). The scholar outlines how Arabism passed through three stages. First was the emergence of Arabism as a contraposition to the historiographic studies which have dominated the Spanish tradition of the study of history, glorifying the medieval past and the times of the Catholic monarchs in the 18th century. Arabism represented the repudiation of more than three centuries of historic triumphalism in Spain. Jose Antonio Conde is considered to be the first Spanish historian to propose this change of approach. The evolution of Arabism or the Spanish version of European Orientalism is intimately linked with the romantic literature of the 19th century, based upon travel books.

The second stage in the approach was institutional development, with the 'Arab issue' being given enhanced prominence by the liberals who promoted the study of the Arabic past of Spain and its relationship with north African countries, by criticising the collective imagination based on the 'Moor' of mainstream schools of thinking. López García highlights the words of Vicente de la Fuente, one of the critics of this new vision, saying that:

> The modern school ... is based on the vision of the Moor, or as it is said now the Arab; this figure, who in his land and Algeria is lazy, idle, a deceiver, a thief and sly, in Spain now we must draw him as a gentleman, gallant, true, a troubadour, a mystic, a poet, an artist, a farmer and even a theologian, of course of sui generis theology. (ibid.: 113)

During this period, colonial expectations also flourished in the Spanish government, which wanted to follow the Europeans' footsteps. It was in this context that the Africanist movement emerged in 1880. While at first the movement garnered members from Arabism, Arab scholars abandoned this line of research following a tendency displayed by some branches of the movement to support Spanish ideological colonial intentions in Morocco with discourses stating a need to 'promote a civilization in Morocco' combined with a pre-existing romantic and exotic view of Islam (Tofiño Quesada, 2003: 143). Parra demonstrates the extent of the presence of this representation of the Maghreb in textbooks, giving the following quote as an example: 'The Universal mission of Spain, its moral superiority, the strategic character of the Maghreb (considered vital to security and national independence)' (Parra in Neila Hernández, 2020: 8).

The third stage of the process began at the end of the 18th century when Arabism was recognised as a school of thought, and a methodology was developed with which to analyse the shared history. In 1932 the first School of Arab Studies was created under the Spanish Republic. At that time, the school focused on the 'Hispanic-Muslim cultural legacy', and later on language, culture and the promotion of international student exchanges. In Fernández Parrilla's terms, 'modern Arabism was born as a historical discipline with the fundamental aim of explaining that unique episode of Al-Andalus ... converted into Spain's "domestic Orient" (Fernández Parrilla, 2018: 233). Later, in 1975, the Autonomous University of Madrid created a new programme of studies to launch the 'contemporary trend of Arabism' in Spain (ibid.: 237). From this renewed approach, scholars have studied the different articulations of identity in the Mediterranean, from the 'Oriental periphery' (McSweeney and Hopkins, 2017: 3) in which Morocco and Algeria represent an oriental space where the identities of the 'Other' from both sides of the Mediterranean were still being reformulated. This concept is addressed in the next section.

The Articulation of the 'Other Moor' from Historical Exchanges

From the perspective of the historical relations between Spain, Morocco and Algeria, with Spain being perceived as a semi-peripheral European country, and the Maghreb as being at the periphery of Orientalism from the ethnocentric point of view of Anglo-Saxon literature, the processes of hybridisation of identity in the region are considered complicated and ambivalent (Aixelà-Cabré, 2020[1]). Martín Corrales (2004) argues that the image of the 'Other Moor' in Spain is not static but dynamic, changing according to political self-interest and context and in any given historical moment[2] (Table 2.1).

An analysis of the historic milestones attributed to, and the adjectives and nouns used to describe the traits of Moors in the literature, demonstrates

Table 2.1   *Evolution of stereotypes associated with the Moors according to Hispanic-Muslim history*

Historical period	Historical events	Traits attributed to Moors
8th to 15th century	Arrival of Muslims in Spain Reconquest (1492)	Fanaticism, savagery, cruelty, lasciviousness, fatalism, sloth
Later 15th century and 16th century	Spanish expansion to North Africa Lepanto War against Ottoman Empire	Cruelty, fearless
16th–17th centuries	Corsair conflicts Expulsion (1609)	Cruelty, fearless, pirates, vengeful, rapists, effeminate
Late 18th century–19th century	Peace and Trade treaties French colonisation of Algeria (1830) Spanish–Moroccan tensions African War (1859–1860)	Demon, barbarian, non-human (beast), savage, lazy, untruthful, misogynistic, against the Spaniards: liberator, progressive
Second half of 19th century	Melilla War (1893)	Savages against liberty, despots Dual vision of Islam: Morocco: static, against modernity Ottoman Empire: Modernity Women: exotic, mysterious, sensual, harem
20th century	French–Spanish Protectorate (1912) Annual War	Savages against liberty, despots Dual vision of Islam: Morocco: static, against modernity Ottoman Empire: Modernity Women: exotic, mysterious, sensual, harem
20th century	Spanish Civil War (1936) Moroccan Independence (1956) Ifni Sahara War (1958–1959)	Dual vision due to the Civil War and the Moroccan inclusion in the war: Fascist vision: ally, friend, sympathy Republican vision: fanatics, bloodthirsty, murderers, rapists, drunkards, traitors
20th century	Algerian Independence War (1954–1962) *Acuerdos tripartitos* (Tripartite Pacts) (1975)	Fear Moroccan: despots Saharawis: friends
21st century	Spanish–Moroccan fishing tensions Perejil Island Conflict Immigration of Algerians and Moroccans	As immigrant: delinquent, uncivil, troublesome Women: submissive to men and religion
21st century	Terrorist attacks (2004/2017) Islamophobia Immigration	As immigrant: delinquent, uncivil, troublesome Women: submissive to men and religion

Sources: Based on data published by Martín Corrales (2004), and information extracted from Aixelà-Cabré and Planet Contreras (2004), Moreras (2005), De Larramendi (2001), Moualhi (2000) and Mateo Dieste (2017).

that in general their representation has tended to be negative. This tendency derives from the needs and intentions of governments in carrying out their historical enterprises. To a large extent, the powerful influence of the Catholic Church, along with the discourse of the Spanish government during the reign of the Catholic Monarchs (who persecuted and expelled the Muslims) gave rise to a dual collective imagination in which goodness was associated with Christianity, while evil and paganism were considered analogous with Islam, thus establishing the dichotomy in the discourse around the 'Moor-Muslim' and the 'Spanish-Catholic' (De Larramendi, 2001).

The category of 'Moor' is a one that homogenises individuals from several origins and regions, regardless of whether they are Muslims. The predominance of Hispano–Moroccan relations through history has promoted this process of homogenisation which tends to lump together a vast number of cultures under the collective image of 'Moroccans', a label that would be inconceivable for Algerians, for example.

If we focus on how Oriental woman are represented in the collective imagination, a duality persists between how the women of the Ottoman Empire are seen as sensual and exotic, while at the same time being dominated by men and religion. Women are considered to be unable to decide on their own destiny, and their subjugation is represented by the burka (because all kinds of head coverings are reduced to the burka in the Spanish imaginary). Aixelà-Cabré and Planet Contreras (2004) argue that research into the role of women in Arab societies has been influenced by, on the one hand, 'prejudices like the biased vision of presupposed axioms (patriarchy, sexual complementarity in the Koran, the hijab), and, on the other hand, a constant comparison between the Arab and European cases without taking into account their different traditions' (ibid.: 150). Aixelà-Cabré and Planet Contreras outline issues on which Spanish society bases its discriminatory discourses: the clitoridectomy, the hijab and polygamy practices, and the Islamic inheritance system. According to Moualhi (2000), these Islam-related issues are misunderstood by Spaniards: the author states that 'the images released are often distorted and/or misleading … They are based on particular or superficial facts and then become generalisations' (Moualhi, 2000: 300). Aixelà-Cabré and Planet Contreras (2004) argue that the real basis for discrimination against women in North Africa is mostly due to inequalities related to status, educational and employment opportunities, and political engagement.

As previously mentioned, the image of the Moors has changed through history depending on political interests, shared economic interests and migration. They were presented as the enemy due to their desire for revenge after losing Granada and the Andalusian kingdom, while General Franco promoted an image of the Moors as friends of the regime to suit his political ends. Following the end of the Dictatorship in Spain, international relations between

Spain, Morocco and Algeria have been characterised by multiple tensions. In 1985, Spain entered the European Economic Community (EEC) agreeing to develop a foreign policy that was oriented towards the Mediterranean, since Spain was to become the 'European door to Africa'. Martín Corrales (2004) identifies three issues that heightened the negative image of the Arab-Muslim on the international arena during this period: the Arab–Israeli War, the Islamic Revolution in Iran and the increase in Arab organisations ideologically linked to radicalism. Following the end of the Cold War there has been an intentional process of bipolarisation in the international arena (De Larramendi, 2001) in which a new villain, 'the Orient', is seen as monolithic and static by the West. The continuation of the negative view of Islam, Muslims, Arabs and Moors is due to ongoing international tensions, which intensified after the terrorist attacks of 9/11 in New York, and later attacks such as those carried out in Madrid in 2004 and Barcelona in 2017. As Neila Hernández (2020: 1) states, 'old images and prejudices of the Southern Neighbourhood rose up from its centre position' and 'racism has served different purposes of domination, control and governance over the other'. This strategy of racist discourse has been adopted by Spain both during and after the dictatorship, internally and internationally. Due to the emergence of international extremist terrorism, links have been made between irregular immigration and security, and debates have been held on the integration of immigrants into Spanish society.

We can find an example even in the usage of the term 'Moor' in the present day. If we look up the term 'Moor' in the *Real Academia de la Lengua* (*RAE*) (an authoritative Spanish dictionary), it can be seen how the language continues to contain stereotypes built on the past. The term 'Moor' is defined as:

> 1. Hailing from the part of North Africa neighbouring Spain; 2. Who professes Islam; 3. Muslim who lived in Spain from the 8th century to the 15th century; 4. Person from certain islands in Malaysia; 5. Informally, a child who is not baptised; 6. Informally, a man who is jealous and possessive and who oppresses his partner; 7. Person with dark skin and black hair.[3]

A COLLECTIVE IMAGINATION FROM THE OTHER SHORE OF THE MEDITERRANEAN: THE ALGERIAN CONCEPTION OF THE 'OTHER SPANIARD'

As the aim of this book is to unveil present and historical connections in the Mediterranean to better understand the Mediterranean migratory system, at this point it is necessary to reflect on the view of Spain from the other shore of the Mediterranean: in this case, focusing on the image Algerians have of the 'Other Spaniard'. The contemporary bilateral relationships between Algeria and Spain have been grounded on economic interests (Cabezón-Fernández,

2018; Cabezón-Fernández et al., 2021). Nevertheless, during their shared history, there were other episodes that favoured a positive view of Spain in Algeria. According to Sempere Souvannavong (2007), one such period is that of the Spanish administration of the Western region of North Algeria between 1509 and 1708, and between 1732 and 1792, meaning that, surprisingly, the city of Oran was under Spanish administration longer than it was under French, Turkish or Algerian administration. This explains features of the city such as its fortresses and military urban design, and the Muslim medina in the oldest part of the city.

Here we refer to the collective imagination of the 'Other Spaniard' constructed upon memories that are 'as individual and collective narratives able to shape national, ethnic, and cultural identities' (Aixelà-Cabré, 2020: 1). Positive elements in the Algerian collective imagination of Spain come from memories from the period when Spaniards moved to an Algeria colonised by France, to repopulate the colony. From the middle of the 19th century to the beginning of the 20th century, the most numerous Spanish diaspora populations settled in the *wilaya* of Oran province. Sánchez Picón and Aznar Sánchez (2002) argue that the flows of Spaniards to Algeria resulted from economic and political instability that hit Spanish coastal regions hardest, due to the economic downturn in sectors such as agriculture and mining. The emigration of Spaniards to French Algeria was encouraged by the Spanish government from 1850 due to the emerging need of workforce in that country, the crisis in Spain, and the fear that the Spanish citizens would emigrate with their properties to the liberated nations in America (Valdés Peña, 2011: 85). This situation promoted the increase of the Spanish emigration to an extent that the phenomenon was labelled the 'Spanish threat' by the French government. These Spaniards worked as farmers, sharing spaces with the Algerians, not only in farms but also in their daily life routines. Moreover, certain Spanish nationals opened their own grocery shops in the cities. Public spaces were shared due to the settlement of this Spanish community in north-west Algeria until the beginning of the Algerian Independence War in 1954. As Sempere Souvannavong (2007) mentions, the strength of the relationship between Alicante and Oran resulted in the official twinning of the cities on 27 June 1985. This long period remains in the collective imaginary of both countries as a time of shared spaces and friendship, reinforced by the fact that the Instituto Cervantes continued to represent Spain culturally in Algeria, and the Spanish consulates in Algiers and Oran were the only ones to remain open during the Algerian Civil War, a time which resulted in the isolation of Algeria from Europe in general (Sempere Souvannavong, 2007). This collective imaginary has prevailed due to the lack of direct conflict between Spain and Algeria, which can be contrasted with the tense relations that have always existed between Spain and Morocco.

In contrast, the view of Algerians in the West has historically been that of a population of warriors, being sometimes translated into a concept of a conflictive society. Sempere Souvannavong (2007) pointed out that the several periods of conflict which the Algerian society has been through promoted an image of the Algerian as a warrior. The author quotes the French proverb, 'Moroccans are farmers, Algerians are warriors and Tunisians are women', to show popular knowledge. As mentioned elsewhere, the Algerian Independence War (1954–1962), the Civil War (1988–1999) and other events which questioned the status quo with Morocco and its allies, have given rise to the imaginary of the Algerians as a conflictive society in European countries, mainly France. Besides, the terrorist attack carried out in 1994, which resulted in its borders with Morocco being closed, intensified the image of Algerian society as conflictive. Furthermore, according to this scholar, the primary source of contemporary Algerian stereotypes in the West is the Civil War:

> The 'black decade' conflict was especially complex and misunderstood by the West, creating even more prejudices in Europe in the era of the global and digital media, mainly in France, where the Algerian issue still is a sensitive subject due to the wounds caused by the War of Independence, the 700,000 Algerian and French of Algerian origin who live in the country, and the intense and controversial relationships that both countries maintain. (Sempere Souvannavong, 2007)

In conclusion, it is worth mentioning that while in general Algerians continue to have a positive image of Spain, for many Spaniards, Algeria is an unknown country that they are sometimes unable to locate on a map, as is shown in Cabezón-Fernández and Sempere Souvannavong (2021).

SPANISH POSTCOLONIAL CONTINUITIES OF THE 'OTHER MOOR': FINAL REFLECTIONS

While the postcolonial or decolonial literature published in Spanish has not achieved the same impact as that in French or English, the use of a colonial lens to analyse social inequalities when studying migration flows is a long-standing tradition in migration studies. From a cultural approach, the academic study of the expression of otherness is impacted upon by cultural difference. The cultural traits that define the 'Other' are projected onto the whole group, essentialising the differences through hierarchical binary assumptions to position the 'Other' in an inferior position in relation to the cultural majority.

It has been demonstrated that cultural difference is in the basis of the formulation of colonial discourses articulated today in Spain towards the 'Other Maghrebi', or the 'Moor'. As mentioned at the beginning of this chapter, from the analysis of the mass media discourses, the discourses towards the non-accompanied minors and, for instance, from the analysis of the adaptation of the adolescent with a migrant background to their Spanish counterpart in the scholar system. Carrasco et al. (2009), Capote Lama et al. (2020) and Cucalón Tirado (2015) have all pointed out how the supposed and stereotyped traits of the Maghrebi families and students (in this case thinking mostly of individuals with Moroccan origin) still promote the deficit theory and other misunderstandings related to communication among the relatives of the students, the students and the professionals from the educational system. Old challenges unsolved in present times. From the results of the project FAMILIA,[4] we have corroborated that these discourses continue to be part of the articulation of the 'Other Moor' towards families and teenagers. As has been highlighted in the research from the 1990s and recent decades, professionals had taken as a cultural trait some aspects that, in reality, are a consequence of the vulnerable socio-economic position of the families with a migrant background.

Another example of the articulation of the 'Other Moor' by the Spaniards, but on the other shore of the Mediterranean Sea in North Africa, is the case of the contemporary Spanish expatriates living transnationally between Algeria and Spain (Cabezón-Fernández, 2018).[5] The economic downturn that resulted from the crisis of 2008 not only led to movements of population from the Global North to the South, with Spaniards migrating to countries such as Argentina, Mexico or Algeria, but also entailed renewed 'intra-European' emigration from Western countries to Northern countries, such as Germany, Switzerland and the United Kingdom (Lafleur and Stanek, 2017).

From the North African shore of the Mediterranean, we find a further example of the articulation of the 'Other Moor': that held by contemporary Spanish expatriates living transnationally between Algeria and Spain (Cabezón-Fernández, 2018). Despite also experiencing an economic crisis due to a decrease in the price of oil (the basis of its gross domestic product), at the time Algeria was immersed in large infrastructure construction projects, as well as investing in the development of other economic sectors to reduce dependence on petroleum. This resulted in Algeria becoming an attractive destination for Spanish and transnational companies and workers, seeking opportunities that had been exhausted in Spain (Cabezón-Fernández and Sempere Souvannavong, 2021). The transnationalisation of Spanish companies encouraged an increase in the mobility of a highly skilled group that, until then, had never moved abroad. The possibility of regular travel between the two countries promoted a circular migration process which has resulted in a minimal degree of social exchange with the local population in Algeria, one that is, in fact, merely instrumental, being oriented to business and business opportunities. Spaniards' relationships with local people are limited to the workplace and rarely enter the personal sphere.

From the discourse and rhetoric on cultural difference that Spaniards construct of the 'Other Algerian' emerge postcolonial continuities (Fechter and

Walsh, 2010). Unlike the research carried out by Yeoh and Willis (2005) into Singaporeans in China, and Korpela (2010) on Westerners in India, according to Fechter and Walsh (2010) the colonial past does not provide such a direct link between coloniser and colonised, as Spain and Algeria do not share a recent historical episode of a colonial regime. To find such a link we must look back as far as the 16th century, when the north-west region of Algeria, comprising the *wilaya* of the current city of Oran, was part of the Kingdom of Spain for almost two centuries.

Currently, in the parts of Spain where the migration that accompanied this colonisation originated from, this history is coming to the surface after years of remaining buried; whereas in the memories of some Algerians it remains fresh. Because of the long history shared between Spain, Morocco and Algeria, discourse in Spain about the 'Moor' is strongly influenced by the colonial division of societies into the Occident and the Orient. The current increase of refugee migration flows, support for extreme right-wing political parties, and the Islamophobia present in European civil society, pose the question of how the conception of the Orient will evolve in the Mediterranean region.

NOTES

1. For a wider overview on the analysis of Spanish postcolonial continuities regarding Morocco and Ecuadorian Guinea, I recommend the works by Aixelà-Cabré, and in particular, Aixelà-Cabré (2020).
2. For an in-depth insight about the articulation of the identity of the Moor, see Mateo Dieste (2017).
3. Entry available on the website of the Real Academia de la Lengua, https://dle.rae .es/moro (accessed 18 October 2021).
4. Project reference: FAMILIA – Famiglie Migranti: Interventi Locali di Inclusione Attiva, by the Fondo Asilo, Migrazione e Integrazione (2017). PI Spain: P. Pumares, University of Almeria, Spain.
5. This chapter is based on some of the information included in the doctoral thesis presented by Cabezón Fernández, M.J. (2018).

REFERENCES

Aixelà-Cabré, Y. (2019). Colonial memories and contemporary narratives from the Rif. Spanishness, Amazighness, and Moroccaness seen from Al-Hoceima and Spain. Interventions. *International Journal of Postcolonial Studies*, 21 (6): 856–873, doi: https://doi.org/10.1080/1369801X.2018.1558093.

Aixelà-Cabré, Y. (2020). Local versions and the global impacts of Euro-African memories: a revision through Spanish colonial imprints. Introduction. *Culture and History Digital Journal*, 9 (2), http://cultureandhistory.revistas.csic.es.

Aixelà Cabré, Y. and Planet Contreras, A.I. (2004). Mujer y política en el mundo árabe. Un estado de la cuestión. *Feminismo/s*, 3 (jun.): 149–159, doi: http://dx.doi.org/10 .14198/fem.2004.3.10.

Ashcroft, B. and Ahluwalia, P. (2001). Key Concepts in *Post-Colonial Studies*. London and New York: Routledge.

Bhabha, H.K. (1994). Remembering Fanon: self, psyche and the colonial condition. In Williams, P. and Chrisman, L. (eds), *Colonial Discourse and Postcolonial Theory*. London: Routledge, pp. 112–123.

Cabezón Fernández, M.J., (2018). North to South. The Spaniards' mobility strategies in Algeria in times of crisis. Postcolonial continuities from contemporary expatriates' bubbles. University of Alicante, Spain, https://rua.ua.es/dspace/handle/10045/90668.

Cabezón-Fernández, M.J., and Sempere Souvannavong, J.D. (2021). The global South as a solution to cope with the crisis: following the transnational itineraries of the precarised Spaniards towards Algeria. *Migration Studies*, 9(3): 423–444, doi: https://doi.org/10.1093/migration/mnz035.

Cabezón-Fernández, M.J., Sempere Souvannavong, J.D. and Mazouni, A. (2021). Spanish–Algerian border relations: tensions between bilateral policies and population mobilities. In Ribas-Mateos, N. and Dunn, T.J. (eds.), *Handbook on Human Security, Borders and Migration*. Cheltenham, UK and Northampton, MA, USA: Edward Elgar Publishing, pp. 250–265.

Capote Lama, A., Nieto Calmaestra, J.A. and Martín Ruiz, N. (2020). Las expectativas sobre el alumnado extranjero en un barrio periférico de Granada (España): trayectorias educativas bajo el filtro del culturalismo. *Aposta*, 85, http://hdl.handle.net/10481/61407.

Carrasco, S., Pàmies, J., and Bertrán, M. (2009). Familias inmigrantes y escuela: Desencuentros, estrategias y capital social. *Revista complutense de educación*, 20 (1), 55, https://revistas.ucm.es/index.php/RCED/article/view/RCED0909120055A.

Coles, A. and Walsh, K. (2010). From trucial state to postcolonial city? The imaginative geographies of British expatriates in Dubai. *Journal of Ethnic and Migration Studies*, 36 (8): 1317–1333, doi: https://doi.org/10.1080/13691831003687733.

Corrales, M.E. (2004). Maurofobia/islamofobia maurofilia/islamofilia en la españa del siglo XXI. *Revista CIDOB d'afers internacionals*, 66–67: 39–51.

Cucalón Tirado, P. (2015). A vueltas con la cultura: Imágenes del alumnado inmigrante en las aulas de enlace de la comunidad de Madrid (España). *Diálogo andino*, 47: 83–92.

De Larramendi, M.H. (2001). Imágenes del islam en la España de hoy. In S. Catalá and Martí, J.M. (eds.), *El Islam en España: Historia, pensamiento, religión y Derecho*. Albacete, Spain: Universidad Castilla-La Mancha, pp. 63–73.

Essed, P. (1991). *Understanding Everyday Racism: An Interdisciplinary Theory* (Vol. 2). New York: SAGE.

Fabbiano, G. (2016). 'Expats', 'settlers', and 'pioneers': contemporary mobilities, social worlds, and the postcolonial dynamics of the French in Algeria. *Autrepart*, 1: 17–33.

Fechter, A.-M. and Walsh, K. (2010). Examining expatriate continuities: postcolonial approaches to mobile professionals. *Journal of Ethnic and Migration Studies*, 36 (8): 1197–1210, doi: https://doi.org/10.1080/13691831003687667.

Fernández Parrilla, G. (2018). Disoriented postcolonialities: with Edward Said in (the labyrinth of) Al-Andalus. *Interventions*, 20(2): 229–242, doi: https://doi.org/10.1080/1369801X.2017.1403347.

Hopkins, C. and McSweeney, A. (2017). Spain and Orientalism. *Art in Translation*, 9 (1): 1–6, doi: https://doi.org/10.1080/17561310.2017.1316039.

Korpela, M. (2010). A postcolonial imagination? Westerners searching for authenticity in India. *Journal of Ethnic and Migration Studies*, 36 (8), 1299–1315, doi: https://doi .org/10.1080/13691831003687725.

Lafleur, J.M. and Stanek, M. (2017). *South–North Migration of EU Citizens in Times of Crisis*. New York: Springer Nature.

Leonard, P. (2010). Work, identity and change? Post/colonial encounters in Hong Kong. *Journal of Ethnic and Migration Studies*, 36 (8), 1247–1263.

López García, B. (1990). *Arabismo y orientalismo en España: Radiografía y diagnóstico de un gremio escaso y apartadizo*. Agencia Española de Cooperación Internacional: Universidad Nacional de Educación a Distancia.

López García, B. (2016). Los arabistas españoles 'extramuros' del orientalismo europeo (1820–1936). Revista de Estudios Internacionales Mediterráneos, 21: 107–117, http://dx.doi.org/10.15366/reim2016.21.009.

Mateo Dieste, J.L. (2017). *'Moros vienen'. Historia y política de un estereotipo*. Melilla: Instituto de las Culturas Ciudad de Melilla.

McSweeney, A. and Hopkins, C. (2017). Spain and Orientalism. *Art in Translation*, 9 (1), 1–6.

Mignolo, W.D. (2000). *La colonialidad a lo largo ya lo ancho: el hemisferio occidental en el horizonte colonial de la modernidad*. Buenos Aires: CLACSO, Consejo Latinoamericano de Ciencias Sociales

Moreras, J. (2005). ¿Integrados o interrogados? La integración de los colectivos musulmanes en clave de sospecha. In M. Hernández Pedreño & A. Pedreño Cánovas (eds.) *La condición inmigrante: exploraciones e investigaciones desde la Región de Murcia* (pp. 227-240). Murcia: Universidad de Murcia.

Moualhi, D. (2000). Mujeres musulmanas: estereotipos occidentales versus realidad social. *Papers: revista de sociologia*, 60: 291–304, doi: https://doi.org/10.5565/rev/ papers/v60n0.1044.

Neila Hernández, J.L. (2020). Imagining the Mediterranean from Spain: Orientalism and modernity in the symbolic universe of the Euro-Mediterranean partnership. *International Journal of Arts and Social Science*, 3 (1): 147–179.

Omar, S.M. (2008). *Los estudios post-coloniales. Una introducción crítica*. Castellón de la Plana, España: Universitat Jaume I.

Peraldi, M. and Terrazzoni, L. (2016). Nouvelles migrations? Les Français dans les circulations migratoires européennes vers le Maroc. *Autrepart*, 1: 69–86, doi: https://doi.org/10.3917/autr.077.0069#xd_co_f=NTc2MGY0NTUtNWM0ZS 00MGIyLThkNDktZDM5ZThjNTE1YTJi~.

Ribas-Mateos, N. (2016). Thinking circularity and gender transversality in contemporary migration. In Sole, C., Parella, S., Marti, T. and Nita, S. (eds), *Impact of Circular Migration on Human, Political and Civil Rights*. Cham: Springer, pp. 111–126.

Ribas-Mateos, N. and Cabezón-Fernández, M.J. (2021). Nuevas fronteras de la movilidad y de las migraciones: un análisis teórico-empírico. *Finisterra*, 56 (117), 253–272, doi: https://doi.org/10.18055/Finis2382.1

Said, E. (1978). *Orientalism*. London: Pantheon.

Sánchez Picón, A. and Aznar Sánchez, J.Á. (2002). Diversidad migratoria en las dos orillas del Mediterráneo. De las experiencias históricas al desafío actual. *Mediterráneo económico*, 1: 152–174.

Sempere Souvannavong, J.D. (2007). El potencial social e histórico de Argelia para la cooperación desde Alicante. Comunicación al II Congreso Internacional de Cooperación al Desarrollo. Migraciones y Codesarrollo, organizado por el Comitè

Universitari Valencià de Relacions Internacionals i Cooperació en la Universidad de Alicante.

Tlostanova, M. and Mignolo, W. (2009). Global coloniality and the decolonial option. *Kult* 6, Special Issue, 130–147.

Tofiño-Quesada, I. (2003). Spanish Orientalism: uses of the past in Spain's colonization in Africa. *Comparative Studies of South Asia, Africa and the Middle East*, 23 (1): 141–148, doi: https://doi.org/10.1215/1089201X-23-1-2-141.

Valdés Peña, A. (2011). Alicantinos en Argelia. Un viaje de ida y vuelta. *Revista de Estudios Internacionales Mediterráneos (REIM)*, 10: 82–101, http://hdl.handle.net/10486/670297.

Walsh, K. (2006). British expatriate belongings: mobile homes and transnational homing. *Home Cultures*, 3 (2), 123–144.

Walsh, K. (2014). Placing transnational migrants through comparative research: British migrant belonging in five GCC cities. *Population, Space and Place*, 20 (1): 1–17.

Yeoh, B.S. and Willis, K. (2005). Singaporeans in China: transnational women elites and the negotiation of gendered identities. *Geoforum*, 36 (2): 211–222, doi: https://doi.org/10.1016/j.geoforum.2003.07.004.

Young, R.J. (2003). *Postcolonialism – A Very Short Introduction*. Oxford: Oxford University Press.

3. The weight of colonial cultural legacy in scholarly and political discourses on migration: for a denationalisation of the migration issue

Mustapha El Miri

WHEN POLITICS INTERFERES WITH THE SCIENTIFIC DEBATE: MIGRATION AND COLONIAL STUDIES, A DIFFICULT PATH TO INDEPENDENCE

The intensity, even the violence, of the debates, polemics and controversies around the question of colonial memory and its impact on representations, as well as the place given to migrants from former colonies, reveals the extent to which colonisation and decolonisation continue to affect French society and, more broadly, Western societies. In recent years, the flow of opinion columns, appeals, accusations, denunciations, support and social mobilisations on these topics has grown to the point of blurring the boundaries between the traditional arenas of political institutions, the media, academia, non-profits, and so on. Moreover, the fact of streaming these controversies on social networks (Twitter, Facebook, YouTube, and so on) has lent them an unprecedented impact which goes far beyond the circle of usual initiates and the national framework in which they are expressed. The globalisation of social mobilisation against police violence, heralded in the United States by the Black Lives Matter and the 'woke'[1] movements, has helped to spread the debate throughout several Western countries: in the United Kingdom regarding the country's colonial and slavery past; in Canada on the fate of indigenous people and racism against Black people; in Germany, Italy, Belgium, the Netherlands, New Zealand and Australia on similar themes; and the list goes on. Far from being limited to former colonial countries, these movements have also reached countries that have no colonial history. This should remind us that colonial memory cannot be considered or analysed solely from the perspective of nation-states, as colonisation was a global phenomenon that has affected representations and social relationships on an equally global scale (Cooper, 1996, 2002, 2005).

Given this context, debates in France have either echoed or, on the contrary, opposed those occurring in the United States – a model that is both attractive and repelling, depending on the context in which our national debates take place – on colonialism, racism, secularity, universalism, 'the French republican model', versus the Anglo-American community model, minorities, multiculturalism, and so on, by reviving dichotomous points of view on colonial history (Stoler and Cooper, 2013).

The blurring of boundaries between scientific and political debates and the resulting circulation of categories used in controversies on colonial memory, their link to migration issues, racism and discrimination phenomena, ethnic and racial inequalities, Islamic terrorism and delinquency, all reveal a confusion in issues, the polarisation of perspectives and the difficult emancipation of the scientific debate from socio-political issues. The difficult extirpation of science from the political debate has also been favoured by the role played by essayists;[2] journalists and writers who have invited themselves to the debating table and often use scientific language to serve political purposes. Whether voluntarily or not, they play a part in the disqualification–requalification of scientific categories by taking great liberties with the imperative precautions of use for any scientific approach and their unavoidable contextualisation. They give common sense to categories that have undergone extensive research precisely to detach them from common sense. In fact, this qualification–requalification operation is necessary to legitimate essays that claim methodological and even scientific credibility, even though they are mainly used to engage in political debates. Such a confusion between the production of knowledge and the elaboration of an opinion has nowadays become the matrix of discussions. In this context, the scale of values is reversed, researchers are ordered to prove their axiological neutrality, whereas essayists become the bearers of a truth that no one else dares pronounce, because they challenge political correctness (Fassin, 1993). Hence, opinion bears the seal of truth, whereas knowledge can only pretend, within the arena of such debates, to analyse a circumscribed fact with limited scope. Moreover, such an inversion of the rightfulness of facts is most conspicuous in debates pertaining to 'immigration' issues, as if this were a field where researchers had never become fully independent.

This is how scientific terms referring to postcolonial, decolonial, intersectional, islamophobia, racialisation, racism and ethno-racial studies were requalified by the politico-scientific debate into categories that refer to their authors and their so-called approach: decolonial, racialist, indigenist, communitarian, anti-universalist, Americanist (promoters of American racial theories), anti-secularity, multiculturalist, promoters of 'cancel culture', going as far as anti-Enlightenment or 'Islamic-leftists'.[3] In December 2020, the

French Minister of Education declared that: 'This intellectual matrix that originated in American universities and in the intersectional theses that seek to essentialise communities and identities' was 'a breeding ground for the fragmentation of societies that converges with the Islamist model' (*Le Monde*, 21 December 2020).[4] The French President himself criticised these studies for producing an 'ethnicisation of racial issues'[5] and dividing the nation. This stance is reminiscent of President Bush's 1991 speech at a graduation ceremony of the University of Michigan in Ann Arbor (Fassin, 1993: 267). At the time, the target was the same, although it bore a different name: the 'political correctness' of anti-racists, anti-sexists, anti-homophobia that threatened universities and divided the nation; a term that has become popular since in Europe, with a semantic shift towards the fight against *la bien-pensance* (form of self-righteousness).

Hence, the political debate has completely crushed the scientific debate, allegedly to defend scientificity and freedom of speech in the face of studies on racism, racialism and postcolonialism, accused of challenging their scientific approach and the freedom to spread knowledge.

But the intensity of the conflicts around a subject that until now in France remained confined to a circle of militant intellectuals or specialists of the field, lecturing halls and academic publishers, can only be understood in terms of the link between the debate regarding colonial memory and the issue of 'immigration'. Whether in scientific or political discourse, the issue of colonial history systematically brings up the issue of migrants from former African colonies (North and sub-Saharan Africa alike). This link suggests that the manner in which the matter of colonial memory is treated conditions the place given to migrants and, in turn, conditions the institutional, legal, intellectual and social accommodations that this entails for 'native' French society. However, in a context of weakening legitimacy of political actors and ensuing authority (Rosanvallon, 2006), the field of migration is the only one where political authority can assert itself without taking too many risks. This largely explains the centrality of migration issues in the political stakes of almost all European and Western countries. Reasserting the authority of the state, the borders of the country and nation (Sayad, 1999), the primacy of modern lifestyles and the identities of Western societies are facts that are easier to express in the light of migratory control than those regarding economic issues, for example. Nowadays, immigration is one of the few areas where a political discourse – tinged with rigour – maintains the illusion of controlling borders, both geographical and in terms of identity, and still enjoys a credit of sorts among the middle and working classes (Bauman, 2016).

Hence, talking about migrations, and more particularly about 'immigrants'[6] and associated stakes in terms of 'challenges for the nation, the Republic' has become a way to build a media footprint and gain political, scientific or editorial visibility, as evidenced by best-selling essays that deal with such issues. This has bolstered the resurgence in scientific and political discourse of the assimilationist model born in the 19th century (Saada, 2005) during the colonial period. The 'French style' Republican model – revisited in the light of contemporary issues with a strong focus on identity in a context marked by terrorist attacks, the theories of civilisational war (Gilroy, 2004) and the crystallisation on 'immigration' – has once again become an ideal in need of reinforcement, even protection, according to certain politicians, academics, intellectuals, essayists and journalists.

This has resulted in a proliferation of public policies, with over 24 items of legislation passed since 1986, restricting migrants' access to the country, ruling on their conditions of settlement and integration. In addition to older measures pertaining to material and health conditions, cultural and moral conditions have emerged, including religious practices, dress (with the veil always triggering Godwin's law in debates), cultural practices, parental education, lifestyles, with some rejected amendments endeavouring to rule so-called community businesses and eating habits as well. The latest ruling, meant to reinforce the respect of the principles of the Republic and the fight against separatism, known as the Separatism Law of 2022, completes the legal arsenal for the institutional reassertion of the assimilationist model.

Thus, to study the links between colonial memory and migratory issues is to expose oneself on the 'front line' of the politico-scientific debate and to risk being caught up in it or pointed out as being responsible for the current 'French angst'. But such a risk is not only the result of the ideological reaction characterising the refusal to go over the history of the French colonial period and analyse its effects on the place of 'immigrants'; it is also the result of a long-standing and porous relationship between science and politics on these issues (Sayad, 1992, 1999).

Either the political debate uses the scientific discourse to put forth its opinions, or certain academics enter the path of political mobilisation in order to further a scientific observation that they feel has been underestimated or dominated.

However, the main observation is that the ubiquity of debates on immigration and the impact of colonisation nowadays is in marked contrast with the academic and political invisibility of such themes that prevailed up to the 1960s and 1970s in France (Tripier, 2004; Liauzu, 2000).

THE SCIENTIFIC AND POLITICAL NON-THOUGHT OF MIGRATIONS IN FRANCE

Although French sociology asserted itself through Durkheim's research on the social integration of individuals in a context where the social fact was institutionalised by the emerging structures of the republican state (education, law, social division of work), it created the illusion of the non-existence of particularities facing the integration of certain populations marked by alterity with respect to the national community (Sayad, 1997). In a way, this posture somehow discredited research on the social relations arising from the colonial system in the homeland, and their impact on the way colonised persons are viewed. The idea that this subject had been treated from the larger perspective of social integration also hid the fact that the racialist approach remained dominant in some areas of social sciences, including for disciples of Durkheim (Saada, 2005). In Durkheim's time, the 700 million colonised individuals, in a global population of 2 billion (Balandier, 2011), were always characterised as inferior races or 'souls' to be civilised. The scientific approach to migratory questions remains strongly influenced by this posture, although it has been updated in line with the current debate and contexts of our times. These studies are marked by the assimilationist perspective, whether fully acknowledged or underlying.

Only after the Second World War, at a time when France was in the midst of building a national narrative based on independence and resistance to Nazism, did the country find itself challenged by its colonial system (Fanon, 2011 [1952]). This period, when the veil of contradictions was partially lifted, opened a space to attempt the writing of another narrative. Hence, some researchers became interested in subjects that were considered as being on the fringe of French academic life at the time. 'The depreciation of the "immigrant" object (non-actor) in the field of research, linked to the social marginalisation of immigrants leads, by "contamination", to the marginali-sation of researchers interested in this specific object', Maryse Tripier (2004: 176) writes. Although nowadays it is common to refer to the work of Césaire (1950), Fanon (2011 [1952]), Memmi (1957), Guillaumin (1972) and Sayad (1978), amongst others, these authors did not enjoy the same academic standing at the time of their research and publications.

Thereby, unlike in the United States where social sciences developed through the study of immigration and its assimilation, and Germany where Simmel and Weber studied the concepts of the foreigner and ethnic groups, respectively, as Maryse Tripier (2004: 173) notes, in France this field was explored at a very late stage. This difference is not only due to the fact that migration issues are more central in American society than in France or in other European countries. It also reveals the political invisibility and academic non-thought on migrations that marked the scientific and political perspectives up to the 1970s. Gérard Noiriel made the following observation regarding the specific case of France:

> When comparing the historiographical production of France and the United States – the other major country of contemporary immigration – the contrast is striking ... Beyond the importance of the issue in historical works, what strikes the French reader is the will to present the immigration process as a problem 'internal' to American society and its past, as a constitutive element of the nation, whereas French textbooks present the opposite perspective: immigration is an 'external' issue (transient, new, marginal) that has nothing to do with the construction of France, nothing to do with the French and their past. (Noiriel, 1988: 19–20)

While there were studies and surveys regarding these issues in the 1950s and 1960s (Girard and Stoetzel, 1953), they remained limited. The idea of migrant labour that intended to 'return home' was dominant among political as well as scientific elites. The foreigner status, whether in its extra-national, identity, or even ethnic dimension, prevailed in the socio-political approach to immigration. This non-questioning of the migratory fact originated, on the one hand, in a stratified conception of the boundaries of identity between immigrants and natives; and on the other hand, in the focus on class relations in socio-political and intellectual debates, with the figurehead of the proletarian 'labourer', relegating migrants to the role of reservists and/or 'supernumerary' figures whose situation could only be grasped in relation to the central figure of the labourer. However, the presence of immigrants from Belgium, Italy, Germany, Spain and Switzerland was already perceptible at the end of the 19th century (Noiriel, 1988). In addition, one should mention the much more invisible presence of immigrants from French colonies and China who did not have access to migrant status because they were considered as indigenous people. At the time, there were close to 500 000 foreign labourers, nearly 220 000 of whom came – sometimes against their will – from various French colonies (Dornel, 2014: 53). This population was essentially composed of Algerians, Moroccans, Tunisians, Malagasy and Indochinese. Between 1914 and 1918, there were nearly 120 000 Algerians workers and 175 000 Algerian soldiers in France (Meynier and Meynier, 2011: 221).

The idea that such migrations had no impact on the host societies, and that they could only be understood through the categories of their arrival, seemed natural. European immigrants, because they were deemed assimilable (close to French culture) were set apart from the immigrants from former colonies, seen as culturally incompatible (Muslims, Asians, Blacks) with the national identity (Noiriel, 1988; Saada, 2005). The historical processes of colonisation and decolonisation strongly participated in the socio-political construction of this racial and cultural classification and segmentation applied to colonised people (Blanchard et al., 2013). Thereby, immigrants from former colonies were categorised as unskilled labourers whose settlement, both on the territory and in the national identity, was neither envisaged nor conceivable. Moreover, the massive arrival of Algerians in France in the aftermath of independence and the Evian Accords gave rise to two opposing interpretations: first summoned the psychological syndrome of 'the dependence complex' of colonised people, as theorised by Manoni (Césaire, 1950), and which supported the idea that decolonisation was a mistake, including for Algerians; the second interpretation saw in this arrival the disguised continuation of colonisation and domination of Algerians (Liauzu, 2004). However, deep down, both interpretations stemmed from the same failure to take the decolonisation of Algeria seriously, as well as from France's military defeat, hence the idea that such a mobility might in fact be the product of the freedom acquired from the former coloniser never occurred to anyone. Algerian immigrants had somehow not yet attained the status of subject per se, and they remained an object in terms of migration studies.

It was not until the 1970s that the question of North African immigration emerged in the public debate, as a public issue. Rooted in the conception of a 'labour migration', with no desire nor vocation to settle, the idea of deporting hundreds of thousands of immigrants was raised by President Giscard in 1974 (Weil and Truong, 2015). But the project came up against a reality that had remained unnoticed until then: the immigrants who had settled in France had chosen not to return to their homeland, despite the incentives of the assisted return plan implemented at the time. Nonetheless, the prevailing qualification of 'labour migration' was never challenged and continued to act as an interior boundary.

The link between migration and labour has essentially been understood unilaterally, as being a shift of labour from Southern to Northern countries. This descending conception posited that migrations were a consequence of the politics of industrialised countries and their development, viewing migrants as subordinated to such logics. Consequently, many studies focused on the living conditions of migrants upon arrival.

In focusing on the arrival of labourers, their inclusion in factories and, more broadly, in the labour market, these studies posit a related and hierarchised link between mobility and work, formalised by the concept of 'labour migration'. Seen as a natural observation, the concept was hardly ever put to discussion and has been taken up since the 1970s by serious and less serious studies alike.

THE NOTION OF LABOUR MIGRATION, A RECONVERSION OF COLONIAL CATEGORIES INTO CONTEMPORARY MIGRATORY CATEGORIES

In my opinion, highlighting the epistemological implications of the notion of 'labour migration' may help to interpret the weight of colonial memory in light of the definition of the immigrant, seen as a body disposed or predisposed to work because of its social, popular, rural and ethnic origins.

It is striking that the social science studies which focused on this type of migration have rarely objectified, theoretically and empirically, this research object. Such a non-explanation is grounded in the understanding of a clandestine epistemology of the labour migration approach. Quite often, the notion of immigration refers to the idea of 'imported' unskilled legal workers – through public policies and national businesses – from former French colonies. As for the term 'labour', it mainly points to the formal menial wage sector in industry, agriculture, construction or services. Usually, it refers to labour market sectors without linking them to the productive system, creating the illusion that they are marginal. It is surprising that this basic assumption, which does not withstand the test of empirical evidence, has not given rise to more questions and investigations.

For example, plural forms of migrations from the former colonies had already appeared as early as the 1970s. Legal and illegal migrants who came of their own accord, female migrants (Morokvasic, 1984), circulants, displaced individuals (Harki), soldiers from North and sub-Saharan Africa who stayed in France, immigrant entrepreneurs, traders from North Africa (Tarrius, 1995), and North African Jews were all part of this immigration. As for the labour market, it was already international, due to the globalisation of the economy (Mabogunje, 1970; Kritz et al., 1992), precisely in the sectors that employed immigrants. Far from being economically marginal, immigrant employment sectors formed the basis of a globalised productive system that already practised a form of relocation from within. Therefore, this cheap labour force benefited not only agriculture, but also the entire food-processing and export industry, the retail sector and the Western consumer. The recruitment of immigrants was no longer based on the logic of importing labour to meet the shortage of native candidates – an idea that was never supported by empirical evidence, although it was regularly relayed as a fact – but it stemmed from the globalisation of the economy of which immigrants were also actors, even informal instigators supporting its foundations (Peraldi, 2001; Tarrius, 2002). Yet, epistemologically wise, a majority of studies favoured the prism of migratory utilitarianism. The issue here is not the integration of migration in the economic strategies of companies. Rather, it is the fact of viewing migratory utilitarianism as a central and decisive dimension of mobility. This approach is part of a conception of 19th-century class relations, between rural and urban areas, in this case extended to the relations between the North and the South. While this idea is not entirely irrelevant, it is nevertheless marked by the performative schema that divides reality into a peripheral, pre-capitalist and poor South, the purveyor of dominated rural migrants, and a central, industrialised, strategic and modern North. It is also partly responsible for the categorisation, within the framework of a racialised form of collective imagination, of the modern white man and the archaic North African, in continuity with the colonial process. This classification reveals the Durkheimian division between rural worlds marked by mechanical solidarity and urban worlds marked by organic solidarity, with the idea that the integration of rural people would necessarily take place through rural flight. This form of clandestine epistemology has permeated empirical surveys on migrations. In this type of work, the social logic of leaving the home country is only captured in the light of socio-economic pressure: fleeing poverty, seeking better living conditions, seeking work. A large body of literature has described the departure of migrants as the result of pressure, and has partly focused solely on the conditions of settlement of these 'uprooted' arrivals (Blanchard, 2018). The migrants have become the new supernumerary individuals (Bauman, 2016) of the 20th century, and studied as marginal in terms of the industrialised productive system and of society.

By falling into this trap, many studies on migrations have endorsed the fact that the official halt put to the importation of labour by France in 1974 marked the end of labour migration and, therefore, this research turned away from the topic at a time when the globalisation of the labour market was becoming effective. Research then focused on family reunification and the integration of 'immigrants' who had settled in France, concurrent with public policy concerns. We have moved from importing labourers to assimilating and/or integrating them to French society. Thus, while it became possible to settle into national identity under certain conditions, North–South relations were reshaped in light of an interpretation of the acculturation, or cultural disorganisation–reorganisation, of immigrants, as used a century earlier by American sociology (Beaud and Noiriel, 1990). Far from breaking away from the approaches of the 1970s, sociology of assimilation is actually an extension of these approaches. Assimilation studies are concomitant with the corresponding state public policies (Gorgeon and Epstein, 2004), and they organise the circulation of concepts between the social sciences and political discourse. Some researchers were even included in the Haut conseil à l'intégration (High Council on Integration), set up in 1980.

Although part of the research work in France moved away from such approaches and opened new avenues in the 1980s and 1990s (Peraldi, 2001;

Tarrius, 2002; Simon, 2002), sociology of labour migration and integration continued to dominate the academic field (Tripier, 2004) and it extended to the children of immigrants, so-called 'second generation' immigrants, a term which is still in use nowadays, more than 40 years later. This term seems not so much to measure factually the generations of immigrants, as it measures the time it took for them to break away from such a representation of extra-nationality.

Not until the 2000s was a renewal in research approaches observed, as well as a profusion of research on migrations with a transnational focus. In that period the state promoted, through earmarked funding, research that broke away from former approaches. 'In 1999, the Research Mission (MiRe) of the Directorate for Research, Studies, Evaluation and Statistics (Drees) issued a request for proposals for a scientific investigation into the various types of mobilities and their implications' (Costa-Lascoux and du Cheyron, 2004: 189).

These studies will help to replace former national approaches in the context of the globalisation of culture and economy (Costa-Lascoux and du Cheyron, 2004). The link between migration and globalisation has given this type of research a certain academic recognition and visibility, and it is now supported by international institutions and researchers, even though traditional general sociology journals still fail to open more space for publications on this theme.

Consequently, the interest in migration topics has considerably increased in the last decade, triggered by three factors. The first, as already mentioned, is linked to the economic globalisation of the labour market in recent years and to the intensification of movements, which highlights the migration phenomenon and removes it from the old North–South patterns.

The second factor is linked to the transnational circulation of knowledge on these issues, to the confrontation of various approaches between national traditions, and to the disciplinary and transdisciplinary institutionalisation of migration studies, through the creation of the Institut Convergence.

The third, which is currently at the heart of every controversy, is the involvement of researchers from migration countries, former colonies, researchers from minority groups (Ndiaye, 2008), foreign researchers recruited in France or French researchers working abroad, young native researchers who are the children of globalisation and hence more receptive to foreign literature, and authors such as W.E.B. Du Bois, Edward Said, Kimberlé Crenshaw, Paul Gilroy, Frederick Cooper and Ann Laura Stoler, among others. These researchers also share a common mastery of foreign languages (academic and colloquial), including English, thanks to an international career (research field abroad, experience working in European or American universities). This new generation, whose sociology should be studied, brings a fresh critical perspective in the tradition of Sayad, nevertheless completed by the approaches developed across the Atlantic that reconnect with French sociology and topics that had been marginalised or rendered invisible in the 1960s. Whereas sociology deemed them marginal, this new generation rejects such approaches and places migrations, postcolonialism, racism, discriminations, ethnicism, sexism, gender, homophobia, sexuality and sexual violence at the centre of the social relations of domination (Fassin and Fassin, 2006; Dorlin, 2008; Belkacem et al., 2019; Mazouz, 2017). These new approaches all qualify the importance of social classes, which become one variable among others, and they investigate the systemic role of the republican state's institutions in the invisibility and transmission of dominations, thus paving the – sometimes conflictual – way for an inventory of Durkheimian and Marxist sociology.

These researchers have begun to deconstruct the myth of the national narrative by reinstating a history of France and of the Republic that unfurled outside 'the Hexagon' (of slavery, colonisation, immigration) as a constitutive element of the nation and of French society on the one hand, and of the social relations at play stressing the alterity of migrants from former colonies, on the other. However, although they bring a fresh approach to research by creating a new dynamic current in the social sciences that controversies and polemics cannot hide, these studies have yet to form a homogeneous corpus or a stable theoretical movement. Mainly occupied with seeking academic recognition, and unveiling hidden forms of domination, or the measure of phenomena such as racism or discrimination, these approaches have not taken decolonisation and its impact on the former coloniser and colonised people very seriously. As a consequence, this research work also struggles to shrug off the weight of colonial legacy which still views the loser, the former coloniser, as the winner (the dominator), and views the winner, the formerly colonised people, as the loser. However, taking decolonisation seriously would allow us to give another interpretation of the issues at stakes, as well as of the tensions and forms of domination and their current representations. Furthermore, taking decolonisation seriously would also mean reinstating the immigrant as a subject.

CONCLUSION: ARTICULATING THE POSTCOLONIAL AND DECOLONIAL TO BREAK AWAY FROM THE NATIONALISATION OF MIGRATION STUDIES

It is as if decolonisation had never happened; or at least not through the action of the formerly colonised people, but only on account of a strategic withdrawal of the former coloniser. And when decolonisation is indeed mentioned, it is only to credit it to the action of the former coloniser. In this sense, the idea that the leaders of the decolonial movements studied in France is regularly brought up. This is a way of insisting on the fact that the desire for freedom was instilled through French schooling, and therefore that the civilisation mission had, in a way, succeeded. And no matter if this blots out the millions of other protesters against colonisation, Algerian or Indochinese peasants alike, who had never set foot in France or in a school, because they were colonised for the most part. The statement made by François Hollande, former President of the French Republic, in Dakar in 2014, is an illustration of this myth at the highest level of the state. He stated that:

> Senghor said that this language, this French language was the language of fighting, of emancipation that it sometimes had the 'sweetness of trade winds', sometimes the 'speed of lightning'. And it was in French that the people achieved decolonisation, in French that they achieved their independence and freedom, and that they most often kept the memory of that language. Not like a legacy, but as a requirement for the whole world. (Statement by François Hollande, President of the French Republic, Dakar, 29 November 2014)[7]

Even in the recognition of decolonisation lies the legacy of what Gilroy calls postcolonial melancholia and the unfinished mourning process of the former colonial empires for their lost supremacy (Gilroy, 2004).

At the time, Césaire had already defended the idea that the study of the impact of decolonisation on the coloniser was as important as studying its impact on the colonised populations (Césaire, 1950). To take this invitation seriously and view decolonisation as a key event in colonial history would mean to study the impact of postcolonialism on former colonising countries. This would allow us to avoid essentialising the relations of domination that are too frequently convened in so-called postcolonial research; the notion that any power interaction between a white European, Westerner and a 'minority' person is a continuation of colonial domination, which in itself is part of postcolonial melancholia that clings to the idea of the structural superiority of the former colonisers, whether from a biological (so-called racial superiority) or a civilisational point of view (that is, cultural superiority, knowledge, education, economy, and so on).

However, it may be precisely the nostalgic yearning for this domination and its factual impossibility that triggers racism, discrimination and postcolonial categorisation of immigrants, as noted by Gilroy in his book *Postcolonial Melancholia* (Gilroy, 2020). Rather than domination, one should mention the efforts made to try and maintain this domination or the illusions of restoring it, and its effects on the categorisation of the Other. The discourse on Christian religious roots, whiteness, incompatibility of civilisations invoked in some far-right political speeches, and increasingly in all conservative (Mudde, 2007) or popular speeches, in order to distinguish themselves from immigrants from former colonies is, in itself, an indicator not of domination, but of its end. This highlights the fact that all the other dimensions are no longer sufficiently divisive to distinguish former immigrants from natives.

In fact, the weight of decolonisation has already been felt by former colonising countries. They no longer have control over the world narrative, which Jack Goody qualified as the 'theft of history' (Goody, 2006), and now they face competition in domains that were once theirs alone, such as the production of scientific knowledge, economic power (France is relegated to the second position in all of its African markets, behind China), cultural and artistic production, and even in the military field (with a succession of defeats on various fields of intervention since the 1960s). Failing to include this context when analysing the postcolonial perspective on immigrants is to deprive oneself of a key to understanding current tensions, as well as to how they are currently being overcome.

What is more, taking decolonisation seriously also means reinstating the Algerian, the Indochinese peasant, the Senegalese forced labourer (Fall, 1993), as subjects and not solely as objects of decolonisation. It means to grant the fact that immigrants from former colonies are also the bearers of the history of decolonisation as much as of colonisation; and that their experience of domination in France, in Europe, cannot be understood otherwise. Furthermore, what was interpreted as docility, as being crushed through domination, can also be interpreted as a form of resistance the effects of which are becoming visible not only in the children of the second, third and even fourth generations, but also in a part of the younger generations of former 'colonisers'. The protests against police violence towards minorities that have marked debates in the United States and spread throughout much of the world were led by both 'white' and 'minority' youth. The protests during what has been described as the Arab Spring, as well as the protests occurring in several sub-Saharan African countries, must be analysed in relation to this decolonisation.

To accept the idea that decolonisation may become a part of the migrants' personal history is to accept the idea that their mobility is also the result of decolonisation. It means considering that migration can also be the product of the link between colonisation and decolonisation, born both of constraints and of acquired freedom. Achille Mbembé spoke of the 'right to move' as a new claim (Mbembé, 2016). Migration may also be interpreted as a claim to this right, and immigrants as its bearers. Hence, migratory mobility itself becomes a test for the forms of domination inherited from colonialism, and contributes to deconstructing them from the base. It contributes to the methodical undoing of geographical, social and socio-racial boundaries erected by the history of slavery and colonialism. Despite the current tensions, pervasive racism, nationalism, the trial of racialisation – and therefore of systemic racism – is open, and the diversity of the French population is at work (Le Bras, 2017).

Hence, we must now elaborate a sociology and a history of the decolonisation experience that is inseparable from colonial history if we wish to strengthen the boundaries between scientific categories and political categories on migration issues.

Consequently, denationalising migration issues means resisting the subjection of scientific analysis to the political agenda, and avoiding the confusion of postcolonial melancholia – expressed through the rejection of immigrants or certain laws restricting their rights – with the domination of otherness. Postcolonial studies, which have opened up a new field for renewing the social sciences through the study of migration, would benefit from opening up a new scientific field: post-decolonial studies.

NOTES

1.   Term which originated in the United States, derived from Afro-American slang, it refers to someone who is awake ('woke') in the face of systemic racism and discrimination against ethnic, religious or sexual minorities.
2.   This category groups various people who have one thing in common: the use of a title (artist, journalist, editorialist, non-academic philosopher, novelist, community activist, political activist, senior civil officer) to gain access to opinion columns in the media and to have the legitimacy to discuss a topic in the same manner as a specialist of the field would. Some academics whose publications are not backed by scientific research and who find it difficult to establish themselves among their peers tend to use this point of entry.
3.   Term used by the French Minister of Higher Education and Research to qualify a school of thought in French research which has been accused of fostering the Islamic radicalisation of part of French youth. A request for an enquiry into Islamic leftism was issued by the minister, but it was not followed through due to the opposition of mobilised institutions such as the French National Science and Research Centre (CNRS).
4.   *Le Monde*, 21 December 2020, https://www.lemonde.fr/m-le-mag/article/2020/ 12/21/genre-identites-cancel-culture-le-fantasme-du-peril-americain_6064150 _4500055.html.
5.   See article published in *Le Monde* on 30 June 2020, https://www.lemonde.fr/ societe/article/2020/06/30/comment-emmanuel-macron-s-est-aliene-le-monde -des-sciences-sociales_6044632_3224.html.
6.   This notion has both a political and a scientific dimension in the French context, because it points to certain populations from North and sub-Saharan Africa and the Muslim realm. It is not correlated to the acquisition of French nationality, and includes both individuals born in France with French nationality and newcomers to the country.
7.   https://www.vie-publique.fr/discours/193133-declaration-de-m-francois -hollande-president-de-la-republique-sur-la.

REFERENCES

Balandier, G. (2011). La situation coloniale: approche théorique. *Cahiers internationaux de sociologie*, 1 (110): 9–29, doi: https://doi.org/10.3917/cis.110.0009#xd_co_f =YTljZDlmZTAtMzdkMi00MmE1LThjYWItOTY2ODU0ZmU4ODM4~

Bauman, Z. (2016). *Strangers at Our Door.* Cambridge: Polity.

Beaud, S. and Noiriel, G. (1990). Penser 'l'intégration' des Immigrés. *Hommes et Migrations*, 1133: 43–53, doi: https://doi.org/10.3406/homig.1990.1487.

Belkacem, L., Direnberger, L., Hammou, K., and Zoubir, Z. (2019). Prendre au sérieux les recherches sur les rapports sociaux de race. Mouvements: des idées et des luttes. https://mouvements.info/prendre-au-serieux-les-recherches-sur-les-rapports-sociaux-de-race/.

Blanchard, E. (2018). Une immigration de *déracinés*? In Blanchard, E. (ed.), *Histoire de l'immigration algérienne en France.* Paris: La Découverte, pp. 23–38.

Césaire, A. (1950). *Discours sur le colonialisme.* Paris: Éditions Réclame, Présence africaine.

Cooper, F. (1996). *Decolonization and African Society: The Labor Question in French and British Africa.* Cambridge: Cambridge University Press.

Cooper, F. (2002). *Africa since 1940: The Past of the Present.* Cambridge: Cambridge University Press.

Cooper, F. (2005). *Colonialism in Question: Theory, Knowledge, History.* Berkeley, CA: University of California Press.

Costa-Lascoux, J. and du Cheyron, P. (2004). Quand la recherche française investit les circulations migratoires. *Revue française des affaires sociales*, 2: 181–205, doi: https://doi.org/10.3917/rfas.042.0181#xd_co_f=NTc2MGY0NTUtNWM0ZS00MGIyLThkNDktZDM5ZThjNTE1YTJi~.

Dorlin, E. (2008). *Sexe, genre et sexualités: Introduction à la théorie féministe.* Paris: Presses Universitaires de France.

Dornel, L. (2014). L'appel à la main-d'œuvre étrangère et coloniale pendant la Grande Guerre: un tournant dans l'histoire de l'immigration. *Migrations Société*, 6 (6): 51–68, doi: https://doi.org/10.3917/migra.156.0051#xd_co_f=NTc2MGY0NTUtNWM0ZS00MGIyLThkNDktZDM5ZThjNTE1YTJi~.

Fall, B. (1993). *Le Travail forcé en Afrique occidentale française (1900–1946).* Paris: Karthala.

Fanon, F. (2011 [1952]). *Peau noire, masques blancs.* Paris: Seuil.

Fassin, É. (1993). La chaire et le canon. Les intellectuels, la politique et l'Université aux États-Unis. *Annales. Économies, Sociétés, Civilisation*, 2: 265–301, doi: https://doi.org/10.3406/ahess.1993.279133.

Fassin, É. and Fassin, D. (2006). *De la question sociale à la question raciale: Représenter la société française.* Paris: La Découverte.

Gilroy, P. (2004). *After Empire: Melancholia or Communal Culture?* London: Routledge.

Gilroy, P. (2020). Postcolonial melancholia. In Seidman, S. and Alexander, J. C. (eds), *The New Social Theory Reader.* New York: Taylor & Francis. pp. 427-434.

Girard, A. and Stoetzel, J. (1953). *Français et immigrés. Travaux et Documents de l'INED.* Paris: PUF.

Goody, J. (2006). *The Theft of History.* Cambridge: Cambridge University Press.

Gorgeon, Catherine and Epstein, Renaud (1999). Les élus locaux et l'intégration des immigrés. *Migrations études*, 86(mars-avril), 12.

Guillaumin, C. (1972). *L'idéologie raciste.Genèse et langage actuel.* Paris: La Haye, Mouton.

Kritz, M., Lin Lean Lim, Hania Zlotnik (1992). *International Migration Systems: A Global Approach.* Oxford: Clarendon Press.

Le Bras, H. (2017). *L'âge des migrations.* Paris: Editions Autrement.

Liauzu, C. (2000). Immigration, colonisation et racisme: pour une histoire liée. *Hommes et Migrations*, 1228: 5–14, doi: https://doi.org/10.3406/homig.2000.3594.

Liauzu, C. (ed.). (2004). *Colonisation: droit d'inventaire*. Paris: Armand Colin.

Mabogunje, A. (1970). Systems approach to a theory of rural–urban migration. *Geographical Analysis*, 2 (1): 1–18, doi: https://doi.org/10.1111/j.1538-4632.1970.tb00140.x.

Mazouz, S. (2017). *La République et ses autres. Politiques de l'altérité dans la France des années 2000*. Lyon: ENS Éditions.

Mbembé, A. (2016). *Politiques de l'inimitié*. Paris: La Découverte.

Memmi, A. (1957). *Portrait du colonisé* précédé de *Portrait du colonisateur*. Paris: Editions Corréa.

Meynier, P. and Meynier, G. (2011). L'immigration algérienne en France: histoire et actualité. *Confluences Méditerranée*, 2 (2): 219–234, doi: https://doi.org/10.3917/come.077.0219#xd_co_f=NTc2MGY0NTUtNWM0ZS00MGIyLThkNDktZDM5ThjNTE1YTJi~.

Morokvasic, M. (1984). Birds of passage are also women. *International Migration Review*, Special Issue 'Women in Migration', 18 (68): 886–907, doi: https://doi.org/10.2307/2546066.

Mudde, C. (2007), *Populist Radical Right Parties in Europe*. Cambridge: Cambridge University Press.

Ndiaye, P. (2008), *La Condition noire. Essai sur une minorité française*. Paris: Calmann-Lévy.

Noiriel, G. (1988). *Le creuset français histoire de l'immigration XIXe–XXe siècles*. Paris: Editions du Seuil.

Peraldi, M. (ed.) (2001). *Cabas et containers. Activités marchandes informelles et réseaux migrants transfrontaliers*. Paris: Maisonneuve et Larose.

Rosanvallon, P. (2006). *La contre-démocratie, la politique à l'âge de la défiance*. Paris: Seuil.

Saada, E. (2005). Entre 'assimilation' et 'décivilisation'. L'imitation et le projet colonial républicain'. *Terrain*, 44: 19–38, doi: https://doi.org/10.4000/terrain.2618.

Sayad, A. (1978). *Les usages sociaux de la 'culture des immigrés'*. Paris: CIEMM – Centre d'information et d'études sur les migrations méditerranéennes.

Sayad, A. (1992). *L'immigration ou les paradoxes de l'altérité*. Bruxelles: De Boeck-Université.

Sayad, A. (1997). 'Le foyer des sans-famille', in *L'Immigration et les paradoxes de l'altérité*. Paris and Brussels: De Boeck Université.

Sayad, A. (1999). *La double absence*. Paris: Seuil.

Simon, G. (2002). Les migrations internationales. *Population et Sociétés*, 382, septembre, 1–4.

Stoler, A.L. and Cooper, F. (2013). *Repenser le colonialisme*. Paris: Payot.

Tarrius, A. (1995). Naissance d'une colonie: un comptoir commercial à Marseille. *Revue européenne des migrations internationales*, 11 (1): 21–52, doi: https://doi.org/10.3406/remi.1995.1442.

Tarrius, A. (2002). *La Mondialisation par le bas: Les nouveaux nomades de l'économie souterraine*. Paris: Balland.

Tripier, M. (2004). L'immigré, analyseur de la société (note critique). *Terrains & travaux*, 2 (2): 173–185, doi: https://doi.org/10.3917/tt.007.0173#xd_co_f=NTc2MGY0NTUtNWM0ZS00MGIyLThkNDktZDM5ThjNTE1YTJi~.

Weil, P. and Truong, N. (2015). *Le sens de la République*. Paris: Grasset.

PART II

BEYOND NATIONAL MIGRATORY DYNAMICS

4.   Migration in Italy: a multiscalar analysis

Fabio Amato

It is not easy to describe and interpret the migration process in Italy in a few words. The task is rendered even more difficult due to constant reports in the media and elsewhere that focus exclusively on migration as a state of emergency. Indeed, for over two decades, but more so since 2015, migration issues have been at the centre of public debate. Particular focus has been placed on the arrivals of boatloads of asylum seekers, reception policies and border outsourcing strategies, which have all made Italy a major player in international agreements. In this historical context, the pursual of a policy of exception and emergency regarding migrants, the re-emergence of nationalism and a resurgence in racism and xenophobia are all manifestations of a difficult relationship with 'the other' that greatly affects the lives of migrants in Italy. At the same time, the policy of allowing border referral[1] in cooperation agreements demonstrates how Italy has chosen to officially close its borders to immigrants and to vet any arrivals (in line with European Community decisions), thereby facilitating ways of exploiting migrant labour.

These issues are essential in order to understand Italian migratory history because they help provide a general picture of the current situation, but they are not sufficient to describe the migrant situation over previous decades, as this may entail the risk of confusing the part with the whole.

According to the sociologist Enrico Pugliese (2008), Italy's migratory model may be defined as Mediterranean. Over the last 50 years, the phenomenon of immigration has also transformed the cultural and socio-economic landscape of the other Southern European states, namely Spain, Portugal and Greece. These countries – once lands of emigration – were seen as mere transit spaces for migrants in the 1970s, but after only a few years it was clear that migrants arrived in these countries in order to stay. This migratory model identifies a general immigration system with the following specific features: immigrants are not explicitly invited; the prevalence of *ius sanguinis* in the acquisition of citizenship; limits and restrictions on the issue of work and residence permits; and scant resources devoted to their integration. However, despite having these common features, Italy, Portugal, Spain and Greece differ significantly in their provision of social welfare according to the main categories of immigrants: immigrants with renewable residence permits; long-term immigrants; irregular migrants; and asylum seekers. Although the Mediterranean migratory model is a useful interpretative model, it must be acknowledged that if we are to go beyond a macro vision in the interpretation of the migratory process and give space to a more complex reading that takes into account race, gender, temporality, individual choice and above all interaction with place, then it is of less use as a common denominator.

Italy, like many major player countries in the 'great game' of mobility, stands out as a country of immigration, because it remains a country of emigration and has also become a transit stop on the way to other European countries. The long history of emigration in this country is perhaps the main element that conditions interpretation. Faced with the increase in arrivals, it is difficult to get away from the idea of exception and anomaly in order to fully appreciate this turning point. Italy is viewed as a state that has gone from being a place of emigration to a place of immigration, despite the fact that emigration has continued, albeit in different forms at different times. This situation has been further complicated by the COVID-19 pandemic, which since February 2020 has had significant repercussions on migrant communities in Italy, with a visible worsening of their living conditions.

Starting from the assumption that Italy, like other countries, is characterised by being at the same time a country of immigration, emigration and transit, the focus below will be on immigration, with a brief reference to emigration and transit. Much has been written about the fact that Italian emigration occurred well before the Unification of Italy (1861) and then exploded in the Liberal age, becoming a mass phenomenon between the last quarter of the 19th century and the outbreak of the First World War, above all to the Americas (Colucci and Gallo, 2015). During the economic boom of post-war reconstruction, there was a significant rise in the numbers of Italians emigrating, especially to other European countries. The 1970s were a watershed when immigration began to overtake emigration. However, contrary to popular belief, the latter did not disappear, merely changing profile. These new emigrants were no longer the proletariat and the peasantry (typified by the emblematic image of the poverty-stricken emigrant with a ramshackle 'suitcase' made of cardboard and tied together with string): instead, they are skilled professionals. This phenomenon was already evident in the 1990s but has accelerated considerably since the economic crisis of 2008 (Pugliese, 2018). These emigrants are an amorphous group including not only the classic 'brain drain' of scientists and researchers, but also qualified people choosing to try their luck abroad, and above all graduate job seekers who are also prepared to accept work in unskilled sectors (catering, call centres, construction, and so on). Although they are heterogeneous, it is possible to define some common characteristics of these migrations that distinguish them from earlier Fordist emigrations, namely youth and education.

Italy is affected not only by migration to other European countries, but also by internal migration. In fact, a key factor in the changes that have taken place over the last 25 years is migration from the south to the north of the country, which has involved an estimated 2 million people over the last 15 years (SVIMEZ, 2019). The so-called 'welfare' migrants, pensioners who choose to leave Italy for countries that ensure a tax exemption policy on their pensions and savings, are also to be included in this scenario. According to the Registry of Italian Citizens Resident Abroad (AIRE) the number of Italians resident abroad has increased from 3.6 million in 2006 to 5.5 million in 2020, 48 per cent of whom are women. There has also been an increase in the number of families moving with children (Fondazione Migrantes, 2020).

However, while the number of people emigrating from Italy to other European Union (EU) countries undoubtedly includes many Italians, it also includes an extremely significant and increasing number of people who were not born in Italy who have been affected by the economic crisis (about 45 per cent of all annual emigration), defined as 'secondary movement' (Fondazione ISMU, 2021).

To date, little has been written about Italy as a transit country for migrants, but its geographical position makes the *Bel Paese* a mandatory transit route for those heading towards France, the United Kingdom, Germany or other Northern European countries such as Sweden, Norway and Denmark. The Dublin Regulation mandates migrancy applications to be filed in the first country of arrival, and therefore those who try to apply elsewhere are forced to return to Italy. Two strategies exist to prevent this: migrants either enter Italy and avoid being detected, or they choose a medium- to long-term project, and once they have obtained their residence permit, try to move on to other European countries. The latter strategy has come to the fore in the news with the ongoing case of migrants awaiting transit to France in Ventimiglia (a city in Liguria on the Italian–French border). In 2015, France reintroduced border controls, in violation of the Schengen Agreement, in order to prevent migrants from crossing the border. Despite attempts by local authorities to alleviate the situation, the living conditions of migrants stranded in the Italian city are extremely harsh (Capitani, 2018). The same policy has been implemented by France at the Alpine border crossing from Clavière in Piedmont to Briançon in France. This border is scarcely mentioned in the French media except for when the body of a dead migrant is found, or when French border patrols invade the area (Pagliassotti, 2019). The news in Italy is full of such stories, for example articles about the vast makeshift encampments set up near Como railway station or the tensions stirred by the Austrian authorities on the Brenner border

line. These are all phenomena that quite clearly define Italy as a transit stopo-
ver point for a variety of migratory projects.

AN OVERVIEW OF MIGRATION IN ITALY

Immigration to Italy can be traced back to the first Chinese communities in
Milan and Rome in the 1920s. Before the 1970s, there are also references
to migrations of colonial origin and to the presence of overseas employees
of multinationals and international military organisations (Colucci, 2018).
However, as mentioned above, there has been a marked increase in the number
of migrants to Italy following the irruption of the post-Fordist economy. The
number soared, above all at the beginning of the new millennium, to 2 million
regular migrants, to then settle at 5.3 million in 2020 (IDOS, 2020). There has
therefore been a rapid growth in regular migration over the last 20 years, but in
recent years it has tended to remain at a steady 8.8 per cent of the total population. In 2019, for the first time in several years, the number of regular non-EU
migrants in Italy decreased. At the beginning of 2020 there were almost 3 616
000 non-EU citizens, a 2.7 per cent decrease compared to 2019. A review of
the number of irregular migrants (now estimated to be around 600 000, which
is 100 000 more than in 2017), to measure the effects of recent migratory
flows, has been called for. This increase is due both to people fleeing reception centres, with almost 100 000 people reported to have escaped from these
centres in 2018 and 2019 (IDOS, 2020), and to laws passed in 2018 by the
centre-right government which prohibit boats carrying migrants from landing
on Italian shores.

Despite the almost obsessive focus on arrivals from Africa, the majority of
migrants are from Europe: 49.6 per cent of resident foreigners, compared to
21.7 per cent from Africa, and 21.2 per cent from Asia. This confirms the fact
that nationality groups in Italy are very heterogeneous.

The opening up of Eastern Europe, following the implosion of the socialist
system at the end of the 1980s, favoured a considerable increase in the number
of migrants from 2000 onwards. Most of these migrants are from Romania (1.2
million, according to the latest available Italian National Institute of Statistics,
ISTAT, figures for 2019), followed by Albania (440 000). The next largest
groups of migrants according to nationality come from Morocco (432 000),
China (305 000) and Ukraine (240 000). Then over 100 000 migrants come
from each of the following countries: the Philippines (157 000), India (153
000), Bangladesh (138 000), Pakistan (121 000), Sri Lanka (104 000), Egypt
(128 000), Moldova (118 000), Nigeria (113 000) and Senegal (106 000). The
fallout events such as the Arab Spring can be seen in the increase in migrants
from sub-Saharan Africa and Asia, in particular the Indian subcontinent, compared to a relative stability in the numbers of both EU and non-EU Europeans.

With regards to territorial distribution, while there are more areas with poles of concentration in the Central and Northern regions, migrants are present throughout all 20 Italian regions. More than 80 per cent of migrants are concentrated in the regions of the Centre-North (83.1 per cent), especially in the North-West (33.8 per cent). At the beginning of 2020, the region with the highest overall number of migrants was Lombardy (1 206 000 resident foreigners – 22.7 per cent of the total). This was followed by Lazio (683 000 – 12.9 per cent), Emilia Romagna (560 000 – 10.5 per cent), Veneto (506 000 – 9.5 per cent) and Piedmont (429 000 – 8.1 per cent). The region of Emilia Romagna also has a high proportion of foreign citizens (more than 12 per 100 inhabitants), with Lombardy and Latium recording slightly lower ratios; while 10.5 per cent of resident foreigners (555 000) are concentrated in the province of Rome alone, 9.2 per cent (488 000) in Milan and 4.2 per cent (222 000) in Turin. Despite an increase in overall immigrant distribution throughout the country, migration is mainly concentrated in large urban areas. The areas with the highest ratios, however, are not necessarily the largest metropolitan cities. In the province of Prato, for example, there are 19 immigrants for every 100 inhabitants, and 15 in Piacenza, Milan and Parma. There are between 12 and 14 per 100 in Modena, Florence, Mantua, Rome, Imperia, Reggio Emilia, Brescia, Lodi, Ravenna, Bologna and Cremona. However, these transformations also affect small municipalities, and there are some cases where migrants make up more than a quarter of the total number of residents: Baranzate (province of Milan, almost 4500 out of a total of just over 12 000 inhabitants – or 36 per cent); Acate (Ragusa, 34 per cent of almost 11 500); Monfalcone (Gorizia, 26 per cent of 29 000 inhabitants); and in Pioltello (Milan) and Telgate (Bergamo), 25 per cent of just over 37 000 and 5000 residents respectively. Italy is not characterised by clear immigrant ghettoisation processes, but the nationality of origin plays an important role in territorial distribution. The main nationalities are widely spread throughout the territory, while at the same time some communities have radiated out from major centres (for example, the Chinese) and others are concentrated in specific areas of the country (for example, Ukrainians are mainly concentrated in Campania).

With regard to gender, household size, labour and territorial distribution, the different communities show a variety of territorial settlement clusters. On the whole, the gender ratio is balanced, although slightly favours women (51.9 per cent at the end of 2019), who perform most of the care work in urban areas. Most migrants are young: at the end of 2019 the average age was around 35 (compared to around 46 for the Italian population), again with significant differences according to when the communities first arrived.

INSIDE THE PROCESSES OF CHANGE

Macro data provides a comprehensive framework from which to analyse immigration. Such data is in itself a reflection of the receiving society and should therefore be interpreted, in all its complexity, by means of examples from the different places where migrants settle. In a strictly geographical sense, the interactions between new arrivals and places of residence constitute different processes of transformation and territorialisation. Even when migrants make choices that lead certain communities to move to specific areas, and in particular specific labour market areas, interactions with different territories play a defining role: for instance, migrating to Pordenone (a city in the North-East) is different from migrating to Catania (a city in Sicily). Due to questions of space, I will limit myself to outlining the rapid evolution of work, housing and educational integration as interpretative matrixes of change that constitute the most significant aggregation clusters. All these factors share commonalities with other Mediterranean countries in Europe. In particular, the Mediterranean welfare system – due to its limits and weaknesses – on the one hand attracts immigrant workers, and on the other hand excludes the majority of them with social citizenship rights (due to its rigidity, that is, reliance on employer-based contributions). In many different ways, these countries have pursued migration policies that are undoubtedly progressive in terms of their basic principles and values, but which are not always implemented. This policy implementation deficit is also due to the complexity of the new international migration framework that emerged in the latter part of the 20th century in response to increased pressure from global migration. However, in the case of Italy there are some particular features that merit being dealt with separately.

Work

The issue of work is a priority because it is the main reason for migrating. In general, for migrants, an improvement in their living conditions is achieved through access to a labour market that allows them to earn a higher income than in the place of departure.

After the 2008 global financial crisis, the Italian economy entered a cyclical slowdown and, despite some signs of recovery, is still very vulnerable. In 2019, according to ISTAT, the total number of hours worked was still lower than before the crisis, with an increase in fixed-term contracts and involuntary part-time work (especially for women). In this critical labour market scenario, migrant labour has taken on an important role with its flexibility, greater mobility and ability to seek out work wherever it may be available, and willingness to work under precarious conditions.

It is worth noting that in 2019 the employment rate in Italy increased with respect to the previous year, and at the same time unemployment fell for the fifth consecutive year (-6.3 per cent). However, this is not a general trend, but is made up of differentiated factors. First and foremost among these is nationality. In particular, the employment rate increase mainly concerns foreign workers (+2.0 per cent compared to +0.5 per cent for Italians), while the fall in unemployment concerns only Italian nationals (-7.5 per cent compared to +0.6 per cent for foreign nationals). According to Laura Zanfrini, in 2018, non-Italian nationals made up 10.2 per cent of the working age population, 10.6 per cent of those in employment, 14.5 per cent of the unemployed, and 8.6 per cent of the inactive population (Zanfrini, 2019).

There are differences on a local level within Italy, with the conditions of foreign workers worsening above all in Central and Southern Italy. While employment for Italian nationals has increased at a similar rate throughout the territory, that of foreign workers has only gone up in the North and has fallen in the Centre and in the South, where access to the labour market is effectively barred to foreign workers, who primarily work in the unskilled/manual sectors: 40 per cent of migrant women are employed in domestic or family care services, while 42 per cent of men are employed in industry and construction. It is clear, therefore, that in 2019 the percentage of migrant workers with respect to the overall number of workers differed significantly by sector, with less than 2 per cent in public administration; credit and insurance; information technology and communication and education. Whereas numbers of migrant workers greatly exceed the average of 10.7 per cent in other sectors: 18 per cent in construction, 18 per cent in hotels and restaurants, 18 per cent in agriculture, and 69 per cent in domestic/care working services (IDOS, 2020). Almost two-thirds of foreign workers (63.3 per cent, compared to 29.6 per cent Italian nationals) work in unskilled or blue-collar jobs, while only 8 per cent work in skilled professions (compared to 38.7 per cent of Italian nationals).

This uneven distribution of labour within the country is made evident by the following figures, with less than a third of foreign workers employed in unskilled labour in the North (28.7 per cent, compared to 6.7 per cent for Italian nationals), compared to almost half in the South (47.8 per cent and 11.8 per cent, respectively). In the Northern regions foreign workers are more likely to work in industry and in blue-collar jobs (23.9 per cent, compared to 6.7 per cent in the South), while in the Southern regions they work in the agricultural sector (18.8 per cent, compared to 3.7 per cent in the North) and in trade (8.3 per cent). Another discriminatory factor is that they are often overqualified for the low-skilled jobs they perform. According to IDOS, 840 000 foreign workers are employed in jobs for which they are overqualified, that is 33.5 per cent, compared to 23.9 per cent of Italian nationals. The gap is particularly significant for women: 42.7 per cent compared to 24.5 per cent of Italians (for men, 26.4 per cent and 23.4 per cent).

With regard to employment, more immigrants work in sectors that employ a higher proportion of non-Italian workers overall: social, welfare and personal service activities (36.6 per cent), followed by agriculture and hotels/restaurants (both 17.9 per cent), then construction (17.2 per cent). Transport and warehousing accounts for 11.1 per cent. This picture replicates the trends found in more advanced countries, although probably with a greater focus on domestic work, which raises the number of people employed in community, social and personal service activities.

These data describe a labour market that tends to automatically reproduce the characteristics of the migrant 'incorporation' model. This model considers foreign workers to be a resource to fill those low-skilled jobs 'in real time' that are essential to the production system (particularly in agriculture), and to provide the domestic help required by families. It would seem, therefore, that nothing is changing, and that in reality – in a context of stifled growth and 'general labour impoverishment' – the hope of seeing some form of rejuvenation of the Italian model of integration remains, for now, thwarted (Zanfrini, 2019). The most sought-after immigrant workers remain those working in unskilled jobs. This became even more evident during the COVID-19 pandemic crisis, as will be seen below.

Housing

After work, access to housing is the next main objective of migrants to enable them to stay in Italy and pursue their migration project. The most effective measure of the transformation process is a house purchase that allows migrants to leave the insecurity of living in rented accommodation behind.

According to the Istituto Scenari Immobiliari in 2019, 63.6 per cent of immigrants in Italy lived in rented accommodation, 21.8 per cent in their own homes, 7.4 per cent at their place of work, and 7.2 per cent with relatives or other compatriots (Toccaceli, 2020). The greatest transformation took place from 2009 to 2019, when 546 000 houses were purchased by non-Italian workers. There has, in effect, been an increase in house sales to immigrants beginning from the new millennium, and increasing between 2004 and 2007 (the year in which foreign workers bought 17.6 per cent of the total 780 000 houses purchased); a dynamism favoured by better access to bank credit which, after the crisis that began in 2008, gradually disappeared for everyone (Toccaceli, 2020).

From 2015 to 2019 there was a new phase of growth with over 230 000 purchases, which increasingly define stabilisation strategies. The majority of purchases are located outside the main cities, although slight increases are also recorded in central and semi-central areas, indicating an improvement for those communities who have been present in Italy for some time. In 2019, 60 per cent of homes were bought by Eastern Europeans. They are followed by Asians from the Indian subcontinent (India and Pakistan) at 14.2 per cent, and then by the Chinese at 13.8 per cent. More North Africans also bought their own homes: up from 4.9 per cent in 2018 to 6.0 per cent in 2019.

In spite of the developments above, renting remains the predominant choice of migrants, albeit with various difficulties in accessing the rental housing market due to owner prejudice and the often vexatious conditions of irregular contracts (higher rents, poor-quality properties, uncertainty about contracts) that confine foreigners to the margins of the real estate market. In this sense, despite some positive signs, living conditions for migrants and their families remain very harsh. By way of example, more than ten years after a survey in the metropolitan area of Naples (Amato and Coppola, 2009), the difficult living conditions of immigrants persist, as they have little choice but to accept bad housing in the most rundown areas of the city, in the worst parts of both the inner city and the outskirts.

School

Schools are the most significant indicators of a society's transformation, and it is especially during the years of compulsory education that a country's most important multicultural challenge is played out. According to the latest available data (Ministry of Education, 2020), in the 2018/19 school year there were over 850 000 non-Italians in schools, making up 10 per cent of the total enrolments in Italian schools, from nursery through to secondary school. In 2009/10 there were 673 000, representing 7.5 per cent of the total. This growth, while not as exponential as was commonly believed, is nevertheless constant, and also compensates for the gradual fall in the numbers of Italians enrolled. The idea of the multicultural transformation of Italian schools has therefore entered a phase of slowdown, due both to the reduction in the intensity of migration flows to Italy, and to the increase in the acquisition of citizenship. In recent years, there has been an influx of children of asylum seekers and refugees, and more significantly, an increase in the numbers of unaccompanied minors (MSNA) who have become important players in migration flows to Italy. However, these growing groups of unaccompanied minors only rarely manage to gain access to the Italian education system.

As a result of immigrant distribution within the country, most non-Italian students are concentrated in the Northern regions (65 per cent). Only 22 per cent of non-Italian students are found in the Central regions and in the South, just over 13 per cent. A more detailed look at individual regions shows the ratio of students with non-Italian citizenship (out of overall enrolments) to be highest in Emilia-Romagna (16.4 per cent), which surpasses Lombardy (15.5 per cent). The ratio also highlights the prominence of the Central regions (Tuscany, 14.1 per cent out of the total number of students and Umbria, 13.8 per cent) in addition to the usual Northern regions (Veneto, 13.6 per cent and Piedmont 13.5 per cent). In the South, the proportion of non-Italian students is below the national average of 10 per cent throughout, and ranges from 2.6 per cent in Sardinia to 7.5 per cent in Abruzzo.

In absolute terms, Lombardy maintains the record for the highest number of foreign students, which in 2018/19 came close to 218 000, followed by Emilia-Romagna with over 100 000, and Veneto (94 000), Lazio and Piedmont (78 000–79 000) and Tuscany (71 000). Campania replaced Sicily as the Southern region with the highest numbers of enrolments, but it remains far behind the figures in the Central-Northern regions (27 000 non-Italian students).

The pattern of nationalities is as follows: in the 2018/19 school year, Romanians were still in first place, with a slight decrease compared to the previous school year (157 470, 18.3 per cent of non-Italian nationality students), followed by Albanians (118 085, 13.6 per cent), Moroccans (105 057, 12.2 per cent) and Chinese (55 070, 6.4 per cent). The real change, however, can be seen in an increase in those labelled 'second generation' students: over 550 000 in the 2018/19 school year, double the number of native Italian students, and who for six consecutive school years have made up the majority of foreign students.

Many school-age non-Italians are subject to delays in completing compulsory education and therefore lag behind their Italian peers. There are various reasons for these delays: there may be a delay accumulated through a refoulement process, or a delay attributable to enrolling minors in classes below their real age group. According to this data, in the same school year, the share of early leavers from education and training (ELET) and not in education, employment or training (NEET) for young people born overseas is amongst the lowest in Europe. Over the last ten years or so, there has been a decline in the proportion of 18–24-year-olds who do not have a higher level secondary education or vocational qualification, and who are not in education or training, for both Italians and foreigners. However, in 2019, foreign-born ELETs accounted for 32.3 per cent of foreigners aged 18–24 (22.2 per cent of the EU28 average), that is, three times the number of native Italians (11.3 per cent). As for NEETs, the data trend over the last decade is broadly stable, with the share of foreign-born NEETs standing at 31.9 per cent of the total number of foreign-born young people aged 15–29 resident in Italy (IDOS, 2020).

2020 ANNUS HORRIBILIS: THE REPERCUSSIONS OF THE CORONAVIRUS PANDEMIC ON THE PLIGHT OF MIGRANTS

The rapid spread of the coronavirus (COVID-19) since February 2020 has had global repercussions in terms of morbidity rates, with such widespread economic, social and psychological effects that it is not yet possible to envisage a return to the status quo. The effects on international migration and on mobility in general were relatively immediate, and repercussions in the living conditions of migrants in Italy were heavily felt, although seldom reported. 'Those who arrived by sea before were just illegal immigrants, now they are infected illegal immigrants, double-dealers. Covid-19, in the language of the media, has fed upon the issue of migration and transformed it into its own image, without altering its negative value' (Cataldi, 2020: 1). It all began by blaming Chinese communities living in Italy for the spread of COVID-19, and then moved on to blaming immigrants in general. Successively, this distrust of migrant communities was manifested through episodes of outright racism. An example is the case of Bulgarian workers in Mondragone (Caserta), in June 2020, who were violently harangued as 'plague-bearers' by the local population at a time when the number of contagions had increased. In the logistics sector, which developed considerably during the pandemic, foreign transport workers were forced to accept degrading working conditions. In addition, migrants rescued in international waters were immediately forced into quarantine, in addition to undergoing the usual delays in rescuing makeshift boats in the Mediterranean.

Migrant communities have been hit harder by the overall widespread consequences of the virus, than by the spread of the virus itself. In terms of work, they were affected more than native Italians; overcrowded housing left little room for social distancing; and online distance learning further increased the educational gap (many migrant students often do not have access to computers and the internet). There was also, of course, a significant decrease in remittances to families in view of a reduction in, or loss of income. Nevertheless, according to the Fondazione ISMU, remittances sent between 1 January 2020 and 30 June 2020 amounted to €3331 billion, compared to €2844 billion in the first half of 2019 and €2722 billion in the same period in 2018 (Fondazione ISMU, 2021). According to Centro studi CeSPI (2020), this increase may be due to the emergence of cash flows that would otherwise have been transferred informally through systems linked to the movement of people and goods between neighbouring countries. The pandemic interrupted such movements, requiring greater use of traceable money transfer services.

In relation to housing, there was a phase of acute crisis for migrants in 2020, mainly affecting home-buying, which more than halved compared to the previous year. This contraction is determined not only by labour market uncertainty, but also by increasing difficulties in access to credit. This sudden downturn interrupts a trend that had seen a move away from areas with a high immigrant population towards neighbourhoods inhabited mostly by Italians: an important indicator of integration that prevents the ghettoisation typical of European countries with a longer history of migration. The aftermath of the economic crisis has affected Asians above all (especially the Chinese and Indians), who are much less able to buy their own homes than they were in the past. The repercussions from the crisis have worsened the conditions of those who live in rented accommodation, and of those who lived in conditions of forced cohabitation and unfit housing even before the crisis.

Conversely, the dramatic consequences of the pandemic have also high-lighted the crucial role of migrants in the Italian economy. Particularly in the lockdown phase, it became evident that serious risks would be incurred if migrant workers were unable to return to Italy or simply access the workplace. In this regard, a new regularisation measure was launched in the summer of 2020, exclusively for the agriculture, livestock and fishing, and domestic care working sectors. There were a total of 207 542 applications, of which 176 848 were for domestic care work and 30 694 for employment in the primary sector. The numbers of workers making such applications according to nationality are as follows (Fondazione ISMU, 2021): from Pakistan (5681 applications), Bangladesh (4275), China (3893), Morocco (3663), Egypt (3146), Albania (2382), India (2354) and Peru (1788). The majority of applications were for domestic care work (85 per cent of the total), the sector for which, in the past, applications had rarely been made.

CONCLUSIONS

In recent decades, Italy has changed radically thanks to the relocation of over 5 million overseas citizens. While conditions have changed over time, neither economic conditions nor the relationship of Italian society with these newcomers have undergone as many transformations. Italy, while sharing characteristics common to other Mediterranean countries, seems to maintain a less open attitude towards migrants when it comes to access to rights and integration processes.

An example of this is the new regularisation promoted by the Italian gov-ernment. This regularisation is a political choice that sees functionalist logic prevail over the protection of migrants in general, the protection of their rights and that of integration processes. The equation between migrant workers and unskilled, underpaid labour seems to be as entrenched in the logic of govern-ment as it is in public opinion. The irregularity of foreign nationals, in all its forms, has become the norm. Many immigrant families manage to survive conditions of extreme hardship, primarily due to the fruits of their undeclared and underpaid labour. This regularisation institutionalises the exploitation of a section of the population in order to ensure the day-to-day survival of the country as a whole. In particular, the domestic care work sector and the agro-food supply chain seem to be unable to do without this systemic exploitation of immigrant labour. At the height of lockdown, it became clear that the work carried out by migrants in the care and agricultural sectors was of prime importance and could not have been done without them. The response to this was a regularisation that would merely protect the demand for cheap plentiful labour, without changing migrants' dire working conditions; on the contrary, it made them permanent.

While acceptance of irregular conditions may be necessary in order to survive the initial phase of the migration project, they are no longer sustainable if projects become long-term: in this way, a situation of chronic social deprivation is established on the basis of nationality. Therefore, a restructuring of the regulatory framework is necessary in order to overcome the outdated rules and practices that currently regulate entry and working conditions and systematically relegate immigrants to a position of social inferiority. These choices require a rethinking of labour policy, especially in certain sectors. This would shift employer behaviour in a cooperative and sustainable direction, be they private individuals looking for care workers, or companies that have to move more operationally towards the principles of social responsibility. Only in this way may the principle of decent work, as set down by the International Labour Organization (ILO), be guaranteed to all.

NOTE

1.   See the agreement of 2017 with Libya and the strategic Italian interest in Niger with the European Union Emergency Trust Fund issue after the 2015 La Valletta meeting.

REFERENCES

Amato, F. and Coppola, P. (2009). *Da migranti ad abitanti. Gli spazi insediativi degli stranieri nell'area metropolitana di Napoli*. Napoli: Guida Editore.
Capitani, G. (2018). *Se questa è Europa. La situazione dei migranti al confine italo francese di Ventimiglia*. Oxfam briefing paper, https://oi-files-d8-prod.s3.eu -west-2.amazonaws.com/s3fs-public/file_attachments/bp-nowhere-but-out-refugees -migrants-ventimiglia-150618-it.pdf (accessed 22 February 2021).
Cataldi, V. (2020). Introduzione. In Carta di Roma, *Notizie di transito, presentazione del VII rapporto della Carta di Roma*, https://www.cartadiroma.org/wp-content/ uploads/2020/12/Notizie-di-transito.pdf (accessed 3 March 2021).

Centro studi CeSPI (ed.) (2020). Focus Migrazioni internazionali. Osservatorio quadrime-strale, N.40, https://www.parlamento.it/application/xmanager/projects/parlamento/file/repository/affariinternazionali/osservatorio/focus/PI0040FocusCeSPI.pdf

Colucci, M. (2018). *Storia dell'immigrazione straniera in Italia. Dal 1945 ai giorni nostri*. Roma: Laterza.

Colucci, M. and Gallo, S. (2015). *L'emigrazione italiana. Storia e documenti.* Brescia: Morcellania.

Fondazione ISMU (2021). *Ventiseiesimo rapporto sulle migrazioni 2020.* Milano: FrancoAngeli.

Fondazione Migrantes (2020). *Rapporto italiani nel mondo, 2020.* Todi: Tau Editrice.

IDOS (2020). *Dossier statistico immigrazione 2020.* Roma: IDOS.

Ministry of Education (2020). *Gli alunni con cittadinanza non italiana. A.s. 2018/19.* Roma: Ufficio Gestione Patrimonio Informativo e Statistica.

Pagliassotti, M. (2019). *Ancora dodici chilometri. Migranti in fuga sulla rotta alpina.* Torino: Bollati Boringhieri.

Pugliese, E. (2008). Il modello mediterraneo dell'immigrazione. *Quaderni Rassegna Sindacale*, 2: 73–87.

Pugliese, E. (2018). *Quelli che se ne vanno. La nuova emigrazione italiana.* Bologna: Il Mulino.

SVIMEZ (2019), *Rapporto SVIMEZ: l'economia e la società del Mezzogiorno.* Bologna: Il Mulino.

Toccaceli, M. (2020). Immigrati e casa: dalla crescita all'emergenza abitativa. In IDOS, *Dossier statistico immigrazione 2020.* Roma: IDOS, pp. 193–200.

Zanfrini, L. (2019). Il lavoro. In Fondazione ISMU, *Venticinquesimo rapporto sulle migrazioni 2019.* Milano: FrancoAngeli, pp. 151–174.

5. The Maghreb of transit, new laboratory of postcolonial migrations

Michel Peraldi

Exemplifying the new, so-called 'autonomous' migration (Mezzadra, 2004; De Gourcy, 2005), the *saoudaa*, dressed in the black abaya worn by Saudi women but with her face uncovered and heavily made up, is a familiar figure in Morocco. She displays the signs of success earned through domestic service in Saudi Arabia, Dubai or Abu Dhabi (Guezzen, 2021). In Tunis, in the back rooms of hairdressing salons, the *femmes valises* ('suitcase women') organise the sale of shopping bags loaded with cosmetics, scarves and jewellery, which they bring back from their regular trips to Istanbul. Peddlers have become familiar figures of daily life in the Maghreb, from the Algerian or Tunisian *trabendo* to the Moroccan *camionnistes* who regularly bring back fabrics and household appliances from their trips to Europe, purchased in the Barbès district of Paris, or in Naples or Milan. The trade routes opened by these initiatives are constantly expanding and now reach the Chinese trading cities specialising in export products (Choplin and Pliez, 2018).

A more tragic urban figure, the *harraga* (Souiah, 2013), a 'border burner', constantly looking for an opportunity to cross, haunts both the quays of North African ports and images of borders on each shore of the Mediterranean. Some barely in their teens, they symbolise the disarray of a supernumerary youth, for whom migration is more of a dangerous and uncertain 'adventure', than a defined and marked-out destiny as a worker. Among these 'adventurers' (Bredeloup, 2008) that Europe hunts down at its borders, are many from sub-Saharan Africa, also seeking clandestine passage towards European shores. We now know (Pian, 2009) that they are the most visible component of a wider movement of which North African societies are becoming aware with some difficulty. Indeed, today, a large proportion of sub-Saharan migrants settle in Morocco, Algeria and Tunisia, reviving the ancestral links woven over the Sahara between Central Africa and North Africa, notably through religious confraternity (Bava and Capone, 2010). This is resulting in a profound economic and social transformation of these societies, which are becoming 'host societies' as much as societies of departure (Peraldi, 2011). Finally, there is an increasing European presence in the Maghreb (Peraldi and Terrazzoni, 2016a).

In addition to retirees who have settled in Morocco and Tunisia, the revival of certain economic sectors, from crafts to tourism, is based in part on small and medium-sized enterprises (SMEs) set up by Europeans (Pellegrini, 2016). These new figures point to a sudden and complex mutation in migration in the Maghreb, rather than a simple change. They have in common their distance, in the imagination and in social terms, from the historical figure of the 'immigrant worker' on which was constructed, throughout the previous century, both the imagination and the institutional frameworks which form the basis of the representation of migration dynamics. This difference can be seen in the following areas. Sending and receiving states are now largely absent from the organisation and management of migratory cohorts, and migration today is primarily a matter of autonomy, either individual or diasporic. The period of migration itself has changed considerably, since although until recently it took the form of exile, it is now mobility, a social period characterised by return journeys and wanderings. Finally, while Europe remains the centre of migratory aspirations and the principal destination, new routes are opening up, at the same time as the Maghreb itself is becoming a migratory space.

THE FRAGMENTATION OF MIGRANT CATEGORIES

In contrast to the era of the mass Fordist migration, we are currently seeing a clear fragmentation of migrant categories and reasons for migration, regardless of the destination of migration. This fragmentation is largely the result of migration policies that have multiplied procedures while at the same time restricting access to visas. Salaried work, while clearly the primary objective of those who migrate, is only one of the reasons to move. In the case of regular North African migration to Europe, and to France in particular, students form a steady flow,[1] and this represents a constantly increasing proportion as visas granted for other reasons are restricted. Family reunification remains the main reason for issuing visas, with the ambiguous consequence of a very visible feminisation of migrant flows over the last 20 years (Rea, 2021). The Organisation for Economic Co-operation and Development (OECD) observes that the proportion of women migrants is now equal to or greater than the proportion of men, although it is not clear, due to a lack of historical research, the extent to which this is due to a late recognition of the hitherto discreet or even secret presence of women in migratory flows, and the extent to which it is the result of changes in employment sectors (Beski-Chafiq, 2014). The increasing demand for migrants in the domestic and personal care services sectors is undoubtedly an important factor in the feminisation of flows (Fine and Puech, 2019; Guezzen, 2021). Numerous research studies have shown that the feminisation of migratory flows also means that professional and personal situations are becoming more insecure. Despite the media's persistent emphasis in recent years on undocumented entry into Europe, empirical research in France shows that most undocumented migrants become irregular after entering the country legally, because irregularity tends to be economically attractive and a condition for obtaining and holding employment. To sum up, while migrant workers in the Fordist era entered illegally and then progressed towards both legalisation and integration, today they enter legally but become irregular, making the lack of regular status no longer an 'accident' but a 'condition' (Fassin, 2010).

Since the establishment of the Schengen procedures (in 1988), European states have constantly developed migration policies that are clearly a reversal of the original intention of the agreement. While previously centred around social issues and integration strategies, state rationales have now evolved towards a position based on the defence of national sovereignty with a focus on border surveillance and control. In short, there has been a shift from the right to reside to the right to move, which states intend to regulate through the combination of an unprecedented strengthening of police controls on migrant populations on the one hand, and the multiplication of procedures and visa bureaucracy on the other. The effects of this change of focus are twofold. First, by widening the sphere of police intervention, they literally criminalise[2] the situation of many unfortunate migration candidates, who are increasingly caught up in a spiral of policing. Moreover, the search for partnerships with 'sending' states[3] and the increase in deportation procedures gives this stigmatisation a transnational dimension.[4] In addition to the repression suffered by 'border burners' in countries of departure, these policies also give rise to situations of serious insecurity, and to the existence of actual transit camps, both at borders and in countries of return (Agier, 2014; Schmoll, 2020). Second, as conditions of access to visas are becoming increasingly selective along social lines, these policies lead to a dual discriminatory effect: between 'established' migrants and 'applicants', when seniority in migration confers an unrestricted right to movement that applicants, subject to the visa procedure, do not have; and in the societies of departure themselves, where obtaining a progressive right to mobility operates as an elitist criterion. In contrast to the starving *harragas* in Algerian, Tunisian (Salzbrunn et al., 2020) and Moroccan ports, there is the figure of the circulating elite, whose easily renewable so-called 'VIP' visa gives them access to medical care, shopping and tourist circuits in France and, since Schengen, across Europe.[5] The paradox is that the shorter the physical distance between the shores of the Mediterranean (in addition to the frequency of flights and the reduction in prices by low-cost airlines; Marrakech[6] is three hours from Paris and Tunis is one and a half hours from Marseille), the greater the social distance from the right to move. In fact, it is now almost impossible for anyone without social capital, financial resources or a stable professional status to travel legally between the Maghreb and Europe.

AND YET THEY MOVE

In fact, despite the viscosity of the procedures, it can be argued on the basis of the most recent research carried out in the past few years in Europe and the United States that migration, understood as relatively long-lasting exile, gives way to very diverse forms of mobility (Rea, 2021). People are migrating for ever shorter periods of time, some even making multiple trips back and forth, depending on opportunities. Moroccan women in the Gulf can only stay in most of the countries where they work for two years. Seasonal agricultural workers are only present in Europe for the duration of the harvesting season. Indeed, the sharpest historical contrast is illustrated by these agricultural workers who, in the 1970s, left their country for the possibility of accessing industrial jobs through agriculture, and who today, strictly regulated by semi-disciplinary schemes, spend seasonal periods in Europe that can barely exceed six months (Morice and Potot, 2010).

The first major phenomenon affecting the Maghreb is the development of significant sub-Saharan migration. Some political actors and experts considered for a time that this migration was in transit to Europe, until it became clear that migrant workforces were clearly taking their place in the economies of the Maghreb countries and settling there. In Algeria, where hardly any research on this subject has been conducted, the number of Chinese workers in the cities of Algiers and Oran alone is estimated at 40 000. They are employed by companies, which are also Chinese, carrying out major post-civil war construction projects (motorways and housing). In Mauritania, Senegalese and Nigerian workers are employed by Senegalese entrepreneurs to revive the dried fish industry (Choplin, 2008). Finally, in Morocco, probably the Maghreb country with the strongest traditional ties with Central Africa, sub-Saharan migrants are present in the construction industry and in domestic service. Women migrants from the Philippines[7] are also becoming visible in the French-speaking press and in call centres. The sub-Saharan presence, which is impossible to measure, is nevertheless currently significant enough for certain neighbourhoods of the major cities – especially Rabat, but also Casablanca and Marrakech – to be referred to as 'black neighbourhoods' (Peraldi, 2018). However, at present it is undoubtedly in Morocco that the participation of sub-Saharan migrants in the country's economy is the most noticeable and widespread, and that the phenomenon is the subject of numerous descriptions and analyses.[8] This is not surprising, since Morocco has the most long-standing, regular, and even the most institutionalised ties with French-speaking Black Africa. The case of the Tidjaniya Muslim brotherhood founded in Fez, its holy city, which spread through sub-Saharan Africa, is not insignificant because it continues to enable regular contacts and circulation from Senegal in particular, to Morocco

(Triaud and Robinson, 2000) and the settlement, in Fez among other cities, of Senegalese members of the brotherhood, married to Moroccan women (Therrien, 2018). Other Senegalese who, benefiting from political agreements dating back to independence, can travel to Morocco without a visa, open businesses and study there. They are certainly the most numerous among the sub-Saharan Africans who are permanently settled in Morocco today. These same agreements exist with other countries, such as Guinea Konakri, and Congo, whose fallen leader came to take refuge in Rabat after his removal, with his entourage and extended family. Indeed, many observers trace the presence of sub-Saharan Africans in the working-class districts of the Moroccan capital back to this event (Peraldi, 2011). Finally, a very long-standing form of Moroccan migration, settled in Senegal, Mali and Côte d'Ivoire, is still today behind the arrival of domestic workers employed by families in Morocco. These hubs of relations are certainly not responsible for, or organisers of, the new sub-Saharan migration to Morocco; however, they have the distinctive characteristic of creating networks and 'bridgeheads'.

A second migration movement, according to the unanimous view of observers, started at the end of the 1990s, when intra-African migration routes, particularly to Nigeria and Côte d'Ivoire, were closing (Marfaing and Wippel, 2004). After a long journey through Niger and then southern Algeria, following a period spent regrouping in the north of the country (Tangiers, Oujda) where these migrants gave the impression that they all wanted to attempt a crossing to Europe, it was in Rabat, Casablanca, and finally Marrakech that sub-Saharan Africans 'settled', giving this term the strong meaning it has in the anthropological tradition. It is true that a large proportion of sub-Saharan Africans living in Morocco are students, currently estimated at just under 10 000, mainly from French-speaking Africa (Berriane, 2009). Their insecure economic status, especially in the case of recipients of scholarships from bankrupt states, and the frequently erratic nature of their study cycle, often make them little different from the 'migrants' whose condition they share. Many of them choose to stay in Morocco once their studies are completed. They find jobs relatively easily in a wide range of fields, from call centres to medical and paramedical careers, from the press to private education and information technology. In many cases, it is their perfect command of French as well as their technical skills that make them attractive to the local labour market. Finally, in Libya, before the political destabilisation of the country, a large majority of the 2.5 million migrant workers acknowledged by the former regime were sub-Saharan Africans (Pliez, 2005), and this remains the case today, even if they are now only in transit (Jacques, 2013). We must also add the sub-Saharan students (Berriane, 2009) to whom universities and specialised schools are increasingly opening up in Tunisia, Morocco (where there are slightly over 10 000 foreign students, almost all of them sub-Saharan Africans) and Algeria.

These students, while clearly socially different from the 'transients', the unfortunate candidates for passage to Europe, are increasingly integrating into local labour markets, particularly in the health and service professions, after finishing their studies.

This is the paradox of new migratory dynamics in the Maghreb, and especially in Morocco, given the diversity and fragmentation of the sectors in which migrants are present. As is well known, Algeria, Morocco and Tunisia have in common significant structural unemployment, which is even more acute among young graduates. In 2012, the unemployment rate of young people (aged 16–25) was almost 22 per cent in Morocco; 22 per cent in Algeria, where this figure is highly contested as it is considered to be an underestimate; and 35.6 per cent in Tunisia.[9] It may therefore seem absurd that young sub-Saharan graduates should find even a narrow path to employment, especially as the political mobilisation of young 'local' unemployed graduates is considerable (Badimon, 2009). These sub-Saharan graduates fulfil the needs of the French-speaking press, where they work as freelancers, as journalists, in call centres where their command of the French language, often spoken without an accent, is a professional skill, and finally, they work informally as school assistants for middle-class children, some of them recruited as teachers in the network of private schools that is developing in Morocco. This raises the question of why Moroccan graduates, who are also French-speaking, do not have access to these jobs, and the predictable answer is fairly obvious: most of the time, it is because they refuse the conditions of insecurity or low pay that are accepted by migrants, because while an unemployed Moroccan graduate can hope to survive while unemployed because they often have the support of their family, migrants are often alone and without support. It is also clear that, insofar as the state regularly sets up recruitment cycles for unemployed Moroccan graduates, waiting for these hiring measures is beneficial. As a result, this division tends to widen the gap between the public sector, which in Algeria, at least, must be described as 'rentier', and the private sector, where conditions of access, through the very possibility of having recourse to migrant labour, tend to diverge from the requirements and expectations of national candidates. This phenomenon has been well described by American sociologists in relation to the 'competition' between young black Americans and new migrants (Waldinger, 1996). However, the hypothesis must be put forward that, in some emerging countries, resorting to migration is not without effects, but is rather a condition (if not the condition) that allows, in certain new and fragile sectors (communication, media, tourism), the emergence of a non-rentier entrepreneurial private sector.

Finally, street vendors, undoubtedly the North African migrants participating in the most pendular form of migration, multiply their commercial trips at the same time as they build diaspora networks in the countries where they travel. These trading activities have evolved considerably since the first studies that shed light on them and described their urban methods of organisation (Tarrius, 2002). These *capitalismes à la valise* ('suitcase capitalists') (Peraldi, 2007), which are concentrated in the former colonial capitals, Marseille and Paris, and continue to widely mobilise informal diaspora networks, have progressively moved to new commercial destinations, such as Istanbul in the 1990s, then Dubai and finally China (Choplin and Pliez, 2018), at the same time as commercial channels and connected circuits were being organised in an entrepreneurial form. This was particularly the case in the second-hand clothing industry (Sandoval Hernandez et al., 2019), dominated by a few major Tunisian companies; in the wedding organisation industry, in which highly organised Moroccan companies are established;[10] and finally in the second-hand car market (Rosenfeld, 2017). Thus, we currently observe not only a reduction in the length of stay, regardless of the professional activity sought by migrants, but also a decline in sedentary lifestyle: even those that are established make multiple trips between their country of origin and their host country, following the example of the *chibanis*,[11] retired Algerian or Moroccan workers who, even though they have moved back to their country, regularly return to the country where they spent their professional life to receive their retirement pension.

Without taking into account the scale of intra-European migration (as of the end of 2014, the Ministry of Foreign Affairs registered 835 255 French nationals in Europe), the migratory movement towards the countries of sub-Saharan Africa and the Maghreb is growing steadily. Figures from French consulates illustrate the trend, although they only partially reflect this phenomenon: 91 092 French nationals were registered in 2006 in the Maghreb (Tunisia, Algeria, Morocco), with 107 103 in 2014. In the case of sub-Saharan Africa, there were 126 573 registered in 2006, and 141 787 in 2014. These Europeans, whether tourists, expatriates or residents, have rarely been the subject of sociological or anthropological research. However, a 'new' migration regime is emerging: the traditional 'expatriates' are being replaced by 'migrants', insofar as a new generation of Europeans, and particularly French people, are settling on the African continent without a 'mission order' or, consequently, any of the privileges hitherto attached to expatriate status (for example, contract, social security cover, expatriation bonus, and so on).

THE NEW MIGRANTS

These new migrants (Peraldi and Terrazzoni, 2016b) are divided into three main types of socio-professional profiles, although the diversity of reasons for mobility and their individual character means that any grouping inevitably fails to take account of some profiles and singularities. The first type groups together those 'not in the labour force', including, but not exclusive to, the many retirees, who often purchase a property in Marrakech, Essaouira or Agadir. Contrary to rumour, this influx is not concentrated in the old medinas alone. In Marrakech, it also concerns the European neighbourhood of Guéliz, the suburbs (Palmeraie) of Essaouira, the districts of the new city (Azlef, Erraounak) and the surrounding countryside (Ghazoua). The second group is made up of entrepreneurs. Some of them are entrepreneurs by trade, but they are most often individuals who come to Marrakech, Essaouira or Agadir and set up a company there, taking advantage of the tourist boom prevailing in these cities. They are sometimes the only people working in these companies, which are very micro and are used to sell services. Local labour laws limit the hiring of foreign employees by local companies. Here again, the media only focus on owners of riads, new small and medium-sized hotel businesses, closer to guesthouses than to hotels. They offer a limited number of rooms and most often include a living area for the owner, who then welcomes tourists 'at home'. Around these new hoteliers, who are the focus of attention, there are however a myriad of entrepreneurs who are socially similar to them and who settle to try out a new career and a new life in the restaurant, service or craft industries.

Finally, the third profile is that of employees, of the entrepreneurs just mentioned, but more generally of companies operating in the tourist industry, some of whom work for Moroccan salaries and sometimes illegally. We have seen some young people working in their compatriots' businesses (showrooms, restaurants, hotels) for the Moroccan minimum wage of 2500 dirhams, equivalent to €250 per month) paid in cash. All these individuals live in Morocco, with one of the following two types of administrative status. Some have a tourist visa, which gives them the right to stay in the country for three months, renewable once but in practice many more times, for which renewal requires leaving the territory. In theory, holders of this visa do not have the right to work and cannot open a bank account to be credited in the local currency, the dirham, as it is non-convertible. However, many live and work in Morocco under this regime. When migrants have a work contract or a company set up in Morocco (which residents can create), or when they are married to a Moroccan national, these new migrants can benefit from a residence permit, valid for one year, renewable on a yearly basis for three years and extendable to five, then ten years. This permit gives them two main rights: to work in Morocco, and to open a bank account that will be credited in dirhams. The process of obtaining this residence permit is not simple and results in the loss of a certain number of advantages, such as social security coverage under the French regime. In February 2008, 21 914 people benefited from this permit, whereas at the end of 2007, 34 097 people were registered in consular registers, according to figures from the National Security Directorate of the Kingdom of Morocco and the

French Ministry of Foreign Affairs. The number of residence permits therefore only reveals the institutionalised part of a population, the majority of whom live under the regime of simple tourists, regularly going back to Europe before the expiry of a tourist visa (three months), which can be renewed without limit.

What these three types of profiles have in common is that they have negotiated the conditions of their mobility and settlement in Morocco themselves without an institutional mediator. In this sense, their experiences differ from those of expatriates, since these migrants are engaged in permanent negotiation with the local society, in terms of both relationships and administration, to fulfil most of the obligations of daily life, whether they are the most complex and cumbersome, such as opening a bank account, drawing up an employment contract, buying a business or a property, or less demanding, such as driving a car, enrolling a child at school, or paying bills. Contrary to the image given by the European press, which is fascinated by the 'jet set' that has included Marrakech in its circuit, the vast majority of these new European migrants come from the least economically and socially protected fringe of the middle classes; these middle classes 'in deficit' lack the necessary economic or social capital to protect them from the hazards of a chaotic economic situation. They include 'heirs' (Boubeker, 2003) without educational capital, people who attended university courses that were abandoned too early in fields of study with no prospects, executives, especially in sales, whose careers were interrupted by a brutal lay-off or a requirement to retrain that was not accepted, commercial failures, precarious careers with one skilled job after another, each of short duration, people without qualifications who have many different jobs, or quite simply professional lives that the interviewees describe as dull. These experiences are a source of dissatisfaction for those who live them, rather than a sign of relegation; the dissatisfaction of those who have acquired cultural capital, but whose living conditions, especially their professional conditions, appear to them to be mediocre and unsatisfactory in light of this capital. There are no figures, no reliable quantitative data concerning the population of study. Informality is widespread, and concerns status as a foreigner in Morocco, as well as professional activity and personal status.

While a number of these French nationals have been living in Morocco for many years, and while their economic activities are visible in the urban centres since they have reshaped the landscape, they remain paradoxically socially invisible, both in terms of numbers and in the urban space, if only because they are confused with tourists in the places they frequent. These migrants do not constitute a community, nor even a set of aggregates, groups, clans or micro-societies, but rather a heterogeneous collection of individuals who are all the more elusive since they are mobile, using their status as tourists and the consequent need to return to Europe every three months as an opportunity to maintain links in their country of origin. Although their 'unprotected' status forces them to constantly mediate with local society, these migrants do not organise as part of a cosmopolitan society, because their relations with local society are minimal. Their contacts with Moroccans are limited, in most cases, to professional relations – whether in associations or salaried employment – and, on a day-to-day basis, to relations linked to the private sphere, since locals often constitute their household staff. Apart from a few elite affinities between French and Moroccans in small intellectual and artistic circles, only members of mixed couples report having friends and acquaintances other than utilitarian ones in local society. Bauman's term is probably the most appropriate to describe the mode of existence of these migrants in Moroccan society: a way of being that can be termed 'liquid' (Bauman, 2006) to characterise both its mobility and its diffuse, fluid character. Migrants do not form a society or neighbourhood, let alone a community or niche. They occupy in a diffuse manner positions which are rarely hegemonic, in the urban space and in the space of activity.

Even Europeans who are settled in the Maghreb are 'mobile actors' before being migrants: either because, in the case of retirees, they live only part of the year in their residence outside Europe; or because, in employment, they play on the status of tourist, imposing on themselves the need to return to their country of citizenship each time their right of residence expires (every two months in the case of Morocco) (Terrazzoni, 2020). It is therefore not unreasonable to suggest that this Euro-Maghreb area, which was a migratory space based on the perpetuation of colonial links, is today being transformed into a circulatory space for multiple social actors who set up their lives and activities either side of the Mediterranean. This is universally accepted as the main characteristic of a transnational space. This very rapid process of transnationalisation can be clarified by another term, that of globalisation. Indeed, as I have briefly mentioned, the Maghreb itself is discreetly becoming a migratory space, open not only to the Mediterranean, or to the former colonial metropolises, but also to the wider area of Central and Eastern Africa, and even to Asia.

CONCLUSION

In conclusion, it should be said that the perception of this dynamic of change in the Euro-Maghreb or Euro-Mediterranean migratory space not only requires the collection of factual elements and monographs, but also to fully understand its complexity we must perform a paradigmatic reversal of perspective. Migratory movements should no longer be seen from Europe, de facto considered as the central, nodal point of arrival of flows, but from their point of departure. This is what researchers cited in this chapter and others have done in recent years. But in performing this reversal, the very world within which these movements take place also changes. For if we are still in a Euro-Mediterranean space, centred on the confrontation between the two shores, this also appears to be a pivotal place, at the core of 'tectonic' migratory plates that link this Mediterranean space to movements from Africa and Asia, until flows, pioneered by North African students going to the United States or Canada, take the direction of the Americas. If we accept that a transformation of the mechanics and dynamics of migration from the colonial to the transnational is taking place here, it is not only migratory modalities that are changing, and new figures that are appearing: it is more fundamentally a change in the relationship to the world, marked by the privatisation of flows, their feminisation, and increased autonomy in journeys. A survey of these new figures and their effects on the societies involved largely remains to be undertaken.

NOTES

1. There were just over 40 000 Moroccan students registered in French universities or prestigious graduate schools in 2018, and 30 000 Algerians and Tunisians in the same year.
2. In an extensive bibliography on this subject, one of the first researchers to develop the notion of criminalisation should be mentioned: see Palidda (2011).
3. An Algerian arrested at customs when attempting to cross the border now faces a nine-month prison sentence.
4. In this area again, the existing bibliography is substantial. Among other works, those in the Babel collection, published by the research programme of the same name directed by Michel Agier, should be mentioned. Other references include Bernardie Tahir and Scholl, 2018, and Migreurop, 2017.
5. The visa is valid for one year and can be repeatedly renewed. It is only available to artists, entrepreneurs and teachers who, through their mobility, ensure the continuity of elite links between France and Morocco. This transcolonial (more than transnational) elite is the lifeblood of restaurants, clubs and media in the city of Marrakech. On this subject, see Peraldi (2018).
6. Before COVID and the restrictions it imposed, Marrakech was one of the favourite tourist destinations of the French, welcoming nearly 3 million tourists, mainly European, each year (see Peraldi, 2018). Tunisia, and its beaches in Djerba and Hammamet, followed closely in the list of French tourist destinations before the pandemic.
7. Bonnes philippines, mauvais employeurs. *Courrier International*, 1 April 2009, http//www.courrier international.com.
8. See Alioua (2005), Pian (2009) and Bava and Capone (2010).
9. Given that the figure for Tunisia relates to the period after the change of regime, the comparison can be made on the basis of 2009, figures when unemployment among 16–25-year-olds was close to that in other Maghreb countries, at 21.6 per cent.
10. On this subject see Rim Affaya's doctoral thesis (forthcoming), EHESS Marseille.
11. This refers to North African retirees who participate in pendular migration between France, where they migrated, and their country of origin where they maintain family ties (Djemaï, 2011).

REFERENCES

Agier, M. (ed.) (2014). *Un monde de camps*. Paris: La Découverte.

Alioua, M. (2005). La migration transnationale des africains subsahariens au Maghreb: l'exemple de l'étape marocaine. *Maghreb-Machrek*, 185: 37–57, doi: https://doi.org/10.3406/horma.2005.2303.

Badimon, M.E. (2009). Les manifestations des diplômés chômeurs au Maroc: la rue comme espace de négociation du tolérable. *Genèses*, 4: 30–50, doi: https://doi.org/10.3917/gen.077.0030#xd_co_f=NTc2MGY0NTUtNWM0ZS00MGIyLThkNDktZDM5ZThjNTE1YTJi~.

Bauman, Z. (2006). *La vie liquide*. Arles: Le Rouergue/Chambon.

Bava, S. and Capone, S. (2010). Religions transnationales et migrations. Regards croisés sur un champ en mouvement. *Autrepart*, 56: 3–15, doi: https://doi.org/10.3917/autr.056.0003#xd_co_f=NTc2MGY0NTUtNWM0ZS00MGIyLThkNDktZDM5ZThjNTE1YTJi~.

Bernardie Tahir, N. and Schmoll, C. (eds) (2018). *Méditerranée: des frontières à la dérive*. Paris: Le Passager Clandestin.

Berriane, J. (2009). Les étudiants subsahariens au maroc: des migrants parmi d'autres? *Méditerranée*, 113: 147–150, doi: https://doi.org/10.4000/mediterranee.3843.

Beski-Chafiq, C. (2014). Femmes en migration: enjeux et défis d'une approche genré. In Poinsot, M. (ed.), *Migrations et mutations de la société française: l'état des savoirs*. Paris: La Découverte, pp. 266–274.

Boubeker, A. (2003). *Les Mondes de l'ethnicité*. Paris: Balland.

Bredeloup, S. (2008). L'aventurier, une figure de la migration africaine. *Cahiers Internationaux de Sociologie*, 2 (125): 281–306, doi: https://doi.org/10.3917/cis.125.0281#xd_co_f=NTc2MGY0NTUtNWM0ZS00MGIyLThkNDktZDM5ZThjNTE1YTJi~.

Choplin, A. (2008). L'immigré, le migrant, l'allochtone: circulations migratoires et figures de l'étranger en Mauritanie. *Politiques Africaines*, 109: 73–90, doi: https://doi.org/10.3917/polaf.109.0073#xd_co_f=NTc2MGY0NTUtNWM0ZS00MGIyLThkNDktZDM5ZThjNTE1YTJi~.

Choplin, A. and Pliez, O. (2018). *La mondialisation des pauvres*. Paris: Seuil.

De Gourcy, C. (2005). *L'autonomie dans la migration. Réflexions autour d'une énigme*. Paris: Karthala.

Djemaï, N. (2011). *Invisibles: la tragédie des chibanis*. Arles: Actes Sud.

Fassin, D. (ed.) (2010). *Les nouvelles frontières de la société française*. Paris: La Découverte.

Fine, A. and Puech, I. (2019). Domestiques d'ici et d'ailleurs. *Travail, genre et sociétés*, 22: 25–114, doi: https://doi.org/10.3917/tgs.022.0025#xd_co_f=NTc2MGY0NTUtNWM0ZS00MGIyLThkNDktZDM5ZThjNTE1YTJi~.

Guezzen, A.N. (2021). *Entre autonomie et assujettissement: les migrations de femmes maghrébines vers les Emirats arabes unis. Cas du Maroc et de l'Algérie*. EHESS Thesis.

Jacques, G. (2013). Migrations en Libye: réalités et défis. *Confluences Méditerranée*, 87 (4): 55–66, doi: https://doi.org/10.3917/come.087.0055#xd_co_f=NTc2MGY0NTUtNWM0ZS00MGIyLThkNDktZDM5ZThjNTE1YTJi~.

Marfaing, L. and Wippel, S. (eds) (2004). *Les relations transsahariennes à l'époque contemporaine*. Paris: Karthala.

Mezzadra, S. (2004). Capitalism, migrations, and social struggles: preliminary notes for a theory on the autonomy of migrations. *Multitudes*, 19 (5): 17–30, doi: https://doi .org/10.3917/mult.019.0017#xd_co_f=NTMzMGI5YTEtMTQ4OC00NjU4LWI5 ZjUtZGIzYmUzMWM0OTNl~.

Migreurop (2017). *Atlas critique des migrations en Europe*. Paris: Armand Colin.

Morice, A. and Potot, S. (eds) (2010). *De l'ouvrier immigré aux travailleurs sans papiers. Les étrangers dans la modernisation du salariat*. Paris: Karthala.

Palidda, S. (ed.) (2011). *Migrations critiques. Repenser les migrations comme mobilité humaine en Méditerranée*. Paris: Karthala.

Pellegrini, C. (2016). Parcours de petits entrepreneurs français à Marrakech. *Cahiers d'Etudes Africaines*, 221–222 (1–2): 81–100, doi: https://doi.org/10.4000/ etudesafricaines.18909.

Peraldi, M. (2007). Aventuriers du nouveau capitalisme marchand. Essai d'anthropologie de l'éthique mercantile. In Adelkhah, F. and Bayart, J.F. (eds), *Voyages du développement. Emigration, commerce, exil*. Paris: Karthala, pp. 73–113.

Peraldi, M. (ed.) (2011). *D'une Afrique à l'autre. Migrations subsahariennes au Maroc*. Paris: Karthala.

Peraldi, M. (2018). *Marrakech, ou le souk des possibles*. Paris: La Découverte.

Peraldi, M. and Terrazzoni, L. (2016a). Anthropologie des Européens en Afrique. Mémoire coloniale et nouvelles aventures migratoires. *Cahiers d'Etudes Africaines*, 221–222 (1–2): 9–28, doi: https://doi.org/10.4000/etudesafricaines.18882.

Peraldi, M. and Terrazzoni, L. (2016b). Nouvelles migrations? Les français dans les circulations migratoires européennes vers le Maroc. *Autrepart*, 77: 69–86, doi: https://doi.org/10.3917/autr.077.0069#xd_co_f=NTc2MGY0NTUtNWM0ZS 00MGIyLThkNDktZDM5ZThjNTE1YTJi~.

Pian, A. (2009). *Aux nouvelles frontières de l'Europe. L'aventure incertaine des sénégalais au Maroc*. Paris: La Dispute.

Pliez, O. (2005). Le Sahara libyen dans les nouvelles configurations migratoires. *Revue Européenne des Migrations Internationales*, 16 (3): 165–182, doi: https://doi.org/10 .3406/remi.2000.1746.

Rea, A. (2021). *Sociologie de l'immigration*. Paris: La Découverte.

Rosenfeld, M. (2017). *Car connection. La filière africaine des véhicules d'occasion*. Paris: Karthala.

Salzbrunn, M., Souiah, F. and Mastrangelo, S. (2020). Parcours migratoire des harragas tunisiens. Entre contrainte et opportunité. In Lacroix, T., Daghmi, F., Dureau, F., Robin, N. and Scioldo-Zürcher, Y. (eds), *Penser les migrations pour repenser la société*. Tours: Presses Universitaires François Rabelais, pp. 167–182.

Sandoval Hernandez, E., Rosenfeld, M. and Peraldi, M. (2019). *La fripe du Nord au Sud. Production globale, commerce transfrontalier et marchés informels de vêtements usagés*. Paris: Ed. Petra.

Schmoll, C. (2020). *Les damnées de la mer. Femmes et frontières en Méditerranée*. Paris: La Découverte.

Souiah, F. (2013). Les politiques migratoires restrictives: une fabrique de harraga. *Hommes et Migrations*, 1304 (4): 95–101, doi: https://doi.org/10.4000/ hommesmigrations.2652.

Tarrius, A. (2002). *La mondialisation par le bas. Les nouveaux nomades de l'économie souterraine*. Paris: Balland.

Terrazzoni, L. (2020). Visibilités et invisibilités des Français à Essaouira et Marrakech. In Lacroix, T., Dahgmi, F., Dureau, F., Robin, N. and Scioldo-Zürcher, Y.

(eds), *Penser les migrations pour repenser la société*. Tours: Presses Universitaires de François Rabelais, pp. 267–280.

Therrien, C. (2018). *En voyage chez soi: trajectoires de couples mixtes au Maroc*. Casablanca: La Croisée des Chemins.

Triaud, J.L. and Robinson, D. (eds) (2000). *La Tijaniyya. Une confrérie musulmane à la conquête de l'Afrique*. Paris: Karthala.

Waldinger, R. (1996). *Still the Promised City? African American and New Immigrants in Postindustrial New York*. Cambridge, MA: Harvard University Press.

6. Gender and emigration: labour market integration and work–life balance strategies of young Spanish female migrants to France and Germany

Belén Fernández-Suárez and Alberto Capote Lama

INTRODUCTION

In the European context, Spain has a long-standing tradition of being one of the leading migrant exporting countries. From 1960 to 1973, it was one of the main labour-providing regions for the most important European destinations in terms of labour market. In these years the most common profile of an emigrant was that of a young male adult, predominantly a factory, construction or agricultural worker (Reques Velasco and De Cos Guerra, 2003). However, it must be remembered that during this period there was an increase in the flow of Spanish women emigrating alone. In the case of France, as indicated by authors such as Fernández Asperilla (2009) and Oso (2009), this phenomenon has previously been overlooked in the research.

Following the economic crisis of 2008, an increase of migratory flows from Southern Europe (severely affected by the loss of jobs and the deterioration of its social fabric) to traditional migrant-receiving European destinations was once again witnessed. These migratory flows were similar across the Southern European region, with its common socio-cultural elements such as high unemployment and a highly unstable labour market, the late emancipation of young people from families, and high educational levels in the younger age groups (Pérez-Caramés, 2017; Capote Lama and Fernández Suárez, 2021; Vázquez Silva et al., 2021). For Dubucs and Mourlane (2017), this process of migration from Southern Europe to Northern and Central Europe can be explained by the delay on the part of young people in achieving employment, housing and stability in this region. There are numerous socio-structural elements in the societies of Southern Europe that might have encouraged this intra-European migration flow, to which the greater impact of economic crises in such territories should be added. To date there has been a lack of research into intra-European migration flows from Southern Europe to Central and Northern Europe (Impedovo and Ballatore, 2019). The academic Kaura Oso (2005) affirms that Spanish female migration in the 20th century has been rendered invisible in migratory studies, despite the fact that recent studies allude to a higher number of women in inter-European migratory flows, as well as a higher probability of university-educated women emigrating (Eremenko and Miyar-Busto, 2020). This chapter asks the question: to what extent might recent female migration flows once again have been considered to have secondary significance in academic studies?

While it is clear is that there is a close link between the economic crisis and the decision made to emigrate (Bygnes and Flipo, 2017; Vázquez Silva et al., 2021), the context in which this more recent phenomenon of Spanish emigration occurs is very different from that of past waves. The signing of the Maastricht Treaty in 1992 established free movement between European Union (EU) member states. Despite the free movement of workers not meeting expectations initially (Dubucs and Mourlane, 2017), in recent years intra-European migratory flows have diversified and intensified. Two overlapping stages can be identified (Benton and Petrovic, 2013): first, the arrival of migratory flows from Eastern Europe after the enlargement of the European Union in 2004; and second, following the economic crisis of 2008, with the increase of migration from Southern Europe (Greece, Italy, Portugal and Spain). EU member states did not all have the same experience of intra-European migration flows either before free movement was introduced or following its introduction. This is a reflection of the inequalities inherent within the European Union (Flipo, 2017; Wihtol de Wenden, 2017), where some have played the role of sending countries and others that of receiving countries. In this regard, there is a broad consensus that recent emigration from Southern Europe has again placed the region in a semi-peripheral role whereby it is once more a provider of labour (Antonucci and Varriale, 2020; Cortés et al., 2020; Della Puppa et al., 2021). Unlike for past waves, labour market integration in destination countries has been characterised to a greater extent by duality, where some of those who have emigrated more recently have found employment in unskilled labour, for example, in the catering and care sectors; and others have found work in more skilled sectors, such as health and engineering, with both markets being subject to international demand in some European countries (Roca and Martín Díaz, 2017). Migrant profiles have been characterised by their diversity (Bermúdez and Oso, 2020), with a certain predominance of young people with a university education. Other characteristics to be highlighted in relation to recent intra-European migration flows are increased mobility, a circular trend, and a potentially temporary nature (King and Williams, 2018). Thus, movement might appear to be a resource for qualified migrants with a view to improving their professional careers (Becker and Teney, 2020). However, more recent studies have shown that some years after the initial momentum of East–West and South–North intra-European migration flows, migrants have tended to choose a degree of permanence or stability in the destination countries, as opposed to the impermanence proposed by the theory of liquid migration (Bygnes and Erdal, 2017; Franceschelli, 2020). The search for financial stability, or the desire to provide a better future for their offspring, would be some of the arguments weighed up by migrants when choosing stability or permanence in the destination country (Herrero-Arias et al., 2020).

In the light of developments in recent intra-European migration flows, the aim of this chapter is to analyse integration into the labour market of this new wave of Spanish migrants to France and Germany, and the impact of gender on the reasons given for migrating. As similar studies have pointed out, there has been a woeful failure to consider the gender perspective in academic research into intra-European migration, and especially with regard to the new wave of emigration from Spain (Cortés et al., 2020). This chapter attempts to compensate for this oversight by addressing this most recent Spanish migratory phenomenon from a gender perspective. It focuses on analysing how gender relations determine integration in the host country, based on two premises: first, the idea that the role of women in recent Spanish emigration has once again been overlooked, both those women who have gained access to the more traditional labour market niches, such as the care sector, as well as young, skilled workers aiming to develop their careers in sectors that have been masculinised on account of their social prestige (Isaakyan and Triandafyllidou, 2016); and second, as pointed out by the feminist perspective on migratory studies, men and women migrate in different ways, insofar as their reasons, the channels they use and their migratory projects are concerned (Visic and Poleti-Cosic, 2018). For the purposes of this analysis, the chapter first provides a summary of the most important contributions on the role of women in international migration. Next, it offers a brief description of the qualitative methodology used to back up the results set out in this chapter, followed by an analysis of the main results. The chapter ends with some brief conclusions.

WOMEN AND INTERNATIONAL MIGRATION

It has been almost unanimously accepted that the proportion of women in contemporary migratory flows in Organisation for Economic Co-operation and Development (OECD) countries has increased, rising to over 50 per cent at the beginning of the century (Castles et al., 2014). This increase in female migration, especially that of highly skilled women, is the result of many factors, ranging from an overall increase in women's professional skills, to appealing factors in the destination countries, as well as the greater possibility of securing a job which makes it easier to achieve a healthy work–life balance. Due in part to a lack of research into the migration of highly skilled women, this increased incidence has tended to accentuate a view of female migration whereby women are seen as passive and dependent individuals, and not autonomous protagonists in their decision to migrate (Oso, 2005; Docquier et al., 2009; Meares, 2010; Dumitru, 2017). González Ramos and Vergés Bosch (2013) point out that the challenges of migration are greater for women than for men who fit the same profile, as women have to consider their migratory decisions and projects more closely, because they need to take their gendered familial roles and life in a couple into consideration alongside their professional aspirations. For women, migration does not always translate into emancipation, and they must often deal with new forms of inequality, to which they are required to generate suitable responses (Riaño, 2011).

In recent years, one of the most commonly used tactics in female migration, particularly intra-European migration, has been to resort to 'au pair' mobility programmes. These mobility programmes emerged in the 1980s with the aim of promoting language learning and intercultural exchange. However, the au pair scheme has been increasingly called into question, given its lack of regularisation and the ambiguity of its legal status, placing care work in a pseudo-familial relationship that falls within the frame of new insecurities related to globalisation (Eldén and Anving, 2019; Oishi and Ono, 2020). A further issue related to the au pair programme is its invisibility, on account of the previously mentioned legal ambiguity it affords workers, and that it takes place in a domestic environment behind closed doors (Sekeráková Búriková, 2020). Despite this, many young women have used this resource as a strategy for pursuing a migration project, developing networks, or simply learning a language (Geserick, 2012; Cox and Busch, 2016). Thus, in a study on young Spanish female au pairs in the United Kingdom, Muñoz-Rodríguez and Santos Ortega (2015) state that many view the move as a springboard towards another job in the future. Having said this, they also underline that this tactic, while accessible, implies a period of significant vulnerability.

The proportion of women in recent intra-European migratory movements, in outflows from both Southern and Eastern Europe, has increased. Bermúdez and Oso (2020) consider this to be the result of an increased demand for workers in female-based sectors, regardless of the level of skill required (in care and domestic service, health, education, and so on). Another feminised sector is that of healthcare, with nurses and physiotherapists choosing to emigrate to other European countries. According to Tanja Visic and Dunja Poleti-Cosic (2018), we can currently talk of a global phenomenon whereby women are emigrating to take on care work and social reproductive work, to the point that this is considered a 'care drain' on sending countries. In the case of intra-European migration, free movement has resulted in the labour demand of cities in the Netherlands and Switzerland being met (Bruquetas Callejo, 2020).

In short, research into the phenomenon of female intra-European migration is sparse within migration studies. Papers on the role of migration flows of women from Southern Europe to EU regions in Central and Northern Europe are beginning to be published now, but are in their early stages, and to this end, this chapter aims to contribute towards meeting such a demand for research and knowledge.

METHODOLOGY

The data analysed in this chapter is part of a research project on recent emigration from Spain to other European countries. The analysis was based on semi-structured, in-depth interviews with a group of Spanish women who emigrated to France and Germany after the 2008 economic crisis, these being two of the countries, along with the United Kingdom, that have recently received the highest number of migrants from Spain. The interviewees were recruited via Facebook groups frequented by Spaniards living in France and Germany's major cities (Paris, Nice, Bordeaux, Berlin and Düsseldorf). Snowball sampling was used to make contact with the interviewees. The typical profile is that of a woman with a high level of education, mainly with intermediate or higher education (A-level equivalent or vocational training). The interviews were conducted individually with questions of an open-ended and exploratory nature, including questions about different aspects of the migratory process: decision-making, the strategies used, social and labour integration in the destination countries, or a definition of short- and medium-term projects. All the interviews were recorded and transcribed with the approval of the participants. A total of 40 interviews with women, 20 Spanish migrants in France and 20 in Germany, were analysed. The names of those interviewed have been changed for purposes of anonymity.

HIGHLY QUALIFIED SPANISH FEMALE MIGRANTS IN EUROPE: GENDER-SPECIFIC MOBILITY STRATEGIES IN A GLOBAL LABOUR MARKET

This section analyses the migratory processes and strategies of young Spanish women who have moved internally in Europe, with a focus on the reasons given for leaving their country of origin, integration into the female labour market, and the different migration strategies adopted on account of the gender division of labour, the relevance of cultural capital in a professional career in the destination society and, finally, the work–life balance of young Spanish women with long-term migration projects.

The reasons Spanish women give for emigrating are often similar to those of men, and allude to job insecurity in Spain, the difficulties involved in progressing professionally, and attaining stability. Those heading the new wave of Spanish emigration are characterised by their refusal to conform to a labour market that prevents them from progressing in their professional careers and personal projects. The mobility of Spanish women is conditioned by the regulatory and cultural gender regimes of the countries of both origin and destination. The difficulties they experience integrating in destination countries are conditioned by cultural capital. Their educational credentials have a different market value in Spain than in France or Germany, possibly leading to increased employability in the destination society. Furthermore, other determining factors regarding labour integration include the level of language skills, the inherent structure of the French and/or German labour markets requiring certain types of female workers, and finally, the gender regimes themselves that limit women's options and equality in the workplace.

Labour Market Integration of Young Women in Europe

First, it should be emphasised that the level of knowledge of the language of the destination country conditions the strategies of many young Spanish women when entering the labour market. As mentioned above, the careers of female Spanish migrants in France and Germany are also conditioned by cultural capital (the market value of educational credentials and knowledge of the language of the destination country) and by the labour market demand in the host society. This gives rise to three migratory profiles within the overall female migration flow: (1) highly skilled, university-educated women in high-demand job sectors in the destination society (the health sector, engineering, telecommunications and research sectors, and so on); (2) highly skilled, university-educated women for whom demand is sparse in the destination labour market (social sciences or humanities); and (3) those with secondary education qualifications, often having worked previously in Spain in the service sector, especially in the catering, retail or care sectors. As the demand for labour in the domestic service sector is markedly gender-based, a relatively common strategy should be added, that is, entry via the feminised niche in the labour market: employment as an au pair. From their country of origin, female Spanish au pairs look for a home which enables them to save on accommodation, receive enough money to live on, as well as giving them an opportunity to learn the language. Moreover, this is a transversal strategy insofar as the social class of the origin families of the migrant is concerned, although as a migratory integration tactic it is much more pronounced in young, working-class, university-educated females between the ages of 20 and 30. In general terms, young women tend to consider this phase of employment to be frustrating, recounting stories of their experiences as au pairs that include the high demands made by the host families, the low wages and, at times, the lack of freedom. However, many of them emphasise that it enabled them to learn the language. Such is the case for Hortensia, who arrived in Paris with an employment contract to work as an au pair, having left Galicia after finishing her studies due to the lack of job opportunities. Her family had suffered the consequences of the 2008 economic crisis, and this undoubtedly influenced her decision to emigrate. She was a part of the Erasmus generation, and it was during this experience that she met her French boyfriend. She chose to work in France as an au pair, but experienced discord within the family unit and suffered from emotional strain as a result. Below is an extract from her interview:

> I came here to work as an au pair. I didn't come to live with him straight away [her French boyfriend] or anything like that, I came to learn about history and improve my level of French. The experience was … I worked as an au pair … in fact, the idea was to stay here for the entire school year but I only lasted eight months … and I stayed mainly for the boy … Things started to become really weird and difficult, there was never any food in the house. (Hortensia, resident in Paris, France)

As an elite sportswoman with a degree in architecture, Aldara's case is different. She had previous experience of working in Spain, none of which she found satisfactory, and also wanted to experience new things. She chose Germany as her destination, but lacking the necessary language skills, she decided to work as an au pair for at least a year. The acquisition of language skills and the value of her qualifications enabled her to find work in her professional field quickly. This is an extract from her interview:

> I could have stayed in Spain working in a different field: being a judo teacher, whatever … I had friends. I mean, I would have had work, that wasn't the problem. The thing is, I had to work really hard for my degree and I wanted to work in my profession at whatever cost. So I came over without knowing any German. I started off as an au pair, a nanny. I found that job in Spain. I was with a family and, well, I had brought over a car and I managed to get the family to pay for German classes, as they didn't pay me very much. 260 euros a month, but of course you didn't have to worry about food or accommodation or anything, as that's included. And, well, I was an au pair for 10 months, studying German, and then I managed to find some work experience which paid 10 euros an hour, undeclared, with an architect. (Aldara, resident in Düsseldorf, Germany)

A significant number of highly skilled Spanish women emigrate with promising work opportunities and possibilities of promotion. For these women the language of the destination country is not always a significant obstacle, because they can work in English. Elvira belongs to this group of highly skilled female migrants who form a diverse group, comprised of, among other professions, healthcare workers, researchers, and employees of engineering and technology companies. She graduated in law and was working in a multi-national information technology company in Madrid. She married a German citizen and moved to Germany to work for the same company there. The professional careers of this kind of highly skilled worker often involve considerable labour mobility: in this case, Elvira's profession took her to Dubai and Switzerland, and although her fixed residence is in Germany, she currently works in Holland. As Pérez Caramés (2017) points out, in the new wave of Spanish emigration, people have found employment in sectors where mobility is a key part of jobs that are embedded in the global economy. For Elvira, this constant movement has affected both her husband and her young daughter. Indeed, as has been reflected in other studies (González Ramos and Vergés Bosch, 2013), sometimes mobility makes it extremely difficult to establish a healthy work–life balance. Elvira's reasons for emigrating were manifold, insofar as opportunities to both develop a professional career as well as form a family with a German citizen are concerned, as can be seen in the following extract from her interview:

> My choice of destination was not for love … we already had a long-distance relationship and it worked. But with regard to your first question, I think it did influence my decision, the fact that he didn't want to move to Spain, as he also had a good job in Germany, so he didn't even look to move. He doesn't speak Spanish and the employment situation there wasn't good. I think that's what led us to decide that he wouldn't move to Spain and that I would look to move abroad, and he could do that too, in order to be together. And that's how we ended up in Stuttgart, in the south. I went there with a work contract, with the same company I'd been working for in Spain, and my work was all in English. (Elvira, resident in Düsseldorf, Germany)

Continuing with highly skilled migration, in the healthcare sector this time, we come across Natalia, who on finishing university became a self-employed physiotherapist. But discontented with the economic situation in Spain, she decided to emigrate to France. The demand for skilled healthcare workers, and especially physiotherapists, is high in France and Spanish physiotherapists are highly sought after. Initial labour integration usually revolves around employment in spas as massage therapists, jobs which are considered tough and badly paid. Natalia currently has her own physiotherapy clinic and is studying a postgraduate course in osteopathy in Spain, where she intends to return in the near future. Thus, it can be seen that, although the demand for healthcare professionals is high, initiating this route is not without obstacles and often involves tough working conditions. Despite this, one of the reasons Natalia gives for emigrating was how much easier it was to practise her profession in France than in Spain, where the economic situation was unpromising:

> I wanted to study another language and spend some time abroad, and going to France was an opportunity to do that and practise my profession at the same time. France is one of the places where it's easy enough to go, the paperwork isn't too complicated … And apart from that, I really did want to go abroad, get away from the situation in Spain, with its Mickey Mouse contracts and so forth. Before leaving, I worked freelance for three companies at a time, coming and going, it was driving me mad. (Natalia, resident in Nice, France)

The labour integration of university-educated Spanish women whose professions are less in demand encompasses a diversity of careers. The success of the migratory projects of these women depends on several factors: their stage in the life cycle, the dynamism and gender-based stratification of the labour market in the destination country, and finally, the number of years as a resident, which would provide certain possibilities for progression. This chapter now turns to consider female university-educated Spanish migrants who are working in feminised labour sectors such as healthcare, catering or retail, and are clearly overqualified to carry out such kinds of jobs. Such is the case of Luisa, a Spanish migrant in France, with a degree in history and a postgraduate qualification in gender studies. Barely able to find work in the catering industry in Spain, which requires few or no qualifications, she arrived in France to work as an au pair and went from job to job looking after children in Spanish families in Bordeaux. She later did a number of different jobs until her French was good enough to do a master's degree in gender studies in a French university, which would enable her to work in this field in France. Hers is a clear example of overqualification in the labour market, in the countries of both origin and destination; with, however, improved expectations after the acquisition of language capital:

> You start looking for a job wherever you can, but you don't seem to get anywhere… I started off by looking after children … in families who lived here … Then I found a job giving out newspapers at train stops. That was 3 days a week, paying 450 euros a month, which was just enough to pay the rent and not much more. In November I found a job as a housekeeper in a hotel. That was for two months, at the start I was cleaning rooms. (Luisa, resident in Bordeaux, France)[1]

The research also uncovered cases of young, university-educated female Spanish emigrants with a very low employability rating in Spain, but who nevertheless managed to carve out a career in the destination country. Such is the case of Elisa, with a diploma in advertising and public relations and a master's degree in marketing management in Spain. In order to learn the language, she also decided to spend a year working as an au pair in Germany.

After that, she found a job in advertising, that is, in the sector she had studied to work in. These female emigrants value not only finding a job related to their area of study, but also the recognition of their skills and the opportunity to build a professional career. Despite being aware that her salary does not equate with those of the host country's own citizens, and the emotional cost of being separated from family, she considers that such an opportunity would not have presented itself in Spain. Elisa is a non-conformist who will not resign herself to accepting a job that is both unrelated to her chosen career and offers unstable working conditions:

> I feel valued. I think that I wouldn't have had the opportunity or projects in Spain that I've found here in Germany. In Spain, you can't even get close because, basically, when you're a junior, like me, you're lucky to get some small projects. Here, I've been able to work on some really important campaigns, for the whole of Europe. And that motivates you a lot, although, having said that, you do get paid less for being a foreigner than if you were German. (Elisa, resident in Düsseldorf, Germany)

The literature has focused almost exclusively on the emigration of young university-educated Spaniards, largely ignoring other educational qualifications, such as increasingly widespread vocational training. This tends to be the choice of families with fewer resources, and who were more severely affected by the economic crisis. Thus, once again, these young people have resorted to working as au pairs. África is a good example of this. She completed advanced vocational training in finance and accounting in Spain. In spite of her young age, before emigrating she had a number of jobs in Spain, some of them without an employment contract. Her first destination as an au pair was Ireland. She then went to France and worked part-time in a hostel where she had free accommodation. Acquiring cultural capital, including language skills, enabled her to climb the professional ladder and she currently works as a receptionist in a hotel. She does not rule out emigrating again in the future, although that would mean a separation from her French boyfriend:

> I've got a boyfriend, but I'm thinking of going to Switzerland or New York. He's going to stay in Monaco because he has an employment contract here. I love him very much, but I have to put myself first. I'll go, I'll continue my professional training and then I'll come back. That's just the way it has to be. (África, resident in Nice, France)

Many female Spanish migrants in Germany and France have a migration project that involves putting down roots in the destination country, partly because they are in a relationship with a citizen of the country or because they have had children there, which means that the decision will be made to stay, at least in the medium term. However, gender norms of the host society, and the absence of a family support network and solid social networks, can result in difficulties in achieving a work–life balance. These issues will be tackled in the following section.

Work–Life Balance in the Migration Projects of Young Spanish Women

The interviews carried out for this study reveal that, in general, female Spanish migrants seek family projects linked to gender norms in Spain. They are therefore in favour of a long period of co-habitation, postpone maternity until a later age and, eventually, send children to nursery to enable the mothers to continue working. Interviewees state that they miss the support of grandparents, frequent support providers for Spanish families trying to find a work–life balance. A good moment to have children is when they have created co-national networks of mothers with whom to share the process, and have found mutual support and understanding with others who share the same cultural baggage. It is also extremely common for these highly skilled women with jobs suited to their qualifications to hire Spanish nannies or au pairs to look after their children, while teaching them their mother tongue and culture. In short, becoming a mother leads women to return to social networks on the basis of ethnicity in order to keep cultural and linguistic identities alive.

Another area of concern for female Spanish emigrants is how to care for their parents in Spain. Managing the emotions involved in separation from the family can be difficult, more so if family members back home fall ill. This can even lead to women rethinking their migration project, some of them either returning or trying to be as close as possible geographically or in terms of travelling time back to their family in Spain. Some of the female Spanish migrants interviewed for this study subsequently paved the way for a family member (brother or sister, mother or father, and even a partner) to join them in the destination country. Such is the case of Alejandra, who followed her Moroccan husband to Germany after losing her job in the construction sector. Once in Germany they separated, and in the meantime her parents' situation in Spain had become more and more difficult. She eventually persuaded them to join her in Germany, although the process of adaptation was hard. Gender norms in Germany make it impossible for her to return to Spain with her children because they would need the father's permission, this being an example of the limits imposed on free movement resulting from legislation affecting migrant motherhood:

> Well, I had to come, otherwise my marriage would not have survived. So I came over with my daughter, but the first year was just awful. I was severely depressed, crying all the time ... I'd been here about a year, I think, maybe two, and we separated ... And in the end, I brought my parents over, that's why they live here now

... And they decided to stay, because I'm an only child, you know? My mum suffers from depression now because it's so different to Spain ... It's affected her a lot, if I'm honest ... I spoke to a lawyer ... The law in Germany states that if the father says you can't leave Germany, then you can't. So I have no choice but to stay. For my children, you know? (Alejandra, resident in Düsseldorf, Germany)

Some Spanish mothers with highly skilled jobs in transnational companies involving a lot of travel, solve their childcare problems with the support of 'flying grandmothers' who fly out regularly to look after their grandchildren when necessary, and form a part of the processes involved in the circulation of care between nuclear family and extended family for brief periods of time (Baldassar and Wilding, 2014; Merla, 2014). Elvira, who was mentioned earlier, is an example of this transnational circulation of care within the family. Both she and her husband have a scant childcare support network in their place of residence, which led them to hire a Spanish au pair to look after their children:

I was travelling a lot for work and had to leave my daughter, so I used to bring my parents over to look after her so that I could go to China ... My daughter has always been really well looked after ... she's gone to nursery, and we had someone to pick her up and look after her until I got home from work, but the travelling made everything so difficult. (Elvira, resident in Düsseldorf, Germany)

The conception of motherhood, and how to approach childcare, changes from country to country and has a strong gender-normative component. France is one of the few European countries that promotes a family policy aimed at sustaining the family as a fundamental social unit, and Germany has a conservative family policy which sees the family as a private institution to be preserved, although it does have some limited public services. The employability of French women is facilitated by childcare policies aimed at children from early childhood onwards. In the case of Germany, it is characterised by maintaining a strict gender division of labour, and is therefore disinclined to support the promotion of gender equality and shared family responsibility. Women are expected to look after their children at home following a traditional family model via long periods of maternity leave, and due to a weak childcare structure, as can be seen by the small number of day-care centres (Rossier et al., 2011). It is common in Spain for children to go to nursery from a very early age, but this is looked upon negatively in Germany. This experience of being considered a 'bad mother' if you send your child to nursery is well known to

Ana, a Spanish emigrant in Germany who works for a transnational technology company:

> I had to put my baby into nursery when he was only four months old, and I found it really hard. A lot of people said to me, 'you're going back full-time?', as if to say, 'what a bad mother you are'! And I would say, 'Well, that's what we normally do in Spain.' And I went back full-time ... German mothers would say 'What, full-time? But you have a baby, how are you going to leave him at nursery until 5 pm?' And I would say that it was normal, that, in fact, some people in Spain have to leave them there until 7 in the evening ... The problem, I mean, the funny thing about this, about maternity leave, that you get paid and everything, hides that fact that, deep down, Germany is very sexist. The men prefer the women to be at home with the baby for three years. I'm an engineer, and if I'm away for three years, by the time I go back mobile phones will have disappeared and we'll be talking through a microchip in our ear! There's no way I can be out of the loop for three years ... There's definitely inequality between the sexes, which I was surprised by ... Because, at the end of the day, here in Germany, if a woman wants to progress in her profession, then it's better if she doesn't have children. There may be some similarities with Spain, but here it's just so obvious! (Ana, resident in Düsseldorf, university educated)

As mentioned above, a strategy used by many Spanish mothers in Germany and France is to create co-ethnic networks in order to share experiences about what transnational motherhood is like. These networks have different functions, from friendship and sharing information, to fomenting the linguistic and cultural knowledge of their offspring by forming friendships with the children of other Spanish emigrants.

CONCLUSIONS

Female Spanish migrants in Spain and Germany reveal a range of educational profiles, which impact upon their labour integration in the destination society. For their part, highly skilled workers, having been employed by transnational companies in Spain, manage to find work in the leading sectors. Being highly qualified is not synonymous with appropriate integration in the labour market, although, as cultural capital theories indicate, it is relevant to achieving this. It is also important that demand in the destination countries exists for the specific skills of the qualified professionals migrating. Furthermore, knowledge of the language is a determining factor when it comes to appropriate labour integration.

The first point of contact for many of these Spanish women who decide to emigrate comes through a means of entry involving childcare, that is, the au pair sector. Access to accommodation, upkeep and at least minimum earnings leads many young Spanish women to choose this option while they improve their language skills. In this regard, Southern European countries provide carers to Central and Northern European countries.

Settling in the destination society and forming a family does not exempt women from taking on traditional roles. It can be complex for female Spanish migrants to experience processes such as motherhood, as they try to balance what it means to be a mother in the country of origin as well as in the host country. Transnational strategies for motherhood are manifold, from asking for support from the family, especially grandmothers who can fly over to help with childcare, to the creation of networks of Spanish mothers to give each other mutual support in child rearing. At times, this view of motherhood and child rearing is at odds with gender norms in the destination society, and with the different political organisation of care and family to the one that exists in Spanish society.

The Southern European migration model would seem to feed off dynamics that attract a foreign workforce to be integrated in secondary labour market niches (as is the case of the care sector). At the same time, it reveals the exodus of highly skilled young people who are not resigned to accepting the conditions of a market characterised by temporary work contracts, job insecurity, and working conditions with clear room for improvement. Both migratory processes are closely connected. In the migratory system that exists in southern Europe, a global labour market niche such as the care sector brings about a significant mobilisation of global care chains made up of non-EU female immigrants and, at the same time, young female Spanish women who emigrate to Central and Northern Europe to work as au pairs, looking after children, while hoping to find jobs more suited to their qualifications. Sometimes, these women may indeed become the very mothers who decide to stay in these regions and who, in turn, require their Spanish compatriots to come and work for them as au pairs or cleaners. In the meantime, welfare states continue to avoid implementing policies favouring a work–life balance; indeed, quite the opposite: they build walls that lead to internal and external migratory movements being considered ever less deserving of reaching Europe's El Dorado.

ACKNOWLEDGEMENTS

The results contained in this chapter form a part of the results of the following R+D+i Projects: (1) 'The new emigration from Spain: profiles, mobility strategies and transnational political activism' (CSO2016-80158R), funded by the Ministry for the Economy, Industry and Competition of Spain; (2) 'Integration and return of the "new Spanish emigration": a comparative analysis of the Spanish communities in the United Kingdom and France' (PID2019-105041RA-I00), funded by the Ministry of Science and Innovation of Spain.

We are also grateful for the financial support of ESOMI through the Aid for the Consolidation and Structuring of Competitive Research Units of the Galician University System (ED431C 2018/25, 2019–2021), funded by the Xunta de Galicia (Spain).

NOTE

1.   The interview was carried out in Galician and the extract translated by the chapter's authors.

REFERENCES

Antonucci, L. and Varriale, S. (2020). Unequal Europe, unequal Brexit: how intra-European inequalities shape the unfolding and framing of Brexit. *Current Sociology*, 68 (1): 41–59, doi: https://doi.org/10.1177%2F0011392119863837.

Baldassar, L. and Wilding, R. (2014). Middle-class transnational caregiving: the circulation of care between family and extended kin networks in the Global North. In Baldassar, L. and Merla, L. (eds), *Transnational Families, Migration and the Circulation of Care: Understanding Mobility and Absence in Family Life*. London: Routledge, pp. 235–251.

Becker, R. and Teney, C. (2020). Understanding high-skilled intra-European migration patterns: the case of European physicians in Germany. *Journal of Ethnic and Migration Studies*, 46 (9): 1737–1755, doi: https://doi.org/10.1080/1369183X.2018 .1561249.

Benton, M. and Petrovic, M. (2013). *How Free Is Free Movement? Dynamics and Drivers of Mobility within the European Union*. Brussels: Migration Policy Institute Europe.

Bermúdez, A. and Oso, L. (2020). Recent trends in intra-EU mobilities: the articulation between migration, social protection, gender and citizenship systems. Introduction. *Ethnic and Racial Studies*, 43 (14): 2513–2530, doi: https://doi.org/10 .1080/01419870.2020.1770828.

Bruquetas Callejo, M. (2020). Long-term care crisis in the Netherlands and migration of live-in care workers: transnational trajectories, coping strategies and motivation mixes. *International Migration*, 58 (1): 105–118, doi: https://doi.org/10.1111/imig .12628.

Bygnes, S. and Erdal, M. B. (2017). Liquid migration, grounded lives: considerations about future mobility and settlement among Polish and Spanish migrants in Norway, *Journal of Ethnic and Migration Studies*, 43 (1):102–118, DOI: 10.1080/1369183X.2016.1211004

Bygnes, S. and Flipo, A. (2017). Political motivations for intra-European migration. *Acta Sociologica*, 60 (3): 199–212. https://doi.org/10.1177/0001699316659909

Capote Lama, A. and Fernández Suárez, B. (2021). La Nouvelle Vague de la emigración española en Francia: proyectos migratorios y tipos de migrantes. *Revista Española de Sociología*, 30 (4): a23, doi: https://doi.org/10.22325/fes/res.2021.23.

Castles, S., De Hass, H. and Miller, M.J. (2014). *The Age of Migration: International Population Movement in the Modern World*. Basingstoke: Palgrave Macmillan.

Cortés, A., Moncó, B. and Barbosa, F. (2020). Young Spanish au pairs in London: migration and gender tensions in the context of intra-EU mobilities. *Ethnic and*

Racial Studies, 43 (14): 2590–2606, doi: https://doi.org/10.1080/01419870.2020 .1774071.

Cox, R. and Busch, N. (2016). 'This is the life I want': au pairs' perceptions of life in the global city. *Nordic Journal of Migration Research*, 6 (4): 234–242, doi: http://doi .org/10.1515/njmr-2016-0029.

Della Puppa, F., Montagna, N. and Korman, E. (2021). Onward migration and intra-European mobilities: a critical and theoretical overview. *International Migration*, 59 (6): 16–28, doi: https://doi.org/10.1111/imig.12815.

Docquier, F., Lowell, B.L. and Marfouk, A. (2009). A gendered assessment of highly skilled emigration. *Population and Development Review*, 35 (2): 297–321, doi: https://doi.org/10.1111/j.1728-4457.2009.00277.x.

Dubucs, H. and Mourlane, S. (2017). Les migrations intra-européennes d'hier et aujourd'hui. *Hommes et Migrations*, 1317–1318: 6–14, doi: https://doi.org/10.4000/ hommesmigrations.3863.

Dumitru, S. (2017). Féminisation de la migration qualifiée: les raisons de l'invisibilité. *Hommes et Migrations*, 1317–1318: 146–153, doi: https://doi.org/10.4000/ hommesmigrations.3914.

Eldén, S. and Anving, T. (2019). Nanny care in Sweden: the inequalities of everyday doings of care. *Journal of European Social Policy*, 29 (5): 614–626, doi: https://doi .org/10.1177%2F0958928719866980.

Eremenko, T. and Miyar-Busto, M. (2020). ¿Billete de ida y vuelta? Perfiles y trayectorias migratorias de los graduados españoles. *Anuario CIDOB de la Inmigración 2020*, 129–166, doi: https://doi.org/10.24241/AnuarioCIDOBInmi.2020.132.

Fernández Asperilla, A. (2009). Trayectorias laborales de las mujeres españolas emigradas en Francia. In Grupo de Comunicación Galicia en el Mundo (ed.), *Un siglo de inmigración española en Francia*. Vigo: Grupo de Comunicación Galicia en el Mundo, pp. 65–78.

Flipo, A. (2017). *Génération low cost. Itinéraires de jeunes migrants intra-européens*. Rennes: Presses Universitaires de Rennes.

Franceschelli, M. (2020). Imagined mobilities and the materiality of migration: the search for 'anchored lives' in post-recession Europe. *Journal of Ethnic and Migration Studies*, doi: https://doi.org/10.1080/1369183X.2020.1840968.

Geserick, C. (2012). 'I always wanted to go abroad. And I like children': motivations of young people to become *au pairs* in the USA. *Young*, 20 (1): 49–67, doi: http://dx .doi.org/10.1177/110330881102000103.

González Ramos, A. and Vergés Bosch, N. (2013). International mobility of women in science and technology careers: shaping plans for personal and professional purposes. *Gender, Place and Culture*, 20 (5): 613–629, doi: https://doi.org/10.1080/ 0966369X.2012.701198.

Herrero–Arias, R., Hollekim, R. and Haukanes, H. (2020). Self-legitimation and sense-making of Southern European parents' migration to Norway: the role of family aspirations. *Population, Space and Place*, 16 (8): e2362, doi: https://doi.org/ 10.1002/psp.2362.

Impedovo, M.A. and Ballatore, M. (2019). Mobility dynamics in South of France: proculturation traces by Italian workers. *Human Arenas*, 2: 291–304, doi: https://doi .org/10.1007/s42087-019-0054-x.

Isaakyan, I. and Triandafyllidou, A. (2016). Female high-skill migration in the 21st century: the challenge of the recession. In Triandafyllidou, A. and Isaakyan, I. (eds), *High-Skill Migration and Recession: Gendered Perspectives*. London: Palgrave Macmillan, pp. 3–21.

King, R. and Williams, M. (2018). Editorial introduction: new European youth mobilities. *Population, Space and Place*, 24 (1): e2121, doi: https://doi.org/10.1002/psp .2121.

Meares, C. (2010). A fine balance: women, work and skilled migration. *Women's Studies International Forum*, 33 (5): 473–481, doi: https://doi.org/10.1016/j.wsif .2010.06.001.

Merla, L. (2014). La circulación de cuidados en las familias transnacionales / The circulation of care in transnational families. *Revista CIDOB d'afers Internacionals*, 106–107: 85–104.

Muñoz Rodríguez, D. and Santos Ortega, A. (2015). Las nuevas precariedades a través de las au pairs universitarias. Del cosmopolitismo a los trabajos de cuidados de bajo coste. *Prisma Social*, 15: 526–561.

Oishi, N. and Ono, A. (2020). North–North migration of care workers: 'disposable' au pairs in Australia. *Journal of Ethnic and Migration Studies*, 46 (13): 2682–2699, doi: https://doi.org/10.1080/1369183X.2019.1571902.

Oso, L. (2005). Femmes, actrices des mouvements migratoires. *Cahiers Genre et développment*, 5: 35–54.

Oso, L. (2009). 'Chambras', porterías, 'pubelas' y 'burones'. In Grupo de Comunicación Galicia en el Mundo (ed.), *Un siglo de inmigración española en Francia*. Vigo: Grupo de comunicación Galicia en el mundo, pp. 79–98.

Pérez-Caramés, A. (2017). Una nueva generación española en Alemania. Análisis de las motivaciones para la emigración bajo el manto de la crisis. *Migraciones*, 43: 91–116, doi: https://doi.org/10.14422/mig.i43.y2017.005.

Reques Velasco, P. and De Cos Guerra, O. (2003). La emigración olvidada: la diáspora española en la actualidad. *Papeles de Geografía*, 37: 199–216.

Riaño, Y. (2011). 'He's the Swiss citizen, I'm the foreign spouse': binational marriages and the impact of family-related migration policies on gender relations. In Kraler, A., Kofman, E., Kohli, M. and Schmoll, C. (eds), *Gender, Generations and the Family in International Migration*. Amsterdam: Amsterdam University Press, pp. 265–283.

Roca, B. and Martín-Díaz, E. (2017). Solidarity networks of Spanish migrants in the UK and Germany: the emergence of interstitial trade unionism. *Critical Sociology*, 43 (7–8): 1197–1212, doi: https://doi.org/10.1177%2F0896920516645659.

Rossier, C., Brachet, S. and Salles, A. (2011). Family policies, norms about gender roles and fertility decisions in France and Germany. *Vienna Yearbook of Population Research*, 8: 259–282. doi: 10.1553/populationyearbook2011s259.

Sekeráková Búriková, Z. (2020). Invisible in homes, visible in cities: visibility and dis/ empowerment in paid domestic work in London. *Gender, Place and Culture*, doi: https://doi.org/10.1080/0966369X.2020.1835832.

Vázquez Silva, I., Capote, A. and López de Lera, D. (2021). La nueva emigración española en Alemania y Reino Unido: identidades migratorias en cuestión. *Revista Española de Sociología*, 30 (4): a24, doi: https://doi.org/10.22325/fes/res.2021.24.

Visic, T. and Poleti-Cosic, D. (2018). Gender and migration re-visited: production of knowledge and feminism (in) between semi-periphery and the core. *Sociologija*, 60 (1): 255–274, doi: http://dx.doi.org/10.2298/SOC1801255V.

Wihtol de Wenden, C. (2017). Les européens dans les politiques européennes d'aujourd'hui. *Hommes et Migrations*, 1317–1318: 45–51, doi: https://doi.org/10.4000/ hommesmigrations.3869.

7. A Southern European model of migrant agricultural labour: two case studies in Andalusia (Spain) and Calabria (Italy)

Francisco Checa y Olmos, Francesco Saverio Caruso and Alessandra Corrado

INTRODUCTION

Over the past three decades many rural areas of the countries bordering the Northern Mediterranean have undergone major changes, particularly as a result of the intensification of agricultural production and market liberalisation at a global level. This has resulted in the industrialisation of the countryside and the transformation of subsistence agriculture. Agricultural industrialisation and entrepreneurship have been promoted by policies and investment: small and medium-sized farms have reversed the trend of being increasingly dependent on long buyer-driven agri-food chains, while many small and medium-sized producers have been forced to convert themselves into agricultural 'entrepreneurs' (Van der Ploeg, 2008) or 'producers as contract workers' (McMichael, 2013), dragged along by the broad context of globalisation. As such, their businesses depend entirely on international markets and the large retail chains that control farms, even before the production process begins (Aznar-Sánchez et al., 2011; Burch et al., 2007). At the same time, an additional transformative factor has appeared in the rural world: the emergence of an immigrant workforce and the dependence of the agricultural sector on the existence and renovation of this source of migrant labour (Cavalcanti and Bonanno, 2014; Corrado et al., 2016; Gertel and Sippel, 2014). In fact, migrant labour is so important to agri-food development in Southern European countries as to inspire the definition of the 'Mediterranean model of migration' (Finotelli, 2007; King, 2000; Pugliese, 2002) or, as applied to the specific migration dynamics in the region, the 'Southern model of migrant agricultural labour'.

This chapter focuses on the processes of agrarian transformation that have affected two regions with similar characteristics: the province of Almería in Andalusia (Spain) and the Sybaris plain in the province of Cosenza, in Calabria (Italy). Both regions are of a similar size and have a population of approximately 700 000 inhabitants, but the most significant similarity is that of a dominant agricultural sector, as indicated by an economic and occupational impact that is among the highest in Western Europe. The chapter addresses the following aspects of the transformation that occurred between 2010 and 2020 in specific agricultural enclaves of these two Southern European regions: technological and organisational innovation, modernisation and the crisis caused by the neoliberal restructuring of agri-food (the influence of large retail chains), and the role played by migrations. The elements that characterise the Mediterranean context are described, taking into account the dynamics of migration and their relationship with changes in agriculture. This contribution aims to highlight the specific development model that characterises these two Mediterranean areas, and the centrality of migrant work in the dynamics of change of the agri-food sector. However, the two regions have experienced different migration dynamics and development pathways, and an analysis of similarities and differences can serve to depict the complexity of migration flows in the changing Mediterranean agrarian setting. The chapter is structured as follows. First, the Mediterranean model, in terms of both the dynamics of migration and its relationship with changes in agriculture, is described. In the subsequent sections the two regions covered in the case studies, Almería and the Sybaris plain, are analysed, highlighting both their similarities and differences. The chapter closes with some conclusions.

THE AGRICULTURAL REGIONS OF ANDALUSIA (SPAIN) AND CALABRIA (ITALY)

The province of Almería has historically been one of the most economically depressed in Spain. Nowadays, as a result of its highly developed intensive agriculture, it has become one of the richest, surpassing even the most prosperous urban and industrial areas in the north of the country in some indicators. The so-called 'Almería miracle' is centred on the exponential growth of the primary smallholder sector. In the two most prominent territories in Almería, Campo de Dalías and Campos de Níjar, agriculture is mainly characterised by horticultural crops grown in sand in greenhouses, on farms that barely exceed 1 hectare, with work operations requiring a considerable labour force that has proved difficult to mechanise (see Checa, 1995; Fernández-Lavandera and Pizarro-Checa, 1981; Jiménez, 2011; Palomar Oviedo, 1994; Rivera Menéndez, 2000; Sánchez-Picón, 2005).

In Italy, following partial agrarian reform and an increase in small and medium-sized farms, together with the modernisation processes of the 1980s and 1990s, the Sybaris plain in Calabria became one of the most prosperous areas in southern Italy. Fundamental to this development have been public investment, the replanting and the varietal reconversion of fruit trees, improvements in the quality of the fresh product, new entrepreneurial actors, and the organisation of small producers into cooperatives to manage work and sales and to support their integration in the vertical chains of organised distribution. However, the drive for modernisation has also faced considerable social, political and structural issues at the local level (Capano and Marini, 1997; Cavazzani and Sivini, 1997a, 1997b), such as dependence on foreign markets, difficulties and disorganisation in the marketing and valorisation of the product, and the consequences of labour informality (associated with fraud against the state, failure to pay social security and pension contributions, taking advantage of irregular migrant work).

For the Spanish region, an analysis is provided of the economic and financial data collected by the Cajamar Foundation, demographic data from the Instituto Nacional de Estadística (National Institute of Statistics) and the annual employment statistics recorded by the Ministry of Labour and Social Affairs. For the Italian region, an analysis is provided of the economic and demographic data collected by the Istituto Nazionale di Statistica (National Statistics Institute) along with employment trends from the Istituto Nazionale Previdenza Sociale (INPS) – Osservatorio Statistico 'Mondo Agricolo' database. Qualitative data was collected by the authors from interviews conducted and direct observation carried out on different dates.

A MEDITERRANEAN MODEL OF MIGRATION: NEOLIBERAL GLOBALISATION AND AGRICULTURE

Northern European countries incorporate migrant workers into their agri-food system (Rye and Scott, 2018), and despite being the source of large migrant flows into Central Europe, Eastern European countries such as the Czech Republic, Hungary, Romania, and Poland (Chierichetti, 2011), employ irregular migrants in agricultural work. Migration flows in the specific contexts of southern Spain (Andalusia) and southern Italy (Calabria) differ to those within the framework of the Southern or Mediterranean model of agricultural exploitation of migrant labour. This model arose in Southern European countries, including Italy, Spain, Greece and Portugal, due to the selective migration policies implemented in recent decades in Europe, in addition to a restructuring of food production processes (King, 2000; Terluin, 2003).

Increasing deregularisation and segmentation of the labour market has resulted in greater demands for a local workforce, especially in low-skilled, poorly paid, dirty, demanding, highly precarious and even dangerous sectors, such as agriculture, construction, care, services, home delivery, cleaning, and irregular self-employment. In order to address the shortage of seasonal agricultural labour in both Spain and Italy, a policy of quotas was introduced, as a mechanism whereby the central government approved the annual quotas of immigrants; however, the figures were derisory and unrealistic. The quotas were never used to regulate the entry of immigrants, but they were used to regularise the status of some of those who were already in the country irregularly (Checa, 1995). The agricultural model promotes productivity and deterritorialisation, basing the management of waged labour on temporary work, subcontracting and, frequently, deregulation (Corrado et al., 2016; Pedreño Cánovas, 1998, 2012, 2014), as can be seen in both Almería and Sybaris. In Spain, particularly in the Andalusian province of Huelva, employers' organisations select and recruit seasonal workers directly in the countries of origin for seasonal jobs, such as picking and packaging, especially in red fruit production (Reigada, 2017), through the practice of recruitment at origin. Demand for this type of employment comes from a small number of young native individuals who have dropped out of education, and from immigrants, mainly from Eastern European countries and non-European countries. Migrant workers need to earn wages to be able to subsist in their country of destination, in addition to sending remittances back home. In both cases, this serves to maintain these labour niches. Due to the price-squeeze dynamics and the competitiveness generated by supplying international markets within the global agri-food system articulated in 'food empires' (Van der Ploeg, 2008), producers resort to leveraging the labour factor and reducing production costs. According to the Cajamar Foundation (Fundación Cajamar, 2015, 2016), new generations of farmers have become employers, and are now experimenting with other ways to increase their profits, especially by means of commercial organisation, reducing the need to severely exploit the labour force in order to maximise profits.

The cumbersome nature of progressively more restrictive migration policies has inevitably led, in both Spain and Italy, to systematic measures of mass regularisation to address the status of the hundreds of thousands of undocumented migrants. However, as Berlan (2002) points out, it is worth noting the role that structural racism plays in social relations and the labour market, in creating so-called 'artificial barriers' which curiously correspond to legal and administrative barriers, created ad hoc in order to contain the mobility of a labour force and thus to guarantee the existence of a 'reserve army' of workers to cover the needs of this intensive agricultural model. This pattern of employment of foreign workers in agriculture has not just affected Spain and Italy; in fact, it has occurred throughout Europe in successive waves (Morice and Michalon, 2009), with Spain, Italy and Greece becoming countries of 'out of control' immigration from 1990. Migration policies that include 'differential inclusion' devices (Mezzadra, 2006) are not neutral; they result in social conditions of exploitation and segregation and produce a climate of social tension that translates cyclically into racist policies, and uncontrolled xenophobia, such as the scenes of racist violence at El Ejido (Spain) in 2000, Castel Volturno in 2008, and Rosarno in 2010 (Italy), among others. In Spain, further racist incidents included that which occurred in Terrassa (Barcelona) in 2003, and the arson attack in Elche (Alicante) in 2004 (Cachón Rodríguez, 2005). And in Italy, the murder in 1989 of Jerry Essan Masslo, a South African refugee employed to pick tomatoes in Villa Literno, and the social mobilisation that followed, led to the adoption in 1990 of the 'Martelli law', the first law regulating immigration. However, these were not isolated incidents: other African migrant workers have died on farms or in informal rural settlements due to brutal conditions of extreme deprivation, marginalisation and exploitation (Corrado, 2011). And in 2006, more than 100 Polish migrants disappeared in the tomato fields of Puglia (Leogrande, 2008).

It is important to highlight the changes that the province of Almería has undergone in the last 15 years, with respect to the recruitment of foreign labour, and the drastic reduction it generated in structural racism and barriers to employment. In fact, agricultural employers now appreciate the need to retain their workers on contract for as long as possible, stabilising the workforce with those who are better specialised in certain tasks, and meeting a demand that they themselves recognised the need for (Aznar-Sánchez et al., 2011). Technical inspections in the field have done the rest, since a small employer who hires undocumented workers can receive sentences of 2–5 years in prison, in addition to sanctions of €10 000 to €12 000 for each undocumented worker. Legislative reforms carried out in Italy in 2016 have also discouraged the use of undeclared employment, criminalising 'illegal intermediation and exploitation of labour' (Penal Code 603 *bis*) with provision for up to six years' imprisonment and the confiscation of businesses. As a consequence of such regulations in both Italy and Spain, in order to increase profits and to cope with the pressures of the market and the value chain, forms of undeclared work are frequently used, where the employment relationship is formalised but contractual provisions regarding working hours, wages, guarantees and workers' rights are circumvented. Despite this, in Almería, there has been a significant incorporation of entrepreneurial immigrant families into the fruit and vegetable sector, with around 8–10 per cent of farms being owned or managed by immigrant families (Galdeano-Gómez et al., 2013; García Lorca, 2010). In contrast, in Italy this dynamic is very limited; as an example, in Sybaris only 1.6 per cent of the farms are owned by people not born in Italy, with more than half of these being children of returned Calabrian emigrants (INEA, 2013).

THE ALMERÍA MIRACLE

The extraordinary development of the local agricultural economy and of the servicing industry that has accompanied it, such as seedbeds, supply warehouses, management and consultancy firms, bank branches, car dealerships, and so on, has had a huge impact on the province of Almería. The impact on the local landscape of this development can be clearly seen: the Poniente Almeriense is a plain of more than 20 000 hectares of greenhouses that can be seen via satellite imagery, and has become known as the 'sea of plastic'. This plain, christened the 'orchard of Europe', produces more than 3.5 million tonnes of vegetables annually. Between 70 and 75 per cent (and up to 80 per cent in 2018) of production is exported, with hundreds of heavy-duty lorries driving to the fruit and vegetable markets of Central European on a daily basis (Fundación Cajamar, 2018, 2019). This historic change, the so-called 'Almería miracle', occurred in just a few decades. Its origins can be found in the policies of expropriation, parcelling and allocation of land carried out in the 1960s and 1970s, first by the Instituto Nacional de Colonización (National Colonisation Institute), and then by the Instituto Nacional de Reforma y Desarrollo Agrario (National Institute for Agrarian Reform and Development), in addition to the construction of wells by the Instituto Andaluz de Reforma Agraria (Andalusian Institute of Agrarian Reform).

As a result of these interventions, land that was unproductive and stony became a fertile and productive oasis. A favourable climate and the continuous innovations in agricultural technology provided the additional factors required for the unique development model (Checa, 2003; Rivera Menéndez, 2000; Sánchez-Picón, 2005; Checa et al., 2018). The consequent need for labour favoured a migratory flow, which arrived first from the nearby villages of the Alpujarra mountains, in the late 1970s. The new settlers, in turn, bought land, seeded it and built greenhouses. These pioneering farmers, accustomed to the economic hardships of their villages and seduced by high economic returns, operated by means of harsh techniques of personal and family self-exploitation. As a result, they saw their productivity and yield rates double every year. Under the plastic of the greenhouses, the farmers not only shortened the ripening times of each product, but they also multiplied cultivation and harvesting cycles. The agricultural boom that resulted led to land being mortgaged to pay for more land, which was then passed on to their children (Molina Herrera, 2002). The constant capacity to produce fruit and vegetables that resulted was so extraordinary that it was able to respond to the non-seasonal demand in European markets. In other words, during the winter months, vegetables from Almería fill Central European supermarkets.

With the entry of Spain into the European Economic Community on 1 January 1986, and the consequent gradual reduction in tariff barriers, the miracle of Almería's agriculture was consolidated. The following data confirms this: in 1980, 100 000 tonnes were exported; five years later the figure was already greater than 250 000 tonnes, reaching 500 000 in 1990, 1.4 million in 1995, and 2.15 million in 2013 (Fundación Cajamar, 2014). The fruit and vegetable sector closed the 2018/19 season with a new record, exporting 2 712 085 tonnes, valued at over €2.5 billion (Fundación Cajamar, 2019), making Almería the leading province for agri-food exports in Spain, representing 20 per cent of the total, surpassing even Valencia and Murcia. Since 1980s, the greenhouses have multiplied in number. From the 300 hectares in the province in 1970, they expanded to 12 000 hectares in 1985, despite measures by the government to contain the construction of new greenhouses and the 'plastification' of the region (Palomar Oviedo, 1994), due to fears regarding groundwater depletion. In the following years, the race for green gold continued, with greenhouse construction reaching 32 045 hectares in 2020. Over the years, greenhouse agriculture has become a kind of chemical laboratory, ever more technologically advanced, aimed at increasing productivity, through achieving total control over the production process. The large transnational firms of agrochemical inputs, seeds and biological control opened offices and branches in the province to support (and control) farmers in the production processes, experimenting with fertilisers and hybrid seeds to achieve a product of greater organoleptic quality. Thus, agricultural entrepreneurs became increasingly dependent on this highly centralised power system, in terms of both sowing and harvesting, and the selling and distribution of the final products.

In total, 168 food traders are responsible for the processing, preservation and selling of all fruit and vegetables produced in Almería, but in recent years the retail system has undergone a major process of coordination and centralisation involving these companies, to the extent that today almost half of exports go through six large aggregations (Única Group, Grupo Agroponiente, Cooperativa Vicasol-SCA, Alhóndiga La Unión, Grupo Agroiris, Murgiverde-SCA). These business groups have become intermediary bodies between the more than 16 000 small producers in Almería, whose average farm size is around 2 hectares, and the few dozen foreign companies that systematically control the export and distribution of all agri-food products (COAG, 2007). These dozen European retail companies belong to large retail chains which agree on a price to pay for tomatoes or peppers. Thus, European retailers have total control over the Almería production processes (Aznar-Sánchez and Belmonte-Urena, 2014). They impose their demands on delivery times, price reductions, verifications and quality protocols. Everything from quality, colour and ripening, to packaging and presentation of products, is defined, in detail, in advance. The farmer is a minor cog in the global production machine (Jiménez, 2008). As a result, it is nearly impossible within this system for the agricultural entrepreneur in Almería to influence intermediate consumption and the cost of materials, time and production methods; and freedom of action is reduced to progressive adjustments to the cost of labour.

Due to fear of labour inspections, in Almería nearly all agricultural entrepreneurs apply to regularise their workers. However, based on our interviews, very few employers pay their workers according to the Provincial Collective Bargaining Agreement for Agricultural Work. It is normal to pay workers as agricultural labourers (fixed/discontinuous or casual labour) the amount of €25–€35 per day, that is, about €600–€660 per month if they work for 20–24 days; instead of the stipulated minimum salary of €778 per month or €5.84 per hour, that is, €46.72 per day. This abuse of the regulations is evident, also considering that overtime, holidays, extra pay, transport, and housing allowances, although covered by the Agreement, are not paid to labourers.

Evidently few native workers wish to be agricultural labourers under such employment conditions, although some returned to work under the greenhouse plastic after their jobs in construction were wiped out when the housing market bubble burst in 2008. The number of native workers in Almería's agricultural sector has remained relatively stable at around 30 000–40 000. These numbers often include the labour of family members: parents, children, and even grandparents, as is typically the case with greenhouse work. The annual statistics for the agricultural sector in the province of Almería give the numbers of workers employed as follows, 42 400 in 2004, 64 090 in 2013, and 74 046 in 2020. This increase is due substantially to the insertion of foreign migrant workers into the family organisation of agricultural production. In fact, manual work in greenhouses has been progressively delegated to them. In 2004, 13 680 foreign workers were registered by the Régimen Especial Agrario (Special Agricultural System), with 22 296 registered in 2013 and 33 436 in 2019.

The migrant labour force is largely composed of migrant workers from African countries. In September 2020, 28 465 non-European Union (EU) workers and 4205 EU workers were registered in the Special Agricultural System in the province of Almería. While numbers of, mainly Moroccan, non-EU workers have increased in a constant and continuous manner, demonstrating the consolidation of a genuine occupational niche of ethnic specialisation, the numbers of EU workers, who are mainly Romanian, decreased by half between 2010 and 2020. Therefore, the belief that African migrants would be rapidly replaced by Eastern European workers, that emerged in the aftermath of the racist violence in El Ejido at the beginning of the 2000s, proved to be unfounded. The growth in the number of Moroccan migrants was reflected in an equally significant demographic at the epicentre of intensive agriculture in Almería: in 2000, El Ejido had around 50 000 inhabitants, of whom 2340 were immigrants; in 2011, the population reached almost 90 000, due to the arrival of immigrants, especially after the regularisation policy was implemented, leading to an amnesty for 28 000 irregular migrants in 2005. In 2016–2020, the trend towards growth has halted and a slight decrease has been recorded, with the migrant population falling to 23 000, a figure in line with the demographic trends elsewhere in Spain and Andalusia (INE, figures taken from the Estadística del Padrón continuo, census of inhabitants).

THE CRISIS OF THE SYBARIS PLAIN

The Sybaris plain in Calabria, a Southern Italian region, is located on the northern Ionian coast, between the Pollino and Sila mountains. It has 33 municipalities and 184 000 hectares of agricultural land. During the post-Second World War period, the region experienced intense economic growth, infrastructure and social renewal, making it one of the most prosperous areas of Calabria. In the 1950s, land reclamation promoted by the Sila Act, and the subsequent (albeit partial) agrarian reform, as well as the consolidation of small and medium-sized subsistence farm ownership, gave rise to significant agricultural activity throughout the area (mainly citrus fruits, olive groves and rice fields), which even encouraged some migration flows from the surrounding mountains and curbed migration towards the industrial areas, in Northern Italy and abroad. The promotion and adoption, in the 1980s, of innovative production techniques and improvements in product quality resulted in integration in the relevant national and international trade circuits (Capano and Marini, 1997; Cavazzani and Sivini, 1997a). The formation of food chains was strictly regulated by the Common Agricultural Policy (CAP) which, from 2000 to 2006, financed the organisation of several Progetti Integrati di Filiera (Integrated Food Chain Projects, IPF). The clementine orange chain (equivalent to 60 per cent of national production), although the most complete at regional level, has shown glaring weaknesses over the years, from the point of view of both integration and competitiveness. Only 20 per cent of clementine production was traded through an integrated retailing system, while 70 per cent remained in the hands of unorganised traders. The awarding of the quality standard Indicazione Geografica Protetta (Protected Geographical Indication, PGI) for Calabria's clementines was designed to enhance the value of the product in national and European markets, but it covered an area of only 800 hectares. The volume of agri-food exports from the entire province of Cosenza is equivalent to only 0.8 per cent of that of Almería. At both the national and the regional level, for many years now the crisis in the olive sector, and more recently that of the citrus sector, has seriously undermined farm income, leading in many cases to their deactivation. Agricultural farmers complain about the lack of investment in research and innovation that, as was the case during the 1980s and 1990s, supported agricultural development, for example by prolonging the harvest periods with early and late varieties, in order to be more competitive with products imported from Spain and from Morocco, the two major suppliers to international markets.

At the provincial level there are some 12 000 hectares of clementine production, approximately half of the total national surface area, with a high concentration (almost 5000 hectares) in the municipality of Rossano-Corigliano alone, at the heart of the Sybaris plain, in addition to 2500 hectares of orange groves. However, the production is fragmented, with the almost 7000 citrus fruit family holdings being on average less than 2 hectares in size. Because of the size and type of crop, producing clementine crops involves extra-family labour for specialised tasks (that is, pruning, irrigation system management), and above all for the harvesting operations. During a very concentrated annual season, during the months of November and December, thousands of workers are recruited to harvest some 350 000 tonnes of clementines. The number of agricultural jobs in the region remains more than three times the Italian average, accounting for almost 90 per cent of the provincial total in terms of agricultural workers. Native Italian workers engaged in this activity in the area are decreasing in number and getting older: while in 2008 there were still 48 676 Italian agricultural workers in the province of Cosenza, by 2018 this number had almost halved to 29 036, and more than half of them were over 50 years old. During the 2000s, Eastern European workers buffered this dramatic decline in the agricultural labour force. Among these, Romanians are the most numerous, representing 50 per cent of the foreign population, followed by Bulgarians, whose presence in Calabria is five times greater than the national average. The settlement of these communities can be clearly seen in the increase in the number of foreign minors, which reached almost 20 per cent of the total foreign population in the province of Cosenza. But their number progressively fell from a peak of 8419 in 2010, to 4226 in 2020 (INPS, 2021). This figure is in line with the more general trend of immigrant 'newcomers' fleeing the Italian countryside in search of better job opportunities in the same period. The dramatic reduction in the numbers of Bulgarians and Poles is striking, as is the decline of the much larger immigrant group of Romanian workers. The trend of 'agrarianisation of migrant labour' has had little impact on the more general rural exodus. The existence of a large pool of undeclared and underground labour, that is not completely regular and therefore is much cheaper, is worth considering. In fact, farmers' organisations in the Sybaris region have estimated that more than 12 000 migrants are needed to cover the harvesting operations during the winter months. The importance of informal labour at the local level can also be inferred from the increase in the foreign population in these areas: in the municipality of Rossano-Corigliano itself there were 7449 foreign inhabitants in 2020, an increase of 800 per cent compared to the 905 residents in 2005 (Italian National Institute of Statistics, ISTAT). Conversely, the numbers of non-EU workers increased from 1109 in 2010, to 2754 in 2020. This significant growth is referred to in terms of a 'refugisation' of agricultural labour (Dines and Rigo, 2015; Corrado and D'Agostino, 2018; Marchesi, 2020), because of the growing recruitment in agriculture of asylum seekers and refugees, mainly sub-Saharan Africans, which followed the so-called 'refugee crisis', and the policy of reception by dispersion in rural areas.

Migrant workers, especially Africans, are characterised by territorial mobility (between the different regions of the South and between the North and the South), as well as by their professional diversification (for example, alternating agricultural work with street commerce or construction). Many still live in the major urban centres of the plain, thus contributing significantly to the maintenance of small commercial activities in the area. The gradual improvement in working conditions and wages for EU workers has in fact produced a slow process of settlement and decrease in circular migration, with fewer returning to their country of origin. Some Eastern European workers cover more specialised and seasonal tasks, including those of tractor driver, irrigation system operator, and mower. Typically, African workers earn an average of €20–€25 per day (or €1 per box of citrus), while Eastern Europeans can reach €35 for the same work; native labourers, especially if experienced, earn around €40 per day. Day labour can mean a 10–12-hour working day.

The outsourcing of harvesting and trading operations leads to greater labour flexibility and simplified management, in addition to the fraudulent obtaining of benefits linked to social security. Fictitious or informal cooperatives operate through agreements with local companies, by signing work contracts between each company and day labourers. At the same time, the development of immigrant networks during working periods has even redefined informal recruitment practices, if they have connections to local gangmasters: a migrant labourer who is employed and a long-time resident in the area can be entrusted with calling and recruiting other nationals. This system is widespread in the Romanian community. In this socio-economic context, it can be seen that the agriculture of the Sybaris plain has a structure that could be defined as 'extensive': not only by virtue of the network of connections that facilitate production, storage, distribution and transformation of fruits and vegetables (also involving, for example, producers in the Gioia Tauro plain, in Calabria); but also, thanks to connections created by the foreign migrants who bring in the labour force, and gangmasters who move the workforce across regional borders, for example, to be employed in agricultural operations in the intensive production system in the neighbouring region of Basilicata. In this way, the district of Sybaris has evolved towards clusters and productive platforms that are much more nuanced and articulated than in the past. The competitive advantages enjoyed now are derived more from the efficiency and effectiveness offered by long productive chains, and functional links with other social, economic, political and territorial contexts, than from the search for low-scale productive arrangements and local markets, which are less established but much less profitable.

CONCLUSIONS

The province of Almería and the Sybaris plain have similar socio-territorial characteristics: the two regions have the highest rates in the EU15 of primary sector activity in the economy and local labour market. Agriculture in Sybaris and Almería developed from a base of a few small and very small enterprises, which experienced a golden phase following the modernisation of the production system in the 1970s and 1980s, and have since travelled two very distinct development paths. While agriculture in Almería has been well embedded in the oligopsony power concertation processes in agri-food buyer-driven chains, and cooperation, vertical integration and innovation have led to an exponential growth of production and added value of an agricultural model oriented to international markets, agriculture in the Sybaris plain has not been able to overcome the fragmentation of businesses and build a system of networks capable of coping with the force of increasingly fierce international competition, driven by large retailers. A comparison in the size of exports from the two provinces is indicative of this: in 2018, Almería's agri-food exports generated €2648 million, the highest in Europe, while Cosenza generated some €20 million, among the lowest in Europe.

Both in the case of a growing and export-oriented agriculture, and in the case of an internal market-orientated agriculture in crisis, it is surprising how the essential component of labour is increasingly composed of migrant labourers, and that the whole agricultural system, whether strong or in crisis, is based on an ethnic and continuously renewed stratification of labour, and on the intensive exploitation not only of land but also of labour. Regardless of the composition of the workforce (mostly Moroccans in Almería, and Romanians in Sybaris) and the economic trend, both regions have registered a slow process of settlement. The rural–urban dimension of the two contexts in the case study seems, in fact, to favour the transition from informal and circular migration to a more stable family migration. The redefinition of migration dynamics as well as of migration and asylum policies, together with the effects of the COVID-19 pandemic on mobility, and the restructuring of agri-food systems, make it important to carry out new research. A comparative perspective would also serve to reach a greater understanding of the factors affecting the transformation of migration flows and their territorial dynamics.

REFERENCES

Aznar-Sánchez, J.A. and Belmonte-Urena, L.J. (2014). The industrial agriculture: a 'model for modernization' from Almería? In Gertel, J. and Sippel, S.R. (eds), *Seasonal Workers in Mediterranean Agriculture*. London: Routledge, pp. 130–138.

Aznar-Sánchez J.A. Galdeano-Gómez E., and Pérez-Mesa, J.C. (2011). Intensive horticulture in Almería (Spain): a counterpoint to current European rural policy strategies. *Journal of Agrarian Change*, 11 (2): 241–261, doi : https://doi.org/10 .1111/j.1471-0366.2011.00301.x.

Berlan, J.P. (2002). La longue histoire du modèle californien. In Forum Civique Européen (ed.), *Le goût amer de nos fruits et légumes. L'exploitation des migrants dans l'agriculture intensive en Europe*. Limans: Informations et Commentaires, pp. 15–22.

Burch, D., Lawrence, G. and Burch, D. (2007). *Supermarkets and Agri-Food Supply Chains: Transformations in the Production and Consumption of Foods*. Cheltenham, UK and Northampton, MA, USA: Edward Elgar Publishing.

Cachón Rodríguez, L. (2005). *Bases sociales de los sucesos de Elche de septiembre de 2004. Crisis industrial, inmigración y xenofobia*. Madrid: OPI-Ministerio de Trabajo.

Capano, G. and Marini, M. (1997). Le trasformazioni dell'agricoltura nella Calabria contemporánea. In Planica, A. (ed.), *Storia della Calabria moderna e contemporánea*. Cosenza: Gangemi, pp. 21–41.

Cavalcanti, J.S.B. and Bonanno, A. (2014). Conclusions: labor between exploitation and resistance. Labor Relations in Globalized Food (Research in Rural Sociology and Development, Vol. 20). In Bonanno, A. and Barbosa, J.S. (eds), *Labor Relations in Globalized Food*. Bingley: Emerald, pp. 269–290. doi: https://doi.org/10.1108/ S1057-192220140000020011.

Cavazzani, A. and Sivini, G. (1997a). *Arance amare. La crisi dell'agrumicoltura italiana e lo sviluppo competitivo di quella spagnola. Soveria Mannelli*. Rubbettino: Soveria Mannelli.

Cavazzani, A. and Sivini, G. (1997b). *Dolci clementine. Innovazioni e problemi di una agrumicoltura sviluppata. La Piana di Sibari*. Rubbettino: Soveria Mannelli.

Checa, F. (1995). Migración, riesgos y beneficios. Los inmigrantes africanos en la provincia de Almería. *Demófilo. Revista de Cultura Tradicional*, 15: 103–134.

Checa, F. (2003). Factores endógenos y exógenos para la integración social de los inmigrados en Almería. In Checa, F., Arjona, J.C. and Checa, A. (eds), *La integración social de los inmigrados. Modelos y experiencias*. Barcelona: Icaria, pp. 103–150.

Checa, F., Corrado, A. and Caruso, F.S. (2018). Territorios en transición. Migraciones y agricultura en el Sur de Europa. *Cuadernos Geográficos*, 57 (3): 1–25, doi: https:// doi.org/10.30827/cuadgeo.v57i3.6407.

Chierichetti, J. (2011). Pays de départ. À chacun son immigration. *Campagnes solidaires*, 262: 3.

COAG (2007). *El poder de las grandes superficies en la cadena agroalimentaria*. Madrid: Coordinadora de Organizaciones de Agricultores y Ganaderos.

Corrado, A. (2011). Clandestini in the orange towns: migrations and racisms in Calabria's agriculture. *Race Ethnicity: Multidisciplinary Global Contexts*, 2: 191–201, doi: https://doi.org/10.2979/racethmulglocon.4.2.191.

Corrado, A. and D'Agostino, M. (2018). Migrations in multiple crisis: new development patterns for rural and inner areas in Calabria (Italy). In Stefan, K., Tobias,

W. and Jelen, I. (eds), *Processes of Immigration in Rural Europe: The Status Quo, Implications and Development Strategies*. Cambridge: Cambridge Scholars Publishing, pp. 272–295.

Corrado, A., De Castro, C. and Perrotta, D. (eds) (2016). *Migration and Agriculture: Mobility and Change in the Mediterranean Area*. London and New York: Routledge.

Dines, N. and Rigo, E. (2015). Postcolonial citizenships and the 'refugeeization' of the workforce. Postcolonial transitions in Europe: contexts, practices and politics. In Ponzanesi, S. and Colpani, G. (eds), *Postcolonial Transitions in Europe: Contexts, Practices and Politics*. London: Rowman & Littlefield Publishing, pp. 151–172.

Fernández-Lavandera, O. and Pizarro-Checa, A. (1981). Almería: la técnica del *enarenado* transforma un desierto. *Revista de Estudios Agro-Sociales*, 115: 31–70.

Finotelli, C. (2007). Italia, España y el modelo migratorio mediterráneo en el siglo XXI. *Madrid: Boletín ARI*, 58: 1–8.

Fundación Cajamar (2014). *Análisis de la Campaña Hortofrutícola de Almería, Campaña 2013/2014*. Almería: Cajamar.

Fundación Cajamar (2015). *Análisis de la Campaña Hortofrutícola de Almería, Campaña 2014/2015*. Almería: Cajamar.

Fundación Cajamar (2016). *Análisis de la Campaña Hortofrutícola de Almería, Campaña 2015/2016*. Almería: Cajamar.

Fundación Cajamar (2018). *Análisis de la Campaña Hortofrutícola de Almería, Campaña 2017/2018*. Almería: Cajamar.

Fundación Cajamar (2019). *Análisis de la Campaña Hortofrutícola de Almería, Campaña 2018/2019*. Almería: Cajamar.

Galdeano-Gómez, E., Aznar-Sánchez, J.A. and Pérez-Mesa, J.C. (2013). Sustainability dimensions related to agricultural-based development: the experience of 50 years of intensive farming in Almería (Spain). *International Journal of Agricultural Sustainability*, 11 (2): 125–143, doi: https://doi.org/10.1080/14735903.2012.704306.

García Lorca, A.M. (2010). Agriculture in drylands: experience in Almería. In Brauch, H.G., Spring, U., Mesjasz, C., Grin, J., Kameri-Mbote, P. (eds), *Coping with Global Environmental Change, Disasters and Security*. Berlin: Springer, pp. 921–934.

Gertel, J. and Sippel, S.R. (eds) (2014). *Seasonal Workers in Mediterranean Agriculture: The Social Costs of Eating Fresh*. London: Routledge.

INEA (2013). *Le imprese straniere nel settore agricolo in Italia*. Roma: Istituto Nazionale di Economia Agraria.

INPS (2021). *Osservatorio sul mondo agricolo*. Available at: https://www.inps.it/os servatoristatistici/3 Last accessed on 14 January 2023.

Jiménez, J.F. (2008). Estudio de caso del Poniente Almeriense. Glocalización de la horticultura. *Papers*, 90: 83-104, doi: https://doi.org/10.5565/rev/papers/v90n0.736.

Jiménez, J.F. (2011). Procesos de desarrollo en el Poniente Almeriense: Agricultores e inmigrados. *Revista de Estudios Regionales*, 90: 179–206.

King, R. (2000). Southern Europe in the changing global map of migration. In King, R., Lazaridis, G. and Tsardanidis, C. (eds), *Eldorado or Fortress? Migration in Southern Europe*. Basingstoke: Palgrave Macmillan Press, pp. 3–26.

Leogrande, A. (2008). *Uomini e caporali. Viaggio tra gli schiavi nelle campagne del Sud*. Milano: Mondadori.

Marchesi, M.E. (2020). *Understanding How Labour Trafficking Networks Exploit Systemic Vulnerabilities in Europe: An Exploration of the Italian Agriculture Sector*. Milano: Università Cattolica del Sacro Cuore di Milano.

McMichael, P. (2013). Value-chain agriculture and debt relations: contradictory outcomes. *Third World Quarterly*, 34 (4): 671–690, doi: https://doi.org/10.1080/01436597.2013.786290.

Mezzadra, S. (2006). *Diritto di fuga*. Verona: Ombre Corte.

Molina Herrera, J. (2002). La inmigración y el modelo de desarrollo almeriense: Una aproximación al modelo de desarrollo almeriense. In Pimentel, M. (ed.), *Mediterráneo Económico (1): Procesos migratorios. Economía y personas*. Almería: Instituto Cajamar, pp. 384–388.

Morice, A. and Michalon, B. (2009). Les migrants dans l'agriculture: vers une crise de main-d'oeuvre? *Études rurales*, 2: 9–28, doi: https://doi.org/10.4000/etudesrurales.8749.

Palomar Oviedo, F. (1994). *Los invernaderos en la provincia de Almería*. Almería: IEA-Diputación Provincial de Almería.

Pedreño Cánovas, A. (1998). *Del jornalero agrícola al obrero de las factorías vegetales*. Madrid: Ministerio de Agricultura, Pesca y Alimentación.

Pedreño Cánovas, A. (2012). Trabajadores y agriculturas mediterráneas en la globalización, Mercados de trabajo en la agricultura mediterránea. *Regiones*, 47: 16–22.

Pedreño Cánovas, A. (2014). *De cadenas, migrantes y jornaleros: los territorios rurales en las cadenas globales agro-alimentarias*. Madrid: Editorial Talasa.

Pugliese, E. (2002). *L'Italia fra migrazioni internazionali e migrazioni interne*. Bologna: Il Mulino.

Reigada, A. (2017). Family farms, migrant labourers and regional imbalance in global agri-food systems. In Corrado, A., De Castro, C. and Perrotta, D. (eds), *Migration and Agriculture: Mobility and Change in the Mediterranean Area*. London: Routledge, pp. 95–110.

Rivera Menéndez, J. (2000), *La política de colonización agraria en el Campo de Dalías (1940–1990)*. Almería: IEA-Diputación Provincial de Almería.

Rye, J.F. and Scott, S. (2018). International labour migration and food production in rural Europe: a review of the evidence. *Sociologia Ruralis*, 58: 928–952, doi: https://doi.org/10.1111/soru.12208.

Sánchez-Picón, A. (2005). De frontera a milagro. La conformación histórica de la economía almeriense. In Molina, J. (ed.), *La economía de la provincia de Almería*. Almería: Cajamar, pp. 43–86.

Terluin, I.J. (2003). Differences in economic development in rural regions of advanced countries: an overview and critical analysis of theories. *Journal of Rural Studies*, 19: 327–344, doi: https://doi.org/10.1016/S0743-0167(02)00071-2.

Van der Ploeg, J.D. (2008). *The New Peasantries: Struggles for Autonomy and Sustainability in an Era of Empire and Globalisation*. London: Earthscan.

8. The care shortage and social acceptance: why the welfare needs of native families subvert immigration policies

Maurizio Ambrosini

The migration of women is often related to care and domestic service needs in native families, both in Southern Europe and globally. The initial phase of inflow of migrants to Southern Europe is often irregular and occurs despite declared policies of border closure and widespread hostility towards immigration. Anti-immigration policies and internal demands for care services are not easy to conciliate, and both phenomena must be placed in a framework of growing social needs connected to the ageing of European societies. Elderly care is a fundamental societal challenge in developed countries, as progress in healthcare has prolonged human life, and care systems need to be adapted to assure suitable assistance for frail elderly persons. In the European Union, this challenge is addressed by means of different arrangements, according to the welfare regime of each state (Esping-Andersen, 1999). Italy, along with most of Southern Europe, follows a welfare regime in which households maintain a crucial role, with public policies and markets playing a lesser one (Ferrera, 2012; Pérez-Caramés, 2014). In this welfare regime it is adult women who are culturally burdened with the responsibility for caring for frail members of their families (Pérez-Caramés, 2014). The aim of this chapter is to demonstrate how the Italian welfare regime has responded to the challenge of a growing demand for elderly care without altering the central role of family households (Moreno, 2002), while incorporating migrant women as care workers in these domestic settings (Bettio et al., 2006). A 'triangle of care' is established, involving frail elderly people, relatives as 'care managers' and migrant 'care workers'. This often occurs outside of the legal framework, through the informal hiring of migrants who lack legal resident status. In contrast to discourse about immigration in other sectors of Italian society, migrant women working at the service of Italian families, and taking care of their frail seniors, are generally tolerated. Due to the irregular status of many of these migrants when they arrive, Italian families have played a crucial role in campaigns aimed at the regularisation of unauthorised migrants (Ambrosini, 2013, 2018). This chapter discusses how this care system operates, how working and personal relationships are shaped, and what problems arise.

DESERVING IMMIGRANTS ARE LESS IRREGULAR THAN UNDESERVING ONES: THE CASE OF CARE WORKERS

In the majority of the more affluent countries in Europe, the family and the private household are still seen as the most appropriate setting for people to receive the care that they need. This expectation remains particularly strong in Southern Europe, and to some extent in Germany, Austria and Switzerland, and more recently in the Netherlands (Bruquetas-Callejo, 2019). This culture of home-care practices and distrust of institutionalisation have also found their way into the conception of good elderly care, with the recent COVID-19 pandemic fuelling this approach to providing care. It should be made clear here that it is the expectation that these tasks are fulfilled by adult women. However, women are overburdened for many reasons, and face growing difficulties in coping with such social expectations within families (Bettio et al., 2006; Bertani, 2013). Two of the main reasons for women being overburdened are the growing participation of adult women in paid employment, and the increasing numbers of elderly people requiring assistance (Degiuli, 2016). To enable care to be provided within family arrangements while both adults participate in the labour market, many households hire migrant women as live-in care workers (Triandafyllidou and Marchetti, 2015). Thus in the past three decades a huge number of Italian households, along with their counterparts in Spain and Greece (León, 2010; Lyberaki, 2008), Germany (Lutz, 2011) and Austria (Weicht, 2010), have shifted from direct care provision to the management of a care system centred around the figure of a paid migrant care worker (Boccagni, 2016; Da Roit, 2007; Tognetti Bordogna and Ornaghi, 2012). This solution has enabled numerous adult women, who for historic cultural reasons are burdened with the lion's share of care for family members, to combine paid employment with looking after elderly parents (Ambrosini, 2015a). This chapter will use the term 'invisible welfare' to denote this system of elderly care operating in parallel with the official welfare system, managed by families and dependent on the work of mainly migrant women, often with irregular resident status (Ambrosini, 2013; Triandafyllidou, 2013). Unlike traditional domestic service, which is mainly associated with the upper-middle classes, ageing and the need for assistance for elderly members affects families of all social levels (Ambrosini, 2013). Thanks to pensions, government benefits and economic assistance from their children, many elderly people in difficult economic circumstances are also cared for at home by a migrant care worker. At the opposite end of the social scale, it is noteworthy that even families which are easily able to afford to place a relative in a good-quality residential facility for seniors consider it more respectful and loving to keep that relative in their own home (for a parallel with Germany, see Lutz and Palenga-Möllenbeck, 2010), hiring a migrant care worker, or even two if necessary.

The desire to maintain the elderly in their home environment, and to ensure them round-the-clock personal assistance, in many cases entails the imposition of a highly restrictive work regime on the workers hired to take care of them (Redini et al., 2020). These working arrangements are underpinned by a racialised vision of domesticity and cultural traditions, with local employers demanding an availability and a flexibility from immigrant women that they can no longer expect from native workers (Calavita, 2005). Furthermore, immigrant women are considered by employers to be 'naturally' apt to perform traditional 'feminine' tasks, such as taking care of their frail family members (Miranda, 2004). A massive unacknowledged restructuring of elderly home care has developed in an essentially spontaneous and informal way, managed directly by households outside the control of the public sector, but tolerated (van Hooren, 2010) and subsidised by the public authorities. Thus, alongside the official welfare system runs another practically invisible parallel system. Contrary to the dominant political discourse on immigration, migrant care workers are considered to perform a crucial task within, and provide a valuable contribution to, Italian families. For this reason, they enjoy higher levels of social acceptance in Italian society, even when they do not possess a regular residence permit (Ambrosini, 2016). An interesting aspect of this dynamic is the fact that these immigrants are free to move in public spaces with the native Italian elderly and children in their care, from parks to supermarkets, without having to fear checks on their legal status. The domestic setting that accompanies care work enables migrant women in the receiving country to solve several issues associated with their lack of legal status: employment, even if it is underpaid, unregulated and lacking social benefits, (supposedly) safe accommodation, food, the possibility to save money and send remittances to family in the country of origin, and protection against (unlikely) checks on legal status by the state authorities. On the other hand, the employment requires the migrant workers to accept constraining living arrangements (co-habitation with their employers/clients), confusion between working time and private life, (often) exploitative working relations, and (sometimes) sexual harassment, or various forms of abuse and violence.

Social acceptance in the private sphere finds some correspondence in public policies. As a general rule in Italy, as in other countries, irregular migrants are more tolerated and even protected if they are women, especially when employed by native families, than if they are men, particularly those who are unemployed and homeless. Domestic and care services are typical work settings for undocumented migrants, not just in Southern Europe but also in countries such as Germany, where they enjoy the silent complicity of public authorities: 'The official policy in Germany is to turn a blind eye to the demand for domestic and care services, neither expanding the public care sector nor creating regular immigration venues for domestic and care workers' (Schwenken, 2013: 135). Lutz and Palenga-Möllenbeck (2010) have called this an 'open secret' of German society. According to Cornelius, in the United States 'individual homeowners do not have to worry about immigration law enforcement, despite the fact that they provide a large share of the jobs that go to unauthorised migrants' (Cornelius, 2005: 786). There is also a thriving demand for domestic care workers in Asian countries such as Singapore and Japan (Huang et al., 2012; Lopez, 2012). This can be described as a 'moral economy' regulating the social acceptance of unauthorised immigrants beyond the terms of the law. Näre (2011) employs this term in analysing the moral norms which characterise domestic and care labour relations and their influence on the negotiation of labour conditions. The nature of domestic care work, and its locus within the household, means that labour relations 'are particularly difficult to separate from moral and familial notions of altruism and dependency' (Näre, 2011: 401). In this context, a labour contract is accompanied by a moral contract 'based on normative notions of good and bad, reciprocity, shared duties and responsibilities' (ibid.). Bonizzoni (2017) also talks of a 'moral economy' in regard to domestic and care services. She argues that the moral economy of domestic work favours 'the creation of close, dyadic and trustworthy relationships' (ibid.: 1657) which can be used for legalisation purposes, albeit at the price of establishing binding and often exploitative relations between domestic workers and their employers. On the other hand, immigrant care workers appeal to their 'deservingness' in the eyes of people with whom they have contact, and later by receiving societies and public institutions. Irregular immigrants make a special effort to demonstrate 'moral qualities' through compliance with the law, hard work, and irreprehensible behaviour, and this is more convincing in the case of care workers at the service of native families and their frail members. The acquisition of legal status is conceived in practice as an achievement based on an effective performance of deservingness (Chauvin and Garcés Mascareñas, 2014; Bonizzoni, 2017). Domestic employers manage key aspects of the experience of migrant care workers and take crucial decisions regarding their settlement. Of paramount importance are the decisions taken by employers about the acquisition of legal resident status by migrant care workers.

Between 1990 and 2010, the Southern European governments of Italy, Spain and Greece engaged in prominent campaigns of regularisation of unauthorised immigrants. The main reason behind this drive for regularisation was informal employment, with employers being key actors in the process due to their investment, especially in Italy, in the decision about who to regularise (Ambrosini, 2018), thus granting the employer the power to decide whether an immigrant worker will acquire the status of a legal resident. In the following decade, Spain and Greece abandoned this policy, while Italy enacted two additional campaigns of immigrant regularisation, in 2012 and in 2020. From 1986 to 2020, Italian governments implemented eight regularisation campaigns, making it the European country with the highest numbers of regularised immigrants. Over the last 20 years, the greatest number of regularisation campaigns have occurred in the domestic and care work sector. The 2009 regularisation campaign was specifically addressed to the domestic and care sector, and 85 per cent of the 207 542 applications made in the campaign held in 2020 came from this sector; while agriculture, the sector for which the procedure was initially conceived, received only 15 per cent of the total number of applications. The crucial step of making an application is regulated by informal negotiations: employers can refuse to apply for regularisation, but workers are able to exert some influence over their decisions. In domestic care services, irregular immigrants have the well-being of elderly people (or children) in their hands, and with time often develop emotional bonds with their clients. It is not easy for an employer to deny a person who has taken care of her elderly relatives for years the right to apply for regularisation, while retaining the same availability and devotion from her (Ambrosini, 2013). Tolerance towards the underground economy and hidden work, the crucial role of families (especially adult women) as providers of care services, the informal employment of irregular immigrants, and subsequent regularisations, have all been identified as playing a crucial role in the Southern European pattern of immigration (King and Black, 1997; Baldwin-Edwards and Arango, 1999). Following the economic crisis of 2008, this pattern seems to have weakened in Greece and Spain. In Italy, despite economic difficulties, a massive politicisation of the issue, campaigns against asylum seekers and non-governmental organisation rescue missions in the Mediterranean, the success of anti-immigrant forces in the general elections of 2018, undocumented migrant women have remained a permanent feature of the labour market in domestic and care services, and political regulation is occasionally required to take account of this fact.

ON THE OTHER SIDE: EMPLOYERS AS CARE MANAGERS

The domestic space is a distinctive workspace, especially if it involves round-the-clock care tasks and co-residence.[1] Work and life, public and private space, work hours and free time, tasks and emotions, often become mixed up. Distinctions become blurred and roles lose their boundaries. Moreover, family members who assume the role of care managers are not used to acting as employers, and they might be reluctant to assume this role (Lutz, 2011), as they are the sons and (more often) daughters of seniors who need assistance, not professional employers. Despite this, they manage key aspects of the experience of immigrant care workers, and take crucial decisions regarding their settlement. Regularisation is the most relevant of these, as the Italian state delegates to employers the decision on whether an immigrant worker deserves a residence and work permit. In the case of domestic and care work this decision is substantially taken by the care manager. Once the employment relationship has been established, the care manager becomes responsible for the supervision and control of the care worker. They leave to the care worker the many practical, time-consuming and often strenuous tasks of direct care for the elderly relative, whilst assuming the new role of management of the care system (Miranda, 2004). Lopez (2012) calls this a 'curoscape', in which the care manager fulfils what are felt to be their 'care obligations', as socially and culturally constructed, by interposing the care worker between herself and the elderly person. The care manager remains involved but defends her private life by being responsible and active, but not 'on the front line', so to speak. The more strenuous activities and tasks of constant supervision of the cared for senior are delegated, with the care manager managing the caring relationship at a distance to provide support and fill the gaps. A gender difference is apparent in this process: male care managers delegate to a greater extent and distance themselves more from the care worker and her needs. Female care managers more often remain at the forefront in taking charge of replacing the worker on her days off or hours of rest, doing activities together with the elderly person, and interacting with the care worker (Ambrosini and Cominelli, 2005; Ambrosini et al., 2010).

The care manager is in the first place the actual employer of the care worker, to whom she give instructions about the work and how to do it. It is from her that the care worker receives orders on aspects such as schedules, the ingredients of meals, rest times and outings with the elderly person, and the administering of medicine or other medical treatment. Moreover, the care manager is the reference point in cases of emergency and for all needs that go beyond ordinary administration. It is the care manager to whom the care worker reports the elderly person's health problems, asks about what should be done, and implements the decisions taken. A second function performed by the care manager is that of mediating between the care worker and the elderly person, balancing their needs and expectations. While the health of the care recipient permits it, they are able to make their voices heard, as they are not merely the passive recipients of a care system, but can express preferences, pleasure or dissatisfaction in regard to the care that they receive. They can decide to maintain their distance, to assume a despotic stance, or they may choose to become emotionally involved in a relationship of confidence and affection with the care worker. Care managers supervise care recipients in their relationships with care workers, moderating their demands in order to reduce strains and conflicts. At other times, the mediation concerns relationships with other relatives, who wish to intervene and often criticise care managers or care workers. A third function of the care managers is to manage the employment relationship at an economic and administrative level. It is usually the care manager who pays the care worker's wages. It is with her that the care worker discusses contractual conditions: wages, working hours, time off and holidays. And it is her permission that the care worker asks for in the process of regularisation, when the opportunity arises. A fourth function concerns the administration of the household of the elderly relative. The care manager deals with various tasks of this kind: making necessary purchases, paying bills and taking care of appliances. She also handles relations with public services, principally with the elderly relative's doctor and the health service. She remains the main link between the care worker and the institutions of society (Ambrosini, 2015b).

AN AMBIGUOUS WORK RELATIONSHIP

As observed in previous sections, perhaps the most distinctive and controversial aspect of domestic care is its mix of work and private life, of the professional sphere and the personal, and with it the emotional sphere. Our latest research study on care work with the elderly in Italy has identified four distinct relational models (Artero et al., 2021). These four models overlap partially with those detected by Colombo and Decimo (2009). The first is defined in terms of professional relations: in this case, a representation of domestic work as analogous to any other paid work, with relatively clear boundaries and well-defined tasks prevails. The exchange of personal confidences is minimal or entirely absent. The parties interact using the formal '*lei*' (you) pronoun, which indicates distance and respect. Employers avoid interfering in the private lives of workers, and at the same time do not involve them in their own personal lives.

The second model is that of reciprocal family relations, in which services are embedded in a context of much more engaging interpersonal relationships involving flows of goods, money, or other aid which extend far beyond the exchange of labour for a wage. The communication flows inhabit the personal sphere and involve the exchange of confidences, generating an ambiguous request for inclusion in the family circle. Thus, a relationship in which the employers seek to secure dedication, loyalty and continuity of the relationship is created, where (women) care workers, especially if newly arrived in the country and legally irregular, feeling lost and distant from their families, can seek protection and support. The most favourable context for this pattern of relationships is the live-in care of elderly people: here, as already noted, listening and companionship are the central dimensions of the relationship. In these cases, the worker is addressed with the informal '*tu*' (you) by the employing family, including the care manager, and often addresses them in the same manner, or at least the elderly family member. The use of affectionate family titles, such as 'grandfather' or 'grandpa', is indicative of the line between work and family relationships becoming blurred; however, this occurs with no concomitant decrease in the asymmetry of status and power (Colombo and Decimo, 2009).

The third model can be labelled exploitative family relations. Families are also a place in which forms of violence, mistreatment and exploitation are sometimes enacted, often at the expense of women. Employers (both seniors and care managers) can use informal manners as a disguise for the exploitation of the care worker. In common with forms of maternalism (Marchetti, 2016), in such cases the employer offers economic and moral support, uses kinship terms, and integrates the worker into the family. However, the employer, either purposefully or unknowingly, takes advantage of this to ask the care worker to perform additional tasks. In this way, care workers are subtly obliged to perform tasks that go beyond their contractual obligations. Exploitative relations emerge most frequently in situations where the care recipient is particularly dependent on the worker or risks suffering a major crisis if left without that particular helper. In these situations, the worker interprets that they form part of the family and feels guilty turning down their employer's requests.

The fourth model is that of abusive relations, which take the form of authoritarian behaviour, prohibitions and controls that affect the worker's private life. Here, employers believe that care workers are naturally inferior and subordinate. Contractual obligations and labour rights are not respected. Indeed, cases exist in this model of relations where the employer has prevented the care worker from bathing 'too often', the elderly person being cared for has prohibited workers from leaving the house even during time off, and care managers have cancelled the workers' days off at the last moment. In our study, extreme abusive relations were often forced upon inexperienced care workers by care managers who do not live in the same house and who avoided developing emotional bonds with the worker (Artero et al., 2021). In this fourth model, employers frequently use the '*tu*' form of address with the worker, with the latter required to respond with the formal '*lei*', thus sanctioning the hierarchical distance between them. Extreme cases, recorded by other researchers, include those in which forms of harassment and sometimes sexual abuse are committed in the domestic space (Boccagni and Ambrosini, 2012).

In our research we have found the second model to be the most frequent and interesting (Ambrosini et al., 2010). Women care managers, dealing with women care workers, often become involved in the problems and needs of the worker, and sometimes those of her family network. The care manager becomes the care worker's point of reference if she has health issues, needs economic help, has romantic problems, or wants to assist with the arrival and employment of relatives. This results in concern and forms of support unthinkable in other labour relations; at the same time, it entails invasions of space, feelings and relationships pertaining to the private sphere. A further aspect which is particularly significant for the second model is intervention by care managers to enable care workers to access public services, especially healthcare. In relationships with public services, where interpretative and discretionary margins can be found, care managers mediate, insist and protest, deploying their knowledge and their ability to influence civil servants, social workers and decision-makers, at times circumventing the rules that restrict access to services for irregular immigrants. The other side of the coin is the expectation of availability of the care worker that goes beyond the terms of the contract. Although arrangements concerning days off and holidays have been regulated more closely in recent years, cases of abuse persist even in formal employment relationships, and not just in the fourth model, that of abusive relations. In the case of exploitative relations, the frequent emphasis by care managers and also by the elderly family member on an almost-familial relationship ('she is a member of our family', 'she is like a daughter for my mother', 'she is like a sister for me') is balanced by the employers much more towards duties and expectations than to rights and freedoms attributed to the care workers.

It should be highlighted, that the blurring of the lines between work and emotions, family relationships and contractual ones, is not simply a strategy used by employers/care managers to obtain greater effort from care workers, or even to exploit them. It may also be solicited by the care workers themselves. Ironically, part of the dissatisfaction expressed by some care workers, recorded in research carried out in the Italian province of Trentino (Boccagni and Ambrosini, 2012), concerned attempts by employers to diminish the emotional component of the relationship. Sometimes, negative associations with live-in care work arise from the aloofness manifested by the elderly person or, perhaps more often, by the care manager, in an environment – the household – which demands human warmth, flexibility, and personal relationships that are very difficult to define contractually. The literal application of the provisions of a contract is unlikely to give rise to a relationship that is satisfactory to both parties. Care workers may also desire to express their care for the elderly person in terms of dialogue and relationship. When the attempt to establish a meaningful bond meets resistance (which is of course legitimate), the experience of care work – reduced to the mechanical provision of a sequence of material assistance – may prove even more difficult to bear.

The frequently made proposal to apply the general model of any employment relationship to domestic work, clashes with the inevitable proximity between the parties that co-habitation entails. While it is necessary, respect for formal rights (salary, schedules, days off), is not sufficient, in many cases, to ensure a satisfactory work relationship. Neither care managers nor care workers, nor elderly care recipients in general, express any great enthusiasm for the idea of cooling the relationship, by adopting the impersonal codes of a standard employer–employee relationship.

MIGRANT CARE WORKERS AS CO-PROTAGONISTS OF THE INVISIBLE WELFARE SYSTEM

Migrant care workers are not passive actors in the construction of the invisible welfare system of domestic care for the elderly. On the contrary, like many other immigrants, including those with irregular legal status, they are actors able to take the initiative, albeit within a system of constraints and inequalities (McIlwaine, 2015). This section will therefore focus on the resources and social practices deployed by care workers: to enter the sector, to cope with living and working conditions that are in many respects onerous, to provide for the needs of their loved ones (in particular, their children) left behind in their country of origin, to obtain regularisation, and perhaps to achieve complete or partial family reunification (Bonizzoni, 2015). These resources consist partly of external support and services provided by charitable organisations, which in the case of migrant care workers are usually religious institutions. They are often sourced through social networks, especially with co-nationals in the host country and the country of origin, and provide support that is partially of a psychological nature: for example, the expectation of eventually being able to achieve residence status. A principal resource available to migrant care workers is in fact political. This paradoxical resource for migrant women in the Italian context (and elsewhere) consists of the lack of effectiveness of the repressive apparatus and the concurrent expectation of accessing some kind of regularisation (Ambrosini, 2013). As previously mentioned, Italian campaigns of regularisation have mainly favoured care workers and the domestic sector: in 2009, the regularisation programme was reserved exclusively for them in explicit and official terms; in other cases (2012 and 2020) they made up the overwhelming majority of beneficiaries.

Of salient importance among these resources is the emphasis on a distinctive aspect of care work: a sense of the social usefulness, even a pride, sometimes explicitly asserted by care workers in contrast to the devaluation of care work culturally prevalent in the receiving society (on this point, see also Bruquetas-Callejo, 2019). Apparently, such work requires no special skills and qualifications, because it is presumed that it consists of the traditional caring and housekeeping activities culturally assigned to women. In reality, however, it comprises various delicate tasks, often relating to health, and it requires specific skills: an ability to listen, to express interest, to share feelings, to raise the morale of the person cared for, and to manage emotions and moods (Stacey, 2011). One aspect of the demanding work of caring is the need for the carer to control her emotions, and even to elicit emotions different from those actually felt: hiding sadness, smiling, listening with interest, talking with pleasure. Migrant care workers sometimes express feelings of pride in the importance of their work, and affirm the honesty, importance and dignity of the work performed (Boccagni and Ambrosini, 2012).

Another crucial aspect of integration for migrant workers is networking and the sponsorship of relatives and co-nationals. Compared with residents with authorised status, migrants with irregular status depend more on their networks to seek employment or to find accommodation, to gather information, and for many other needs (Bloch et al., 2014). The arrival of unauthorised migrants is primarily championed and organised by such networks, providing varying degrees of help with different levels of self-interest, depending on whether they are close relatives, friends or strangers. In sociological terms, it can be said that social capital is of paramount importance for irregular migrants (van Meeteren et al., 2009). In research concerning transnational and reunited Latin–American families carried out by the authors in the Liguria region, of the 300 women interviewed, eight out of ten had arrived alone, relying on the support of a social network consisting of relatives and compatriots, with around half of them relying on relatives, the other half on friends and acquaintances (Erminio, 2010). A further key process concerns what may be called 'familisation': that is, the tendency mentioned above of many employers to seek to attenuate the asymmetry of status by attributing to the worker, at least in words, the status of an adjunct member of the family, and frequently developing an emotional attachment to her (see also Miranda, 2004). The density of the relational dimension and the overlap between labour relations and family relations emerges with particular force in the case of the care of elderly people. The elderly expect their care workers to relieve them of loneliness and depression, to be a substitute for children and other relatives who cannot be as close to them as they would like. Generally crucial from the point of view of workers is the relationship established with the care manager, a point already made in the previous section. Care managers thus also become supports, resources and confidants in regard to issues that extend beyond the employment relationship, home management or the relationship with the person receiving care. At other times the supportive relationship extends beyond the end of the employment relationship when the elderly person cared for dies or is hospitalised and family members maintain a sense of gratitude and obligation towards the care worker. In several cases, they help her to find a new job. Moreover, the workers can draw on advantages and resources from these semi-familial relations that enable them, for example, to meet pressing demands made upon them by family members in their country of origin (Boccagni and Ambrosini, 2012).

CONCLUSION: DOMESTIC CARE WORK, THE SOCIAL ORDER AND IMMIGRATION POLICIES

This chapter focuses on the contrast between the political rejection of irregular immigration and the acceptance of migrant care workers, regardless of their legal status. It can be concluded that various strategies are employed to reduce the cognitive dissonance between general norms and particular behaviours, including the following: isolating the individual deserving case as an exception in a generally disorderly and threatening situation; seeing oneself as a benefactor to a person in need; assuming responsibility, by drawing on resources and relationships, for the needs of a care worker which cannot be satisfied by a public institution; and treating the irregular job given to a care worker as a sort of trial period, with a pledge to regularise her position at the earliest opportunity.

Hiring a domestic care worker can also be seen as a way to save the social order: a care regime in which families (but in reality, adult women) take direct care of the frail members of the household, resisting entrusting them to an external institution. However, inevitably tensions and contradictions arise between the emphasis placed on households as the correct locus for care, and the closure of borders to immigrants wishing to work. As families are no longer able to perform their traditional tasks, they hire domestic care workers who frequently have irregular status. In this way they extend their capacity for caring, without modifying the frame of domesticity as the appropriate site for care of relatives (see, for the Austrian case, Weicht, 2010).

In contemporary Italy, and various other countries, the increasing numbers of women employed outside the home, as well as their desire to achieve emancipation from very burdensome care workloads, entails reliance on the work of migrant women. Families, and the adult women within them, confirm the central social importance of women migrant workers in supplying care and services to frail persons, widening their range to include such external subordinate persons in the familial relationships. This process can be described as 'asymmetric modernisation', in which adult Italian women are able to access paid employment and at the same time maintain the roles socially expected of them by devolving the most burdensome tasks to other women. These private arrangements have a political aspect. Confirmation of the centrality of the family as the locus of care and response to fragility exists in opposition to immigration rules which limit the arrival of migrant workers, where effective compliance with restrictive immigration policies would upset the 'curoscape' (Lopez, 2012) based on the family. Adequate provision of services by the state to meet these needs would require a much greater deployment of public services of various kinds, as well as a change in cultural paradigms regarding the most appropriate sites and methods for meeting social needs, especially for elderly care. This social and cultural framework explains the resistance to possible new solutions for the challenge of an ageing Italian society. Beyond the problem of nursing home costs, most families are convinced that providing care at home is the best response to the needs of their elderly relatives. At the same time, the Italian state saves money by letting families solve the issue of elderly care privately, without providing more public services. Italy occupies the third to last position in the Organisation for Economic Co-operation and Development (OECD) classification,[2] with about 4000 nursing homes for the elderly, providing 280 000 places; in comparison to 5400 homes with 373 000 places in Spain, 10 500 homes with 720 000 places in France, and 12 000 homes with 876 000 places in Germany.

More recently the pandemic has led to more questions regarding the quality of assistance provided by nursing homes to frail seniors, and domestic solutions have further increased in popularity. Innovations resulting from this trend could include a greater distinction between the role of care receiver (and her family members) and that of employer. Many ambiguities and much mistreatment of care workers arise as a result of the overlap between these two roles in the experience of the households involved, given the extreme privatisation of assistance to frail elderly people. Therefore, the rationale behind social innovation in this field would consist of some form of deprivatisation of elderly care. A possible improvement in this sector would consist of regulations bringing it under the umbrella of standard working arrangements, where immigrant care workers are hired by conventional employers and provide services to seniors who would become their clients and not their direct employers, or by the close relatives of their employers. In this way the emotional implications and personal bonds involved in care services could be more clearly distinguished by clarifying employment duties and rights. New immigration policies are required, to allow native households, immigrant care workers and possible intermediaries to combine their reciprocal needs in open and formal ways. The tolerance and social acceptance of the irregular immigration of women to perform domestic care is a pragmatic option, but is not the most appropriate solution to the issue of elderly care in developed and democratic countries.

NOTES

1.   The following observations derive from a series of research studies conducted in Northern Italy: Ambrosini and Abbatecola, 2010; Ambrosini and Boccagni, 2007; Ambrosini et al., 2010; Ambrosini and Cominelli, 2005; Ambrosini and Salati, 2004; Boccagni and Ambrosini, 2012. Another recent study (project INNOVACARE) has updated previous results with new empirical materials, consisting of 86 interviews with migrant care workers, elderly, and family

members responsible for the organisation of care (care managers) (Artero, Hajer and Ambrosini 2021).
2. https://www.secondowelfare.it/innovacare/quale-futuro-per-le-residenze-sanitarie-per-la-lungodegenza.html (accessed 12 December 2019).

REFERENCES

Ambrosini, M. (2013). *Irregular Migration and Invisible Welfare*. Basingstoke: Palgrave.

Ambrosini, M. (2015a). Irregular but tolerated: unauthorised immigration, elderly care recipients, and invisible welfare. *Migration Studies*, 3 (2): 199–216, doi: https://doi.org/10.1093/migration/mnu042.

Ambrosini, M. (2015b). Employers as 'care managers': contracts, emotions and mutual obligations within Italy's invisible welfare system. In Triandafyllidou, A. and Marchetti, S. (eds), *Employers, Agencies and Immigration: Paying for Care*. Ashgate: Aldershot, pp. 17–34.

Ambrosini, M. (2016). From 'illegality' to tolerance and beyond: irregular immigration as a selective and dynamic process. *International Migration*, 54 (2): 144–159, doi: https://doi.org/10.1111/imig.12214.

Ambrosini, M. (2018). *Irregular Immigration in Southern Europe: Actors, Dynamics and Governance*. Cham: Palgrave.

Ambrosini, M. and Abbatecola, E. (eds) (2010). *Famiglie in movimento. Separazioni, legami, ritrovamenti nelle famiglie migranti*. Genova: Il melangolo.

Ambrosini, M. and Boccagni, P. (2007). *Il cuore in patria. Madri migranti e affetti lontani: le famiglie transnazionali in Trentino*. Trento: CINFORMI (Centro informativo per l'immigrazione), Provincia di Trento.

Ambrosini, M., Bonizzoni, P. and Caneva, E. (2010). *Ritrovarsi altrove. Famiglie ricongiunte e adolescenti di origine immigrata*. Milano: Osservatorio regionale per l'integrazione e la multietnicità, Regione Lombardia.

Ambrosini, M. and Cominelli, C. (eds) (2005). *Un'assistenza senza confini. Welfare 'leggero', famiglie in affanno, aiutanti domiciliari immigrate*. Milano: Osservatorio regionale per l'integrazione e la multietnicità, Regione Lombardia.

Ambrosini, M. and Salati, M. (eds) (2004). *Uscendo dall'ombra. Il processo di regolarizzazione degli immigrati e i suoi limiti*. Milano: FrancoAngeli.

Artero, M., Hajer, M. and Ambrosini, M. (2021). Working with a family: how a family-oriented welfare system opens the border for migrant care workers. *Revue Européenne des migrations internationales*, 37 (1): 117–138, doi: https://doi.org/10.4000/remi.18282#xd_co_f=NTc2MGY0NTUtNWM0ZS00MGIyLThk NDktZDM5ZThjNTE1YTJi~.

Baldwin-Edwards, M. and Arango, J. (eds) (1999). *Immigrants and the Informal Economy in Southern Europe*. London: Routledge.

Bertani, M. (2013). Families in Italy in the face of the crisis of 'Mediterranean' welfare. *Italian Sociological Review*, 3 (2), 85–100, doi: http://dx.doi.org/10.13136/isr.v3i2.53.

Bettio, F., Simonazzi, A. and Villa, P. (2006). Change in care regimes and female migration: the 'care drain' in the Mediterranean. *Journal of European Social Policy*, 16 (3): 271–285, doi: https://doi.org/10.1177%2F0958928706065598.

Bloch, A., Sigona, N. and Zetter, R. (2014). *Sans Papiers. The Social and Economic Lives of Young Undocumented Migrants*. London: Pluto Press.

Boccagni, P. (2016). Searching for well-being in care work migration: constructions, practices and displacements among immigrant women in Italy. *Social Politics: International Studies in Gender, State and Society*, 23 (2): 284–306, doi: https://doi .org/10.1093/sp/jxv031.

Boccagni, P. and Ambrosini, M. (2012). *Cercando il benessere nelle migrazioni. L'esperienza delle assistenti familiari straniere in Trentino*. Milano: FrancoAngeli.

Bonizzoni, P. (2015). Uneven paths: Latin American women facing Italian family reunification policies. *Journal of Ethnic and Migration Studies*, 41 (12): 2001–2020, doi: https://doi.org/10.1080/1369183X.2015.1037257.

Bonizzoni, P. (2017). The shifting boundaries of (un)documentedness: a gendered understanding of migrants' employment-based legalization pathways in Italy. *Ethnic and Racial Studies*, 40 (10): 1643–1662, doi: https://doi.org/10.1080/01419870 .2016.1229488.

Bruquetas-Callejo, M. (2019). Long-term care crisis in the Netherlands and migration of live-in care workers: transnational trajectories, coping strategies and motivation mixes. *International Migration*, 58 (1): 105–118, doi: https://doi.org/10.1111/imig .12628.

Calavita, K. (2005). *Immigrants at the Margins: Law, Race and Exclusion in Southern Europe*. Cambridge: Cambridge University Press.

Chauvin, S. and Garcés-Mascareñas, B. (2014). Becoming less illegal: deserving-ness frames and undocumented migrant incorporation. *Sociology Compass*, 8 (4): 422–432, doi: https://doi.org/10.1111/soc4.12145.

Colombo, A. and Decimo, F. (2009). *Spazi di confidenza: la regolazione della distanza sociale nella collaborazione domestica*. In Catanzaro, R. and Colombo, A. (eds), *Badanti & Co. Il lavoro domestico straniero in Italia*. Bologna: Il Mulino, pp. 253–278.

Cornelius, W. (2005). Controlling 'unwanted' immigration: lessons from the United States, 1993–2004. *Journal of Ethnic and Migration Studies*, 31 (4): 775–794, doi: https://doi.org/10.1080/13691830500110017.

Da Roit, B. (2007). Changing internal solidarities within families in a Mediterranean welfare state: elderly care in Italy. *Current Sociology*, 55 (2): 251–269, doi: https:// doi.org/10.1177/0011392107073306.

Degiuli, F. (2016). *Caring for a Living: Migrant Women, Aging Citizens and Italian Families*. Oxford: Oxford University Press.

Erminio, D. (2010). Dalla maternità transnazionale al ricongiungimento: la molteplicità dei percorsi. In Ambrosini, M. and Abbatecola, E. (eds), *Famiglie in Movimento. Separazioni, Legami, Ritrovamenti nelle Famiglie Migranti*. Genoa: Il melangolo, pp. 17–90.

Esping-Andersen, G. (1999). *Social Foundations of Postindustrial Economies*. Oxford: Oxford University Press.

Ferrera, M. (2012). The South European countries. In Castles, F.G., Leibfried, S., Lewis, J., Obinger, H. and Pierson, C. (eds), *The Oxford Handbook of the Welfare State*. Oxford: Oxford University Press, pp. 616–629.

Huang, S., Yeoh, B.S.A. and Toyota, M. (2012). Caring for the elderly: the embodied labour of migrant care workers in Singapore. *Global Networks*, 12 (2): 195–215, doi: https://doi.org/10.1111/j.1471-0374.2012.00347.x.

King, R. and Black, R. (1997). *Southern Europe and the New Immigration*. Brighton: Sussex Academic Press.

León, M. (2010). Migration and care work in Spain: the domestic sector revisited. *Social Policy and Society*, 9 (3): 409–418, doi: https://doi.org/10.1017/S1474746410000126.

Lopez, M. (2012). Reconstituting the affective labour of Filipinos as care workers in Japan. *Global Networks*, 12 (2): 252–268, doi: https://doi.org/10.1111/j.1471-0374.2012.00350.x.

Lutz, H. (2011). *The New Maids: Transnational Women and the Care Economy*. London: Zed Books.

Lutz, H. and Palenga-Möllenbeck, E. (2010). Care work migration in Germany: semi-compliance and complicity. *Social Policy and Society*, 9 (3): 419–430, doi: https://doi.org/10.1017/S1474746410000138.

Lyberaki, A. (2008). *Deae Ex Machina: Gender, Migration and Care in Contemporary Greece*. GreeSE paper n. 20. London: Hellenic Observatory, London School of Economics.

Marchetti, S. (2016). Citizenship and maternalism in migrant domestic labour: Filipina workers and their employers in Amsterdam and Rome. In Gullikstad, B., Kristensen, G.K. and Ringrose, P. (eds), *Paid Migrant Domestic Labour in a Changing Europe: Questions of Gender Equality and Citizenship*. Cham: Palgrave, pp. 147–168.

McIlwaine, C. (2015). Legal Latins: creating webs and practices of immigration status among Latin American migrants in London. *Journal of Ethnic and Migration Studies*, 41 (3): 493–511, doi: https://doi.org/10.1080/1369183X.2014.931803.

Miranda, A. (2004), Une frontière dans l'intimité. La confrontation culturelle entre femmes étrangères et femmes autochtones dans l'espace domestique. *Les cahiers du CEDREF*, 12: 115–135, doi: https://doi.org/10.4000/cedref.551.

Moreno, L. (2002). *Mediterranean Welfare and 'SUPERWOMEN'*. UPC Working Paper 02-02. Madrid, www.iesam.csic.es/doctrab.

Näre, L. (2011). The moral economy of domestic and care labour: migrant workers in Naples, Italy. *Sociology*, 45 (3): 396–412, doi: https://doi.org/10.1177%2F0038038511399626.

Pérez-Caramés, A. (2014). Family policies in Spain. In Robila, M. (ed.), *Handbook of Family Policies Across the Globe*. New York: Springer, pp. 175–194.

Redini, V., Vianello, F.A. and Zaccagnini, F. (2020). *Il lavoro che usura. Migrazioni femminili e salute occupazionale*. Milano: FrancoAngeli.

Schwenken, H. (2013). 'The EU should talk to Germany'. Transnational legal consciousness as a rights claiming tool among undocumented migrants. *International Migration*, 51 (6): 132–145, doi: https://doi.org/10.1111/imig.12118.

Stacey, C.L. (2011). *The Caring Self: The Work Experiences of Home Care Aides*. Ithaca, NY: Cornell University Press.

Tognetti Bordogna, M. and Ornaghi, A. (2012). The 'Badanti' (informal carers) phenomenon in Italy: characteristics and peculiarities of access to the health care system. *Journal of Intercultural Studies*, 33 (1): 9–22, doi: https://doi.org/10.1080/07256868.2012.633312.

Triandafyllidou, A. (ed.) (2013). *Irregular Domestic Workers in Europe: Who Cares?* Aldershot: Ashgate.

Triandafyllidou, A. and Marchetti, S. (eds) (2015). *Employers, Agencies and Immigration: Paying for Care*. Aldershot: Ashgate.

van Hooren, F. (2010). When families need immigrants: the exceptional position of migrant domestic workers and care assistants in Italian immigration policy. *Bulletin of Italian Politics*, 2 (2): 21–38.

van Meeteren, M., Engbersen, G. and van Sal, M. (2009). Striving for a better position: aspirations and the role of cultural, economic, and social capital for irregular migrants in Belgium. *International Migration Review*, 43 (4): 881–907, doi: https://doi.org/10.1111%2Fj.1747-7379.2009.00788.x.

Weicht, B. (2010). Embodying the ideal carer: the Austrian discourse on migrant carers. *International Journal for Ageing and Later Life*, 5 (2): 17–52, doi: http://dx.doi.org/10.3384/ijal.1652-8670.105217.

9. Lebanese migration policy since 2011 and its role in the Syrian refugee movement

Kamel Doraï and Imad Amer

INTRODUCTION

Forced migration is not a new phenomenon in the Middle East but is a necessary factor in an analysis of the changes that have occurred in the socio-political context of the region. From population movements from the Caucasus and North African regions to the Levant since the beginning of the 20th century, and the large dispersion of Palestinian refugees following the creation of the State of Israel, to recent waves of Syrian and Iraqi refugees, migration plays an essential role in structuring the socio-economic, political and demographic landscape of the region. Thus, contemporary refugee movements can only be understood in connection with the dynamics of cross-border migration that have been formed over the years.

Middle Eastern migration has been radically transformed by the Syrian crisis of 2011. In the past, most Syrians who left their country of origin did so to find work, mainly by moving to Lebanon. However, following the crisis, Syrians have constituted one of the largest refugee populations since the Second World War. The principal consequence of this large influx of refugees has been the ending of the region's open-door policy, with neighbouring countries implementing restrictive migration policies. The mass arrival of forced migrants concentrated in certain areas (such as border cities and villages, and poor neighbourhoods in the main cities of the host countries) has had a significant local impact on host societies. This massive refugee movement follows others, such as the forced exile of Palestinians after the creation of the State of Israel in 1948, that of the Lebanese following the outbreak of civil war in 1975 until the restoration of the government in 1990, and the fleeing of Iraqi refugees following the outbreak of war in the early 1980s (Chatty, 2010). Refugee movements are one of the major consequences of the political crises that have occurred in the Middle East in recent decades.

Despite not being a signatory of the 1951 Geneva Convention, Lebanon is host to one of the largest per capita refugee populations in the world. The region is also characterised by a long history of significant human migration resulting from regional economic disparities and transnational social ties. Today's forced migration movements appear to be linked to previous cross-border migration at a regional level. In the Middle East, where conflicts have generated large refugee groups, the existence of structured and ancient diasporas is a key element in understanding current refugee mobility. Based on research conducted in Lebanon in the framework of the Migration Governance and Asylum Crises (MAGYC) project which seeks to assess how the governance of migration has been influenced by recent refugee crises and how crises in general shape policy responses to migration, this chapter explores the impact that changes in Lebanon's migration policy have had on the migration process of Syrian refugees in Lebanon. The conflict in Syria has resulted in one of the largest movements of refugees and internally displaced persons in recent history. Since 2011, according to the United Nations High Commissioner for Refugees (UNHCR) more than 5 million Syrians have found refuge in countries bordering their country of departure. The scale of this exodus, and its long-term nature, has profoundly modified the regional and national balance and has led to a redefinition of the modes of governance of migration, of access to the labour market and of residence in Lebanon. Lebanon's migration policy has always been linked to the country's economic interests as well as to the special relationship that the state maintains with its Syrian neighbour. Since the end of the civil war, Lebanese migration policy has been shaped by the balance of power between the various political parties and their link with the Syrian authorities. External interventions, such as the role played by the UNHCR and the European Union, are also central to understanding the evolution of Lebanese asylum policy since 2011 (Fakhoury, 2020). In this chapter, after a reminder of the specific migratory relations that Lebanon maintains with Syria, we focus our analysis on the internal political dynamics that led to the implementation of a restrictive immigration policy. Following the 2015 refugee crisis, the European Union (EU) developed a new cooperation with Eastern Mediterranean states to turn the Syrian refugee crisis into a development opportunity. The EU signed two agreements (the Jordan and Lebanon compacts) in 2016. Both states became central actors, in cooperation with European states and international donors, in the implementation of containment policies based on tools to control Syrian refugees' mobility at both national and Euro-Mediterranean levels. The Lebanon compact is one step in the implementation of European Union migration policies, with other agreements such as that signed with Turkey post-2015.

MIGRATION POLICY OR ASYLUM POLICY?

Following multiple crises and wars, including the Israeli–Palestinian conflict, and those of Lebanon, Iraq and Syria, which produced several million forced migrants, the countries of the Middle East now host the largest population of refugees in the world, as well as a large number of internally displaced persons. Given the fact that none of these Middle Eastern host countries, with the exception of Turkey, is a signatory to the 1951 Geneva Convention – which defines the term 'refugee', outlines their rights as well as the legal obligations of States to offer them protection – migrants fall into a legal vagueness which has significant consequences on their movements and activities. The question of the migration policies of the host countries must therefore be analysed over time and placed in their regional and Euro-Mediterranean context.

The absence of specific refugee legislation in host countries in the region does not reflect an absence of migration policies implemented in response to the arrival and settlement of people fleeing conflicts; various measures to regulate entry and rights of residence have been adopted. The migration policies of states in the Middle East are often thought of as the product of constraints imposed by the European Union. Recent studies have highlighted the crucial role of EU policies in shaping national migrations and asylum in Middle Eastern countries (Bank and Fröhlich, 2021; Fakhoury, 2021; Seeberg, 2018). While this dimension is fundamental in understanding the ways in which migratory and refugee flows are managed, it is nevertheless necessary to analyse the internal political dynamics of each country, and in particular their responses to each of the successive crises. European Union policy tends to promote local integration of refugees in their host countries, whereas local state authorities promote temporary solutions to avoid refugees' integration in the long term.

The non-resolution of the Palestinian question, which resulted in camps created in the early 1950s becoming a permanent fixture, strongly conditions the current treatment of new flows of refugees in the region. One result of this is that following the fall of Saddam Hussein's regime in 2003, the main host states in the region did not open refugee camps on their soil. While the establishment of camps permits the operational management of a humanitarian crisis and facilitates the control of the resulting refugee populations, their existence also poses various questions. By creating obstacles to mobility, camps can generate pockets of poverty that are partially disconnected from the socio-economic environment of the host country. In the long term, restricting the movement of refugees generates an increase in dependence on humanitarian aid organisations. It can also create a form of stigmatisation that leads to the segregation of refugee populations in their host society. As mentioned above, the reluctance of the authorities of host states to open refugee camps is partly based on fear of repeating the long-term settlement of refugees on their soil as happened with Palestinian refugees. Conversely for Jordan, Syria and Lebanon (to varying degrees), the absence of camps combined with fairly unrestrictive forms of entry and stay following the Iraqi crises of 1990–1991, and then post-2003, have demonstrated increased refugee mobility and therefore greater possibilities for their re-emigration to third countries (Chatelard and Doraï, 2009).

As Lebanon, like the other Arab countries in the region, is not a signatory to the 1951 Geneva Convention on refugees, or the 1967 Protocol Relating to the Status of Refugees, with the exception of Palestinians who are recognised as refugees in the state where they have their permanent residence, the category of refugee does not exist as such (Zaiotti, 2006). While most states in the Middle East do not have a formal asylum system, there are asylum procedures developed by the UNHCR in place. As noted by Michael Kagan: 'The systems that exist on the ground for refugees in the Middle East are essentially off the radar screen of conventional thinking in the field of international law because they rely on shifting responsibility from the state to the UN' (Kagan, 2011: 9). Following the fall of Saddam Hussein's regime in Iraq in 2003, hundreds of thousands of Iraqi refugees found asylum in neighbouring countries, with a few thousand arriving in Lebanon. In response, the Lebanese authority wrote its first asylum policy in conjunction with the UNHCR. Given that it was not part of the 1951 Convention, the UNHCR signed a memorandum of understanding (MOU) with the government of Lebanon (Directorate of General Security) on 9 September 2003.[1] The memorandum of understanding stipulated that: 'Lebanon does not consider itself to be a state of refuge', and that the 'only durable solution for refugees registered with UNHCR is their resettlement in a third country'. The MOU served to provide 'temporary humanitarian solutions for people who are illegal residents in Lebanon and apply for refugee status at UNHCR'. This agreement between the UNHCR and the Directorate of General Security constituted the legal and operational infrastructure for the management in Lebanon of the later Syrian refugee crisis, and allowed the UNHCR to exercise a direct role with regard to displaced Syrians from 2011 up until 2014, when the Lebanese government implemented the UN refugee registration processes.

Pre-2011, a Migration Policy Rooted in Syrian–Lebanese Relations

The Lebanese authority's response to the Syrian refugee crisis of 2011 is related to the lengthy history linking these countries. The Syrian occupation of Lebanon began in 1976 and ended in 2005, following the assassination of the former prime minister Rafiq Hariri (Meier, 2016). Since then, Lebanese political factions have been divided on the nature of their relationship with the Syrian authorities. Several bilateral agreements have been signed that include regulations concerning access to residency and the labour market for Syrian migrants. The Taef Accord, signed in 1989, marked the cessation of armed conflict and cemented the role of the Syrian regime in Lebanon as a guardian authority, entrenching its absolute control on the inner workings of the Lebanese state institutions (Picard, 2016). On 22 May 1991, the governments of Lebanon and Syria signed the Treaty of Brotherhood, Cooperation and Coordination between the Syrian Arab Republic and the Lebanese Republic,[2] establishing the Syrian Lebanese Higher Council[3] to implement agreements reached. The signing of the treaty was accompanied by a series of other agreements between the states regarding security, military and defence arrangements. However strained the Syrian–Lebanese relationship has been over time, agreements based on the relatively free circulation of workers highlight the importance of the role played by Syrian labour forces in the post-war reconstruction of Lebanon (Chalcraft, 2008). Despite a lack of precise statistics, the magazine *Le Commerce du Levant* estimated that in 2003 there were a total of 400 000 Syrian workers in Lebanon in the construction and agricultural sectors. In 2005, before the assassination of the Lebanese Prime Minister Rafiq Hariri and the Syrian military exit from Lebanon, Amnesty International estimated their total number to range between 400 000 and 600 000.[4]

In 2005, following the assassination of the Lebanese Prime Minister, Rafiq Hariri, the March 14 bloc[5] mobilised massive protests and demonstrations against the Syrian regime and the joint Lebanese–Syrian security apparatus. In parallel, the March 8 coalition mobilised support in favour of the regime, which in turn resulted in a vertical political division of Lebanon's political scene. The demonstrations ended with the withdrawal of the Syrian regime from Lebanon on 26 April 2005. The military withdrawal was accompanied by a wave of revenge attacks perpetrated on Syrian workers and Syrian nationals by affiliates and supporters of political parties opposing the Syrian regime. The consequences of such events were felt on both sectarian and regional levels. The four pro-Syrian regime security officers were imprisoned in what, to a large extent, consisted of a process of dismantling the military regime.[6] This major event ended the direct role of Syrian nationals in Lebanese political and social life, and began a new era marked by different dynamics between the Syrian and Lebanese people.

In June 2005, after the parliamentary elections, a new government led by Prime Minister Fouad Siniora from the Future Movement was established. This government took the first step towards managing the presence of Syrian workers in Lebanon, establishing the Department of Syrian Workers' Welfare within the Directorate for Employment in the Ministry of Labour.[7] The role of the department included 'reviewing and registration of application for work permits for Syrians in accordance with the laws and effective rules and the specific accreted systems for the work of Syrians', in addition to 'the coordination with the joint work offices regarding the Syrian Lebanese borders and the exchange of information on all that pertains to the Syrian workers in Lebanon'. The department was established in parallel with the government of Syria's tightening of the conditions under which Syrian workers were allowed into Lebanon. For example, the government of Syria increased the border crossing fee from \$4 to \$18, and prohibited the transport of goods, food and cars with more than 20 litres of diesel from Syria. However, further steps in this direction were not taken by the governments of Syria and Lebanon because of the common interest both states have in the presence of the Syrian labour force in Lebanon. For instance, the movement of the Syrian labour force into Lebanon reduced the unemployment figures in Syria. This labour force also resulted in approximately \$1 billion being spent annually in Syria's consumer markets (Chalcraft, 2006). In Lebanon, farmers, industrialists, real estate brokers, as well as the owners of cafes and hotels, rely heavily on the relatively cheap Syrian labour force, especially considering that they can be dismissed at no cost, given that the Lebanese Labour Code does not grant foreign workers social security benefits.

Post-2011: From an Open-Door Policy to Restrictions

Concerning the Syrian refugee crisis, Lebanese migration policy is not an exception in the region. The policies of neighbouring states towards refugees from Syria have changed over time. Initially marked by the opening of their borders, these policies evolved towards an increasingly pronounced closure, with the introduction of visa requirements for Syrian nationals in all bordering countries. The year 2014 proved to be a turning point in Lebanon, with the suspension of the bilateral employment agreement governing the Syrian labour force that had been in place since 1994 (Longuenesse, 2015). At the same time, labour migration and refugee mobility intensified, with more than 300 000 refugees being registered by the UNHCR in 2014. While the conflict in Syria has resulted in the forced migration of several hundred thousand refugees, economic migration has not disappeared between the two countries. Most migrant workers stayed in Lebanon, some of whom could not return home and became de facto refugees and registered with UNHCR. The blurring of categories, and the coexistence within the same population of different legal statuses is one of the features marking migration in the region.

The open-door policy: 2011–2014
Conflict in Syria began in 2011, following massive peaceful demonstration against the regime which quickly escalated to widespread armed conflict

between Syrian government forces and armed opposition groups. The spread and intensification of the armed conflict and widespread violence led thousands of Syrians to flee to Lebanon. The government of Lebanon took no measures to respond to the influx of refugees to its territories until 2014, when political disagreement in Lebanon increased between those groups affiliated to the Assad regime and others opposing it. This political division has had a significant impact on the management of the Syrian refugee crisis in Lebanon. A considerable number of these refugees originated from opposition-controlled areas in Syria, resulting in concerns resurfacing about the potential alteration of a fragile demographic balance with political ramifications, and the return of historical divisions based on sects. In light of the lack of any legal solutions for Syrian refugees in Lebanon, the Lebanese Security Forces took control of the situation and implemented a security-driven approach to deal with refugees. This resulted in the Lebanese Security Forces (LSF) and Lebanese Army Forces (LAF) detaining Syrians at checkpoints and conducting raids on their houses.[8]

As the conflict in Syria intensified, it spilled over into Lebanon. In response to the kidnapping of a Lebanese individual in Syria in 2012, a series of kidnappings of Syrians and other foreign nationals were carried out, hinting at a potential spillover of conflict and tension into Lebanon's internal political scene.[9] The LSF also intervened in the deportation of Syrians back to Syria under the pretext of a judicial decision, while denying that there was any political basis for the deportations.[10] The deportation of Syrian refugees by the LSF triggered a series of local and international condemnations. The European Union representative condemned the decision to deport the refugees at a press conference[11] held on 4 August 2012. Human Rights Watch and Ruwad Frontiers Association[12] also condemned the actions of the LSF. Human Rights Watch published an open letter stating the following:

> I am sending you this message to inform you that we have received on the first of August a credible source report on LSF's deportation of four Syrian nationals forcibly back to Syria after they have expressed their concern of oppression in their country. Any forced return for individuals susceptible to oppression or any other form of mistreatment is a revocation of Lebanon's commitment against forced return as per the international law.[13]

Palestinian refugees from Syria, the first group experiencing restrictions in Lebanon

Although the current conflict has generated new refugees, it has also forced tens of thousands of Palestinian refugees already in Syria to seek asylum in a third country. Before becoming one of the countries producing the highest number of refugees, Syria was the primary host country for several hundred thousand Iraqi refugees fleeing the chaos and violence that followed the fall of Saddam Hussein's regime in 2003, not to mention the presence on its soil of nearly 500 000 Palestinian refugees.[14] The current conflict has had dramatic consequences for the Palestinian population in Syria. Before 2011, Palestinians enjoyed access to education and the labour market in Syria without experiencing significant discrimination (Shiblak, 1996); while the outbreak of the Syrian conflict returned Palestinians to being stateless. This can be viewed as replicating a scenario that occurred with Palestinians in Iraq during the aftermath of the fall of Saddam Hussein in 2003 (Doraï and Al Husseini, 2013). Due to their specific status, Palestinian refugees are not covered by the UNHCR mandate (Feldman, 2012). Even if some of them are in receipt of assistance from the United Nations Relief and Works Agency for Palestine Refugees in the Near East (UNRWA) in Lebanon, they lack legal protection, transforming them de facto into illegal migrants subject to potential deportation to Syria. Palestinian refugees tend to be transformed into asylum seekers by conflicts, and as they are stateless, they cannot even seek the protection of their country of origin.

The policy governing entry and residency for Palestinian refugees from Syria has evolved over time. Prior to 2013, Lebanon had adopted a flexible policy and hosted more than 75 per cent of the total number of Palestinian refugees from Syria. As of August 2013, while transiting through Lebanon remained permitted, Palestinians from Syria were required to prove that they had family ties there, or that they were coming for a medical appointment, or to an embassy. A few exceptions to these rules, at the discretion of the General Security Directorate, could be observed. Since 3 May 2014, faced with an ever-increasing influx of refugees from Syria, the Lebanese General Security Directorate has considerably tightened the conditions of entry for Palestinian refugees from Syria, resulting in the majority being denied entry to Lebanon. At the same time, the Lebanese authorities have implemented restrictions to the renewal of residence visas for Palestinians from Syria already present on its soil. Many reside illegally in Lebanon, which results in limitations to their mobility, access to services and assistance, and administrative procedures such as birth registration. Along with difficulties related to their residency status, Palestinians from Syria face significant economic hardship. Lacking access to the labour market, families live mainly on economic assistance provided to them by UNRWA, as well as food assistance distributed to them. According to a study conducted by UNRWA and the American University of Beirut, 90 per cent of them live below the poverty line, being unable to cover their basic needs (Chaaban et al., 2016). The absence of a legal framework for Palestinian refugees who are forced to leave their country of residence, as well as the political treatment of Palestinian refugees by states in the region, raises the problem of secondary migration during conflict.

From 2014 to the present day: the implementation of a restrictive migration policy

On 15 March 2014, a new government led by Tammam Salam was formed in Lebanon after a political coalition between various political factions was enforced. Seats within the government were distributed among three blocs: 'March 8', 'March 14', and a bloc consisting of the President and Druze leader Walid Jumblatt. After the formation of the government, the LSF prohibited the entry of Palestinian refugees (Doraï, 2015), issuing a circular for all airline companies to refrain from transporting any Palestinian refugees from Syria to Lebanon. The circular was accompanied by the deportation of 30 Palestinian refugees on 4 May 2014.

On 23 June 2014, for the first time since the beginning of the conflict in Syria, the government of Lebanon established a ministerial committee to tackle all matters related to Syrian refugees. The committee was headed by the Prime Minister and included the Minister for External Affairs, the Minister for Internal Affairs and Municipalities, and the Minister of Social Affairs. The importance of the Syrian refugee crisis and the need to reach consensus is reflected in the membership of the committee, with representatives from the three blocks of the 'National Consensus government'. The committee was commissioned to take the necessary steps to respond to the influx of Syrian refugees in coordination with the relevant administrations. The membership of this committee and its process of formation is indicative of the importance of the Syrian refugee crisis, hence the government's need for the consensus of all political blocs. The government of Lebanon issued *The Syrian Displacement to Lebanon Policy Paper*, an unprecedented step of its kind since the start of the war in Syria. The policy paper represented an official guide for managing the refugee flow into the country, cancelling the open-door policy, and putting an end to the relaxed procedures in welcoming Syrians. Instead, the aim of the policy was to decrease the number of Syrian refugees in the country through halting their registration with the UNHCR and encouraging their return to Syria. The policy paper did not explicitly state the government's aim to completely close the borders, or stipulate any outright forcible steps to that end. Rather, it allowed the entry of refugees, albeit on an exceptional basis and for urgent humanitarian situations. The policy paper was issued against the backdrop of Lebanon's participation in the Geneva Conference on the plight of Syrian refugees, convened less than two months prior to its announcement. International support agreed upon at the Conference entails not only monetary support (of which Lebanon has so far only received 44 per cent), but also, in accordance with the principles of international solidarity and sharing of responsibility, the facilitation of the entry of Syrian refugees to other countries and their residence in these countries.

The government of Lebanon sought to pressure other countries to take in Syrian refugees and to increase the international community funds allocated for host communities. Indeed, in December 2014 the United Nations called for funds of up to $55 million to support the lives of millions of Syrian refugees and as well as to provide support for host communities. According to an article published in the *Legal Agenda*[15] on 9 December 2014, by stating its intent to 'decrease the number of Syrians registered with the UNHCR', the government has indirectly admitted the right of Syrians to refugee status, albeit conditionally and temporarily, despite having previously denied such rights. For only with the status of refugee and its associated rights can a distinction be made between those eligible and those not, those in need of protection and those not, according to internationally recognised criteria (Saghieh and Frangieh, 2014). From August 2014, the LSF action took that distinction into consideration as it started to document people according to the categories 'displaced' and 'not displaced'. Notably, the Syrian displacement policy paper indicates that if an individual breaks Lebanese law or fails to meet the conditions of entry into the country, the award of the category of 'displaced' would be revoked. Such regulations are vague and potentially dangerous, given that a considerable number of Syrian refugees have lost their identification cards and their residency permits. In the formulation and implementation of this policy paper the government of Lebanon has adopted an approach of 'soft power' to reduce the numbers of refugees in a policy that, at least ostensibly, accepts the existence of the right to asylum.

A similar mechanism was adopted in measures aimed at decreasing the numbers of 'displaced people' in Lebanon, in a policy which opened with a statement 'encouraging the Syrian displaced to return to their country or to other countries through all available means'. The use of the term 'encouraging' is very telling in this context and can only be understood as the government's intention to adopt non-coercive measures, or at least appear to, in its implementation of the policy. By the use of the term, it is clear that the government lacks the capacity to implement such measures, having few tools at its disposal to force the return of refugees, and is therefore primarily dependent on the willingness of refugees to return, preferring this to deportation or coercive measures.

In the same way, coupling this 'encouragement' with emphasis placed on 'strictness in the implementation of the Lebanese law' and the threat of 'removal of the "displaced" category' makes it fairly evident that the government's intention is to mobilise all available 'soft' means to pressure Syrian refugees to leave Lebanon. One of the primary means employed by the government since the onset of its mandate has been refraining from renewing residency permits.

The policy paper on Syrian refugees was followed by several procedures (decision number 197/1, December 2014) implemented by the Ministry of Labour that sought to specify employment open exclusively for Lebanese nationals, indirectly reducing the categories of employment opportunities available to foreigners, including Syrians.

SYRIAN REFUGEES AT THE MARGINS OF LEBANESE SOCIETY

Along with the tightening of entry requirements and limitations to access to the labour market, Lebanese authorities have developed restrictive policies affecting Syrians in informal settlements leading to their marginalisation (Kikano et al., 2021). These policies relate to a decision, made at the very start of the refugee crisis, not to open camps for Syrian refugees, based in part on the fear of permanent settlement stemming from both the state and the refugees themselves. In Lebanon, this refusal to officially open camps for Syrians on its territory derives from the fear of repeating the complex relationship and history of conflict that resulted from the presence of Palestinian refugee camps. By contrast, the Iraqi crises of 1990–1991 and post-2003 demonstrated for Jordan, Syria and Lebanon that the absence of camps, combined with a relative freedom of entry and residence at the beginning of the crises (this has to be nuanced according to the countries and periods concerned), a fairly easy access to public services and employment in the informal labour market, have increased the possibility of mobility of refugees and therefore their re-emigration to third countries (Chatelard and Doraï, 2009). However, the decision not to open refugee camps involves both state policies and logics developed by the refugees themselves. Lebanon, where the Palestinian presence – and therefore the camps – is marked by a history of conflict and a complex relationship with the Palestinian refugees, has so far refused to officially open camps for Syrians on its territory. The fear of creating 'Syrian' spaces in Lebanon, which might lead to the development of political and/or armed movements, remains strong for Lebanese political leaders. Political parties are also deeply divided on the Syrian conflict, with some groups supporting Assad's regime and others supporting opposition groups.

In January 2017, the Lebanese government and the United Nations approved the Lebanon Crisis Response Plan 2017–2020. In contrast to the *The Syrian Displacement to Lebanon Policy Paper* in 2014, which aimed to stop the Syrian exodus and encourage return by all available means, the new plan dealt with the various humanitarian and development aspects of the Syrian refugee crisis in Lebanon. The plan outlined issues related to refugee status, the difficulty in obtaining legal residency, and the impact of this on the lives of Syrian refugees in Lebanon, in addition to reviewing and amending the applicable

policies in order to remedy this situation. Also included were various infrastructure development plans for the refugees and the host communities, including water, energy, sanitation, education, food security, health and housing. It
was estimated that these sectors required an investment of $2.8 billion, to be
sourced through grants and soft loans from the World Bank along with funding
from the Lebanese government, non-governmental organisations, and other
donors. In recognition of the prolonged duration of the Syrian refugee crisis
and its repercussions on the host communities, the 2017–2020 plan focused on
both short- and long-term development, with projects counting on the involve-
ment of the following ministries: the Ministry of Social Affairs, the Ministry
of Energy and Water, the Ministry of Health, the Ministry of Agriculture, the
Ministry of Education and Higher Education, and the Ministry of Economy
and Trade. It coincided with the beginning of the financial crisis in Lebanon,
where warnings of the unstable financial situation in Lebanon explained the
importance of the financing plan for the Lebanese government and its official
bodies, as concerns regarding liquidity resulted in the Banque du Liban insti-
tuting various financial engineering operations in 2016 to attract capital from
abroad at very high interest rates.

In response to the plan, the Lebanese General Security Directorate issued
new instructions to grant residency, exempt from fees and delays, to a category of Syrian refugees. This included all Syrian refugees registered with
the United Nations High Commissioner for Refugees before 2015, regardless
of their legal status (illegal entry, overstaying, or obtaining residency based
on registration with the UNHCR after 2015); it excluded refugees who had
obtained residency after 2015 not based on registration with the UNHCR (such
as a pledge of responsibility, a lease contract, or other categories).

In parallel with the development of the Crisis Response Plan, the Lebanese
President Michel Aoun pressed for the 'safe' return of displaced refugees,
expressing this concern in several statements and during a meeting with the
President of the UNHCR on 3 February 2017, where the President said that
Syrian refugees cannot stay in Lebanon. An appeal was also made to the international community to facilitate the return of the displaced by establishing safe
areas inside Syria.

In March 2017, the Lebanese General Security Directorate issued new
instructions to grant free residency to a category of Syrian refugees and
exempt them from delay and residency fees as a translation of the Lebanon
Crisis Response Plan 2017–2020. The decision included all Syrian refugees
registered with the United Nations High Commissioner for Refugees before
2015, regardless of their legal status (illegal entry, overstaying, or obtaining
residency based on registration with the UNHCR after 2015). It excluded from
this decision the refugees who obtained after the year 2015 a residency that is
not based on registration with the UNHCR (such as a pledge of responsibility,

a lease contract or other categories). However, during the same period in March 2017, the Lebanese army evacuated more than 80 camps in the Bekaa Valley near the Rayak al-Askari airport by a military decision, the reasons for which are unknown, as is the party that issued the instructions. A suicide bombing led to a massive raid carried out by the Lebanese army on camps in Arsal on 30 June 2017, resulting in extensive arrests.

In 2018, the Lebanese government took several steps that had a direct impact on Syrian refugees, including the issuing by the Ministry of Labour of Resolution No. 29/1 on 18 February 2018, restricting some professions to the Lebanese, and the launch by the General General Security Directorate on 20 April 2018 of a campaign to close all shops and institutions managed or operated by Syrians. This campaign was repeated at the end of 2018. In addition to these measures, the Ministry of Foreign Affairs requested that the UNHCR not issue any statements related to Syrian refugees, and withdrew residency from UNHCR workers in an attempt to pressure the organisation, accusing it of working against facilitating the return of refugees. On 6 June 2018, Foreign Minister Gebran Bassil issued the UNHCR an ultimatum, giving it two weeks to draw up a plan for the return of Syrian refugees. The President of the Lebanese Republic added to the conflict by issuing statements criticising the UNHCR and demanding the assistance of Arab countries to facilitate the return of Syrian refugees. An international 'Friends of Syria' conference was held in Brussels, during which donor countries pledged to provide $4.4 billion to neighbouring countries hosting refugees.

Policies exerting pressure on Syrian refugees continued in 2019, as the Ministry of Labour tightened working conditions for Syrian workers and enforced stricter procedures, paperwork and higher fees. The Supreme Defence Council, headed by the President of the Republic, also intervened in the refugee situation, calling for a halt to unauthorised labour. On 1 July 2019, the army demolished 20 shelters for Syrian refugees under the pretext that they were violating the construction laws, following the prohibition of the building of any concrete facilities by Syrian refugees and only permitting the use of removable materials.

CONCLUSION

In 2020, Lebanon entered a stifling political and economic crisis that led to a rapid and dramatic collapse of the local currency. The country also suffered from the outbreak of coronavirus which exacerbated the impact on those businesses that had remained economically viable. The economic crisis has had a huge toll on Syrian refugees in Lebanon. Due to the restrictive policies pursued over the past decade, and given their fragile economic and legal situation, refugees have been subjected to enormous pressure with regard to their livelihoods, residence and health. Alongside this difficult economic situation, the General Security Directorate implemented measures to prevent the entry of some categories of refugees to Lebanon, and on 28 July 2020 circulated a decision to facilitate the exit of Syrians residing in Lebanon legally or illegally; and the Ministry of Labour launched a campaign to regularise the conditions of foreign workers, requiring payment of fees due.

Through the years, the Syrian and Lebanese people have to varying degrees shared existential threats, as their access to the basic requirements of daily life has dwindled in the light of the worsening economic crisis. In a statement to the United Nations High Commissioner for Refugees on 8 January 2021:

> Nine out of every ten Syrian refugee families in Lebanon are currently living in extreme poverty. This percentage reached 89% in 2020, up from 55% only one year previously. Families are currently on less than 308,728 Lebanese pounds per person per month, which is less than half the minimum wage in Lebanon.

Fears have become centred on the food insecurity of refugees, and these fears are supported by the nearly threefold increase in food prices in Lebanon in the transition from 2019 to 2022. At the same time, opportunities to find work have diminished due to the severe economic collapse in the country. This reality leads families to depend on financial coping mechanisms that are detrimental, including child marriage, abandoning schooling, and reduced spending on education and health. It is also expected that the rates of child labour will rise significantly due to poor access to educational services and financial difficulties.

The high concentration of Syrian refugees in Lebanon can be partly explained by the historical and previous migratory links existing between Syria and Lebanon. Regional mobility pre-existed the independence of states in the region. When national borders were created at the beginning of the 20th century, this circular migration transformed into transnational networks. Since the end of the civil war in Lebanon, bilateral agreements have been signed to facilitate the circulation and employment (with restrictions) of people. In 2011, labour migration turned into asylum seeking, relying on pre-existing cross-border networks. The settlement of Syrian refugees is also the result of an open-door policy during the first two years of the conflict. Changes in the Lebanese asylum policy are related both to internal political issues and to international pressures. The Lebanese political scene is divided, with some political actors opposing the Syrian regime, others supporting it. Lebanese authorities have oscillated between support to Syrian refugees and imposing constraints, with some observers calling it 'a policy of no-policy'. In this chapter we have tried to analyse the genealogy of Lebanese asylum policy through the evolution of the migration pattern, from labour migration to refugees' settlement.

ACKNOWLEDGEMENT

This chapter has been written in the framework of the MAGYC Project funded by the European Commission's Horizon 2020 Research and Innovation Programme (Grant agreement number 822806). The MAGYC (Migration Governance and Asylum Crises) project seeks to assess how migration governance has been influenced by the recent 'refugee crises', and how crises at large shape policy responses on migration. The general objective of the project is to appraise policy responses in light of the 'crisis' and to assess their efficiency for the long-term governance of migration.

NOTES

1. Lebanese President, Decree n:11262, 30/10/2003.
2. Treaty signed on 22 May 1991. The Treaty resulted in a leap in the relationship between the two states. Within the framework of this Treaty, many objectives were determined. To accomplish these objectives, several joint organisms were established on the authority of this Treaty to watch over the implementation of its provisions and any others that might be issued.
3. The Higher Council shall set up the general policy of coordination and cooperation between the two states in all fields (political, economic, social and many other fields), and shall supervise its implementation and adopt the plans and decisions taken by 'the Follow-Up and Coordination Commission', 'the Foreign Affairs Committee', 'the Committee for Economic and Social Affairs', 'the Committee for Defense and Security Affairs', or any committee established subsequently.
4. Amnesty International (2005).
5. Since 2005 the Lebanese political scene has been divided into two main blocs, the 'March 8' gathering politically affiliated to the Syrian regime, and the 'March 14' for the political parties opposed to the Syrian regime.
6. United Nations Security Council (2005).
7. *Lebanese Official Gazette* (2005), Decree n: 15488, 17/10/2005.
8. Human Rights Watch (HRW) (2011).
9. Human Rights Watch (HRW) (2012a).
10. Human Rights Watch (HRW) (2014).
11. EU Representative (2012).
12. Ruwad Frontiers Association was founded by a group of Lebanese human rights activists active on refugee issues through the Ad-Hoc Committee in Support of Refugees and Asylum-seekers (ACSRA) (1999–2002) and for one year with a civil company called Frontiers Center (FC) (2003). Building on this history, FC's mandate is to defend and advocate on behalf of refugees, asylum seekers and stateless persons. FC is developing a professional quality legal counselling and advocacy programme. Its staff and partners are trained and advised by experts with experience in international human rights and refugee law and legal aid development and includes counsellors with backgrounds in law and social sciences.
13. Human Rights Watch (HRW) (2012b).

14.   United Nations Relief and Works Agency for Palestine Refugees in the Near East (UNRWA) (2022).
15.   An English version has been published by the Heinrich Böll Stiftung.

REFERENCES

Bank, A. and Fröhlich, C. (2021). The governance of Syrian refugees in the Middle East: lessons from the Jordan and Lebanon Compacts: Special Issue (SI) of *Digest of Middle East Studies*, ed. by Kelsey Norman: Contribution to 'Taking Stock of Middle East Migration since the Arab Uprisings'. *Digest of Middle East Studies*, 30 (4): 256–261, doi: https://doi.org/10.1111/dome.12247.

Chaaban, J., Salti, N., Ghattas, H., Irani, A., Tala, I. and Batlouni, L. (2016). Survey on the Socioeconomic Status of Palestine Refugees in Lebanon 2015. American University of Beirut, UNRWA.

Chalcraft, J. (2006). Syrian workers in Lebanon and the role of the state: political economy and popular aspirations. In de Bel-Air, F. (ed.), *Migration et politique au Moyen-Orient*. Beyrouth: Presses de l'Ifpo, pp. 81–103.

Chalcraft, J. (2008). *The Invisible Cage: Syrian Migrant Workers in Lebanon*. Stanford, CA: Stanford University Press.

Chatelard, G. and Doraï, K. (2009). The Iraqi presence in Syria and Jordan: social and spatial dynamics, and management practices by host countries. *Maghreb-Mashreq*, 199: 43–60.

Chatty, D. (2010). *Displacement and Dispossession in the Modern Middle East*. New York: Cambridge University Press.

Doraï, K. (2015). Les Palestiniens et le conflit syrien. Parcours de réfugiés en quête d'asile au Sud-Liban. *Revue européenne des migrations internationales*, 31 (3–4): 103–120, doi: https://doi.org/10.4000/remi.7392.

Doraï, K. and Al Husseini, J. (2013). La vulnérabilité des réfugiés palestiniens à la lumière de la crise syrienne. *Confluences Méditerranée*, 87: 95–108, doi: https://doi.org/10.3917/come.087.0095#xd_co_f=NTc2MGY0NTUtNWM0ZS00MGIyLThk NDktZDM5ZThjNTE1YTJi~https://doi.org/10.3917/come.087.0095#xd_co_f= NTc2MGY0NTUtNWM0ZS00MGIyLThkNDktZDM5ZThjNTE1YTJi~.

Fakhoury, T. (2020) *Refugee Governance in Crisis: The Case of the EU–Lebanon Compact*. https://www.magyc.uliege.be/wp-content/uploads/2021/01/D2.3-v1December2020.pdf.

Fakhoury, T. (2021). The external dimension of EU migration policy as region-building? Refugee cooperation as contentious politics. *Journal of Ethnic and Migration Studies*, 48 (12): 1–19, doi: https://doi.org/10.1080/1369183X.2021.1972568.

Feldman, I. (2012). The challenge of categories: UNRWA and the definition of a 'Palestine refugee'. *Journal of Refugee Studies*, 25 (3): 387–406, doi: https://doi.org/10.1093/jrs/fes004.

Kagan, M. (2011). 'We live in a country of UNHCR.' The UN Surrogate State and Refugee Policy in the Middle East. UN High Commissioner for Refugees (UNHCR). http://www.refworld.org/docid/4d8876db2.html.

Kikano, F., Fauveaud, G. and Lizarralde, G. (2021). Policies of exclusion: the case of Syrian refugees in Lebanon. *Journal of Refugee Studies*, 34 (1): 422–452, doi: https://doi.org/10.1093/jrs/feaa058.

Longuenesse, É. (2015). Travailleurs étrangers, réfugiés syriens et marché du travail. *Confluences Méditerranée*, 92: 33–47, doi: https://doi.org/10.3917/come.092.0033

#xd_co_f=NTc2MGY0NTUtNWM0ZS00MGIyLThkNDktZDM5ZThjNTE1YTJi
~.

Meier, D. (2016). L'occupation syrienne du Liban avait pour objectif son annexion. In Meier, D. (ed.), *Liban. Identités, pouvoirs et conflits: Idées reçues sur un État dans la tourmente*. Paris: Le Cavalier Bleu, pp. 103–108.

Picard, É. (2016). *Liban Syrie, intimes étrangers. Un siècle d'interactions sociopolitiques*. Paris: Sindbad/Actes Sud.

Saghieh, N. and Frangieh, G. (2014). *The Most Important Features of Lebanese Policy Towards the Issue of Syrian Refugees: From Hiding Its Head in the Sand to 'Soft Power'*. Heinrich Böll Stiftung, https://lb.boell.org/en/2014/12/30/most-important-features-lebanese-policy-towards-issue-syrian-refugees-hiding-its-head.

Seeberg, P. (2018). EU policies concerning Lebanon and the bilateral cooperation on migration and security–new challenges calling for new institutional practices? *Palgrave Communications*, 4 (1): 1–9, doi: https://doi.org/10.1057/s41599-018-0192-7.

Shiblak, A. (1996). Residency status and civil rights of Palestinian refugees in Arab countries. *Journal of Palestine Studies*, 25 (3): 36–45, doi: https://doi.org/10.2307/2538257.

Zaiotti, R. (2006). Dealing with non-Palestinian refugees in the Middle East: policies and practices in an uncertain environment. *International Journal of Refugee Law*, 18 (2): 333–353, doi: https://doi.org/10.1093/ijrl/eel006.

Reports and Official Documents

Amnesty International (2005). Lebanon: stop the attacks on Syrian workers and bring the perpetrators to justice (published in Arabic), https://www.amnesty.org/ar/documents/mde18/004/2005/ar/.

EU Representative (2012). *Statement by the Spokesperson of High Representative Catherine Ashton on Expulsions by the Lebanese Authorities of Syrian Nationals to Syria*, United Nations, https://www.consilium.europa.eu/uedocs/cms_data/docs/pressdata/EN/foraff/132115.pdf.

Human Rights Watch (2011). *Lebanon: Stop Detaining Syrian Refugees*, https://www.hrw.org/news/2011/05/20/lebanon-stop-detaining-syrian-refugees.

Human Rights Watch (2012a). *Lebanon: Investigate, Prosecute Kidnappers*, https://www.hrw.org/news/2012/08/20/lebanon-investigate-prosecute-kidnappers.

Human Rights Watch (2012b). *Letter to Lebanese Officials Regarding Deportation of Syrians*, https://www.hrw.org/news/2012/08/04/letter-lebanese-officials-regarding-deportation-syrians.

Human Rights Watch (2014). *Lebanon: Syrian Forcibly Returned to Syria*, https://www.hrw.org/news/2014/11/07/lebanon-syrian-forcibly-returned-syria.

Lebanese Official Gazette (2005). Creation of a Labour Welfare Department, 48, 27 October, pp. 5160–5161, http://legallaw.ul.edu.lb/LawArticles.aspx?LawTreeSectionID=214079&LawID=211840&language=ar.

Memorandum of Understanding between the General Directorate of General Security and the Regional Office of the United Nations High Commissioner for Refugees on dealing with asylum applicants at the Office of the United Nations High Commissioner for Refugees in Lebanon (2003), Lebanese President, Decree n: 11262, 30/10/2003, Official Gazette n: 52, 13/11/2003, p. 6070 (published in Arabic(, http://77.42.251.205/Law.aspx?lawId=8774.

The Syrian Displacement to Lebanon Policy Paper, 23/10/2014, Cabinet session decisions, Lebanese Government (published in Arabic).

Treaty of Brotherhood, Cooperation and Coordination between the Syrian Arab Republic and the Lebanese Republic (1991). Syrian Lebanese Higher Council (published in Arabic), http://www.syrleb.org/SD08/msf/1507751751_.pdf.

United Nations Security Council (2005). *Letter dated 20 October 2005 from the Secretary-General addressed to the President of the Security Council*, https://undocs.org/S/2005/662.

UNRWA (2022) UNRWA Registered Population Dashboard, Syria, www.unrwa.org.

10. Repoliticising gendered vulnerability: the blind spots of vulnerability-focused humanitarian programmes in Greece

Alice Latouche

INTRODUCTION

The Southern European Migration Model emphasises the changes which happened in Europe between the 1970s and the 1990s, when Italy, Greece, Portugal and Spain were transformed from countries of emigration to ones of immigration. The model focuses on the analysis of the flows of new migrants who came to live in these countries to join their undeclared labour force in a context of economic growth. In terms of gender analysis, the model deconstructed preconceived ideas of mainly male migration flows, by revealing how women came to Europe, not necessarily to follow their husbands, but driven by their own agency. In particular, the model provided a new perspective on the gender and racial division of labour in Southern European countries, by highlighting the gendered opportunities given to migrant women, mainly in domestic work and the sex trade (King, 2000; Lazaridis and Psimmenos, 2000; Miranda, 2010). Following these analyses focused on the experience of migrant women, gender-based violence was gradually taken into account in European migration policies as a specific source of vulnerability, thus acknowledging the specific needs of gender-based/sexual violence survivors in terms of protection and healthcare (Freedman, 2018). However, the focus on migrant vulnerabilities came in a context where the emphasis was put on the extension of camps as a means to control the borders (Akoka and Clochard, 2015), and on the criminalisation of migrants (Rodier, 2008).

A striking example is Greece, in which the hardening of border policies went hand in hand with the growing significance of the identification of 'vulnerable groups'[1], which would have access to special guarantees refused to others. In 2015, after more than 850 000 people (mainly from Syria, Afghanistan and Iraq) crossed the Aegean Sea to reach Europe, new policies to control migrant flows were implemented on the closest islands to Turkey: the 'hotspot approach' (in 2015) formalised the retention of migrants who came by the Aegean Sea in Kos, Leros, Chios, Lesbos, Samos and Kos during their asylum procedure (Tassin, 2019), and the European Union (EU)–Turkey deal (in 2016) introduced a new 'fast-track procedure' aiming at reducing the number of asylum seekers coming to Europe. Following this procedure, migrants coming from Syria, or from countries with a protection rate of more than 25 per cent, have to go through a 'admissibility procedure'[2] in which it is evaluated whether they can be sent back to ask for asylum in 'a safe third country', namely Turkey. Only vulnerable groups are allowed to bypass the geographical restriction of the islands to reach the mainland, avoid expulsion to Turkey, and for those deemed the 'most in need', to access proper accommodation through the Emergency Support to Integration and Accommodation (ESTIA II) programme (Papada, 2021; Spathopoulou et al., 2020).

In this context, the inclusion of gender-sensitive polities cannot be analysed without taking into account the fact that the guarantees given to vulnerable groups are based on a selection, and the exclusion of those deemed 'non-vulnerable' (Sözer, 2019). But how do we identify who is vulnerable? How can one prove vulnerability, especially in a case where there are no scars attesting the previous violence? Which kind of practices does it provoke for people in charge of identifying vulnerability, and for those who are assessed? How can one mitigate 'vulnerability'? In the hotspots, the assessment of vulnerability relies on a medical examination which will determine whether one belongs to a specific category of vulnerability (non-accompanied minors, gender-based/sexual violence survivors, pregnant women, and so on). But the identification of 'vulnerable persons' often relies on the selection of predetermined groups, such as women and children, associated with victimhood and powerlessness (Butler et al., 2016; Fineman, 2008), which neglects the political and social dimension of vulnerability. Indeed, if the integration of gender violence in European policies attests to a consideration of the specific violence suffered by women on the migratory journey, it neglects a real analysis of the relations of gender and racial domination (Freedman, 2018). In direct opposition to this gender essentialist conception of vulnerability, recent feminist theories have pointed out how, on the contrary, the concept of vulnerability could be used to analyse situations of self-deprivation, where individuals are subject to such power relations that they are no longer able to act wilfully, or to be safe (Garrau, 2021), in order to draw the attention of the state in the fight against social inequalities (Fineman, 2008). 'Vulnerability' can be linked to the concept of 'precarity', a condition of insecurity linked to the failing social and political supports which are expected to mitigate the risks inherent in human life.

Following this research, I propose a critical analysis of the concept of 'vulnerability' as it is used in the hotspots, by focusing precisely on the practices provoked by the assessment, and the long-term precariousness of women included in accommodation programmes for vulnerable groups. The aim is to explore how migration policies focused on vulnerable groups work hand in hand with exclusion and military policies at the borders, by restricting humanitarian assistance to a small portion of 'deserving' migrants (Sözer, 2019). Furthermore, this analysis will provide a critical point of view on the new relations of power that are paradoxically produced by gender-sensitive policies. To achieve that end, I shall first examine how the assessment of 'vulnerability' heavily relies on stereotypes of gender that exclude men, and force women to 'perform' their vulnerability according to the implicit expectations of the evaluators. I shall then focus on the experiences of vulnerable migrant women, by demonstrating how the accommodation policies actually reinforce their precariousness by forcing women to accept undeclared jobs within the same gendered and racialised sectors of employment, a dynamic already analysed by the Southern European Migration Model in the 1990s. The continuity of these relations of power, reinforced by the anti-migrant policies, will provide new elements to understand how the very definition of gendered vulnerability is, in itself, deeply political.

This chapter comes from an ongoing sociology thesis, focused on the trajectories of exiled women, from the hotspots to Athens. This chapter is based on research work carried out over three months on the island of Chios (from March to May 2019), and four months on the island of Samos (August to November 2021). I interviewed 15 women and kept in regular contact with them, including those I met in Chios, for over two years. These women are of different nationalities (Afghanistan, Cameroon, Democratic Republic of Congo, Syria, Equatorial Guinea), and an average age of between 23 and 40 years old (the age group which represents 62 per cent of adult migrant women in Greece). The wish to carry out a multi-sited ethnography by 'following' migrant women recognized as vulnerable during their journey is motivated by the will to restore the complexity of their experience according to the spaces they cross.

THE IMPACT OF THE HARDENING OF BORDER POLICIES ON GENDERED VULNERABILITY

A Gendered Selection on the EU's Doorstep

Since the EU–Turkey deal, ratified in March 2016, being recognised as vulnerable has become a key element of the asylum procedure. Indeed, all asylum seekers from Syria, Somalia, Pakistan, Bangladesh and Afghanistan who come to Greece by the Aegean Sea are to be sent back to Turkey unless they can prove that they would be endangered if they claimed asylum in this 'safe third country', or if they are deemed vulnerable. As said before, only the vulnerable asylum seekers can be transferred on the mainland and be integrated into the ESTIA II programme in order to be accommodated in social housing (Kourachanis, 2020). The assessment of vulnerability is therefore based on a new selection, which will distinguish those who will be detained on the islands during the whole process, or sent back to Turkey, and those considered in need of assistance and protection. According to the International Protection Act (IPA) adopted in January 2020 in Greece, vulnerability is defined by easily identifiable criteria (elderly people, pregnant women, people suffering from a serious illness), but also by less tangible elements, linked to past violence (people who have suffered torture, or gender, sexual or psychological violence). These vulnerabilities are then categorised according to their degree of gravity by doctors from the Hellenic National Public Health Organization (EODY, formerly KEELPNO): 'high vulnerabilities' (A), 'non-vulnerable with special needs of hospitality' (B), and 'non-vulnerable persons' (C). Vulnerabilities can be identified at any time during the procedure, whether during the admissibility procedure supported by the European Asylum Support Office (EASO), or during the examination of the asylum application by the Greek Asylum Service (GAS). The 'high vulnerabilities' include visible, 'self-evident' vulnerabilities, that can be assessed through a medical examination, or which are considered obvious (pregnant women, minors, elders) (AIDA, 2019), while the 'non-vulnerable with special needs of hospitality' category focuses on invisible vulnerabilities, often psychological conditions that need to be followed up and monitored. In this particular case, when vulnerability is not self-evident, the subjectivities of social workers come into play to determine who shall benefit from the programme. As an example, Alia Spathopoulou, Anna Carastathis and Myrto Tsilimpounidi emphasised how the assessment relies on racialised perceptions of nationality, and stereotypes of the economic migrant perceived as the embodiment of strength and independence (Spathopoulou et al., 2020). Therefore, those identified as 'Pakistani men' are immediately considered as belonging to the category of the 'economic migrant', and if they do not have any physical proof of their vulnerability, they will be perceived as potentially driven to Greece for financial reasons. This example highlights how the assessment of vulnerability is, in itself, a selection which happens in a broader context of filtering at the borders, and the intertwinement of humanitarian aid and migration control policies.

Following on their analysis, I would like to underline the gendered stereotypes that intervene in the selection: first, men are often perceived as non-vulnerable unless they can prove that they are suffering from a severe disability or a mental illness (Keygnaert and Guieu, 2015). This phenomenon is not new in itself: traditionally, humanitarianism has often based its inter-ventions in war zones on the gendered division between women and children, considered as helpless and vulnerable, and men, perceived as a potential threat (Carpenter, 2005). For the anthropologist Hande Sözer, the gendered selection of vulnerable groups of asylum seekers in Turkey implies that those who gain access to a 'paternalistic form of care' (namely women and children) will go through 'a paternalist control' which put their behaviour under surveillance to see whether they deserve special aid: the necessity to show their gratitude, to avoid wearing make-up and staying up late at night, are assessed to check whether they fit the stereotype of a proper 'vulnerable' person (Sözer, 2019). In the case of the assessment selection, not all women are deemed vulnerable: only those who fit the stereotypical representation of gendered vulnerability will be recognised as such. To illustrate this point, I would like to describe the experience of Gloria, from Cameroon, who explained how, during her vulnerability assessment on the island of Chios, she tried to look 'fierce and determined' so the social workers would not assume she was 'crazy' and to indicate that she could easily fit into the Greek community. She was suffering from a post-traumatic disorder linked to her previous experiences of sexual violence, and was given drugs to prevent nightmares and panic attacks. Nevertheless, she was worried that her psychological health would be a problem during the interview with EASO, which she thought would determine whether she could be accepted in Europe or not. She tried to look strong, but she was taken aback when the social worker told her 'she looked well enough' and expressed doubts about her medical condition. At the end of the interview, she thought she had failed, and that she 'should have cried' so that they would have believed her.

This example reveals how it is expected of women to fit the stereotypical image of the powerless victim. Gloria, who wanted to show her strength, was doubted precisely because she did not use the stereotypical narrative of a helpless victim. In line with this point, migrant women can be forced to adopt a 'strategical essentialism' (Spivak, 1988), that is to say, they tempo-rarily put aside their agency to fit the 'mould' and what is expected of them. Otherwise, the risk is to be viewed with suspicion and, if we follow this theory in the case of the vulnerability assessment, to be detained in poor living con-ditions in the hotspots, or to be sent back in Turkey. A gender-based violence (GBV) expert in a Greek non-governmental organisation (NGO), in charge of training social workers working with migrants, explained the importance of the stereotypes associated to victims of gender-based violence during the vulnerability assessment: wearing make-up, and laughing, are not considered to be the proper conduct of someone who has been raped. On the contrary, begging, speaking slowly, crying, are perceived as a self-evident 'sign of vulnerability' (Spathopoulou et al., 2020). It is therefore expected that migrant women perform vulnerability in order to be convincing, even though this 'universal', self-evident image of victimhood is in fact a cultural and historical construction (Ticktin, 2011). In this context, the emphasis is therefore put on the identification of symptoms of vulnerability (crying, shaking, and so on) and it contributes to depoliticising gender-based violence by focusing on the identification of victims in need of rescue, without taking into account the social context in which they are happening. But gender-based violence cannot be addressed as a pathology that requires humanitarian aid: it is, in itself, a political issue linked to relations of power happening in a certain space, and in a certain context.

Turning a Blind Eye to Border Violence

Likewise, the identification of categories of 'vulnerable groups' neglects a real comprehension of the social and political conditions which produce vulnerability. It is therefore not surprising that migrant women living in the hotspots are not considered to be in a situation of vulnerability, even though numbers of NGOs' reports have pointed out the risk of gender-based violence in the camps (HRW, 2019; UNHCR, 2018). On the contrary, the focus on the symptoms of previous gender-based violence relays the idea that it only happens in the countries of origin, and ends at the threshold of Europe. Indeed, the assessment relies on the Country of Origin Information (COI) database on the political, cultural context and the gendered relations of power of the country of departure, in order to verify that the gendered violence relayed in women's testimonies is in line with what is known of their country of origin (Keygnaert and Guieu, 2015). This phenomenon is not new, as gender policies and women's rights have often been used to stigmatise countries of the South (Dorlin, 2008). Moreover, focusing on the violence that happened 'there' often equates to turning a blind eye to the violence produced at the borders, 'here'. A striking example of this is the refusal to take into account the effect of pushbacks on migrants who have tried to cross the Aegean Sea. Pushbacks – in other words, the informal return of migrants against their will – are deemed illegal by the Geneva Convention and the EU Charter of Fundamental Rights. But since March 2020, when Turkey announced that it would no longer prevent migrants from crossing the borders, pushbacks have been a recurring practice to send back people who came by the Aegean Sea. During these pushbacks, migrants go through sexual, psychological and physical violence which should, theoretically, be assessed as a vulnerability. As an example, Antoinette, who came from the Democratic Republic of Congo, took a boat from Turkey and reached the island of Samos with 30 other people. Greek coastguards found them hiding in the woods and took them on their boat, where they had to give their phones and money. They were asked to undress and were subjected to a body cavity search; an experience accounted as a rape. They were then left drifting for several hours in an inflatable boat until Turkish coastguards found them. After Antoinette finally managed, after another attempt, to reach Samos and be registered in the camp, she tried to explain during the vulnerability assessment what she went through, but she said they did not want to hear about it. Far from being an exception, other interviewees related the difficulty to talk about push-backs and be heard. This example highlights not only the will to turn a blind eye to the violence happening at the borders, but also how vulnerability is conceived and assessed. The necessity to perform a vulnerability that happened 'there' in order to be able to leave 'here', the camp and the space where they suffered physical and sexual violence, is the embodiment of the intertwining of humanitarian policies and border control.

Therefore, the assessment of vulnerability implies new relations of power linked to the context of anti-migrant policies through the necessity to perform gendered vulnerability; the evaluation procedure replays the symbolic relations of power between the one in need and the one able to help. I would like to point out how helping vulnerable migrants, and especially families, women and children, reinforces the fiction of European goodness and empathy, while turning a blind eye to the effects of border policies on migrants' lives. To understand the long-term consequences of depolitisation of gender-based violence and vulnerability, I suggest to focus on the journey of women who have been deemed vulnerable, and who have been able to get social housing in Athens, through the ESTIA programme for vulnerable asylum seekers. Analysing the everyday experience of their social position, at the intersection of gender, race and class relations, will produce new insights to comprehend what is gendered vulnerability in migration flows, and whether the new paradigm of the humanitarian government has changed the power relations analysed in the Southern European Migration Model (Agier, 2013).

BEYOND A HUMANITARIAN CATEGORY: THE LONG-TERM PRECARITY OF VULNERABLE WOMEN

Reinforcing Dynamics of Power Analysed in the Southern European Migration Model

I have examined earlier how gender-based vulnerability was tackled, in the hotspots, as a pathology which could be identified, and which implied some special needs that could be taken care of by humanitarian aid. From this point forward, by focusing on migrant women's experiences during the programme and what happens at the end of it, I would like to repoliticise gendered vulnerability and point out how the lack of consideration for the social dimensions of vulnerability inevitably contributed to reinforce the dynamics of power analysed in the Southern European Migration Model.

To analyse the impact of the ESTIA programme on vulnerable women's lives, I suggest adopting the methodology developed by Dina Vaiou and Maria Stratigaki (2008). A distinction is made in the research between the concepts of integration and settlement: with 'integration' referring to the formal practices linked to state institutions, such as access to childcare and health services; while 'settlement' focuses on the informal practices involved in building a life in the host country such as finding a job, becoming familiarised with the neighbourhood, and creating a network. This distinction was devised as a way to analyse both the difficulty that migrant women experience in accessing social services (integration), and the power relations they encounter in their day-to-day life in Athens as a result of their gender and race. As mentioned in previous sections, vulnerable migrants are able to apply for accommodation and cash assistance through the ESTIA programme (renewed in June 2020 as ESTIA II), a programme financed by the Greek government and the EU Asylum, Migration and Integration Fund. ESTIA was previously managed by the Office of the United Nations High Commissioner for Refugees (UNHCR) and is now managed by the Greek government. Assistance from the ESTIA programme is reserved for asylum seekers who are deemed to be vulnerable. These programmes form the core of policies aimed to assist migrants in their phase of integration in Greece (Papatzani, 2020). Of the social housing provided by the organisation, 54 per cent is located in the capital, Athens (UNHCR, 2019), in the most economically deprived neighbourhoods deserted by the local population in the 1980s, and which became very attractive for migrants arriving in the 1990s. Nevertheless, far from producing a new kind of residential segregation, these neighbourhoods stimulated solidarity between migrants and Greeks (Papatzani, 2020).

In terms of integration, women deemed vulnerable are provided with social housing and cash assistance by the ESTIA programme. They are assigned professionals who will guide them through the administrative procedures necessary to access state services, such as getting a social security number (AMKA), which is a requirement for access to healthcare. These services were not available during the 1990s, and most of the Albanese women who arrived in this migration flow relied on their networks of friends or relatives to find a place to stay, and struggled to legalise their job in order to get access to the Greek National Insurance system (IKA). Whilst it is an improvement on this, the support given by the ESTIA programme is far from sufficient: a report by the NGO Mobile Info Team points out that most of the vulnerable migrants in the ESTIA programme do not get enough support to obtain the documents required for long-term integration and to be able to work legally in Greece. Only 6 per cent of asylum seekers in the ESTIA programme have a Greek bank account, 49 per cent have an AMKA, and 55 per cent have a tax number (AFM) (MIT, 2021). Moreover, migrant women encounter difficulties gaining access to cash assistance, as this is provided in the form of prepaid cards and often given to the man of the household. But most of all, its focus on the integration of migrant women conceals the very question at the centre of their settlement in Greece, turning a blind eye to the daily social exclusion that women face in their experience of the city, as both women and migrants.

Focusing instead on the informal practices that migrant women need to negotiate sheds light on the power relations that women face at the intersection between gender and race, and also questions the limits of understanding gendered 'vulnerability' as a humanitarian issue. Indeed, on the one hand, migrant women walking through the city streets are often associated with sexual availability, a stigma linked to the gender segregation of public spaces, the consequences of which are the perception that their bodies are 'out of place' (Tyner, 2011). In other words, the public space is often experienced by women as a place where they do not belong, because of the risk of harassment and gender-based violence. As the geographer Martina Low (2006) explains, the arrangement of bodies in space reproduces the structural principles of society, including those of gender. To avoid this feeling of vulnerability and of gender-related fear, women often rely on strategies that enable them to feel safer, such as taking public transport at night (Lieber, 2008). However, migrant women, often considered the embodiment of otherness, are additionally at risk of racist aggressions, which limit their ability to walk as freely in the city as local women (Miranda, 2020) or to use the same strategies to avoid violence. As an example of this, while I was walking with a young Afghan woman, down the streets she usually walked to get to work, she told me that she was used to being followed and that she often had to take refuge in open shops along the way. She managed to find a job on the night shift at an NGO working with isolated minors, and was afraid to walk through the city at night, but she was unable to take public transport as she had suffered in the past from several racist assaults on the buses. This example highlights the gendered and racialised experience of migrant women in Greek cities, and how the public gaze produces boundaries which determine who does and who does not have access to public spaces. The 'integration' of vulnerable women who suffer gender-based violence is therefore determined by the way 'vulnerability' is conceived in the first place: as a pathology, or a powerlessness linked to gender, and not a political issue linked to racism and sexism.

The difficulty migrant women experience settling in Greece is therefore not addressed in the programme, which merely offers temporary relief during the examination of asylum claims. As soon as the women leave the programme, the support provided by the state to promote integration also ends, and they have to rely on informal practices and networks to negotiate a place for themselves in the country. Not genuinely integrated, nor fully settled, they often find themselves in a state of limbo. Since the asylum law reform of March 2020 (4674/2020) refugees have up to 30 days following receipt of international protection, after which they will be forced to leave their accommodation as they are no longer eligible for the aid. Following this reform, thousands of refugees were evicted, and organised a sit-in in Victoria Square in protest (Rafenberg, 2020). There are no bridges between the ESTIA and HELIOS refugee programmes. HELIOS is designed to provide ongoing support, but places are scarce, and it is quite difficult for refugees to be accepted into the programme, as they must be living in accommodation managed by the ESTIA programme, or registered in a camp, or hosted in a centre run by an NGO. Thus, leaving the ESTIA programme often results in homelessness.

An in-depth examination of the consequences of the transience of this programme reveals the same gender dynamics identified in the Southern European Migration Model, specifically the gendered and racialised division of labour. Indeed, as women considered vulnerable often find themselves in extremely precarious situations, forced to live on the streets on leaving the programme, working is often the only way to survive. Leah, from Cameroon, is an example of this. Leah was living in a flat provided by the ESTIA programme, until she was afforded international protection, she was then forced to leave her flat after one month, during which time she stayed for several days at the apartment of a friend in Athens. While trying to join the HELIOS programme, she started to look for work as she did not have access to financial help. She worked for free in a hostel, a job which came with accommodation, before she found an opportunity, through an acquaintance, to work in a hotel on an island close to the Port of Piraeus. She then worked from 8 a.m. to 9 p.m., and on the weekends to midnight, without any days off. Her salary was to be €300 in the first month, and then €600 in the second, a little under the minimum wage of €758 a month. She was sleeping in a room shared with other refugees, above the boiler room.

This example resonates with the analysis of Gabriella Lazaridis and Iordanis Psimmenos (2000) in their research into the gender division of labour in the framework of the Southern European Migration Model. Indeed, they point out how gender and racial stereotypes played a huge role in the job opportunities afforded to migrant women. In the 1990s, migrant Albanese women in Greece were only able to find, through their networks, undeclared 'female jobs' in the domestic sector, or in the sex trade, in which the risk of exploitation and gender-based violence was high. Furthermore, racial stereotypes intervened in the process of recruitment, whether in enhancing the supposed submissive, nurturing nature of migrant women, in the case of Filipino women, or in the case of Arab women, 'othering' them by considering them to be completely at odds with the Western European model of womanhood (Anthias, 2000).

The stereotypes of the female gender (nurturing, gentle, compliant) underline the power relations between the employer and migrant employee, and how migrant women from the Middle East are perceived, more than others, as alien. These gender dynamics are still current more than 30 years after they were first examined. The new paradigm of humanitarian government and policies that require assessments of vulnerability indirectly lead to the reproduction of the dynamics of the Southern European Migration Model: the often undeclared gendered and racialised division of work, which puts women in a situation where they are dominated by others and where their ability to protest is minimal (Lazaridis and Psimmenos, 2000; Anthias, 2000). Moreover, women forced to live on the streets following their involvement in aid programmes experience a precarity that puts them at risk of gender-based violence and racist attacks; some of them no longer have any choice but to rely on their own networks, despite the patriarchal gender relations within their families and community (Vaiou and Stratigaki, 2008). However, in contrast to the female migrant flow of the 1990s, they are often forced to return to camps located on the outskirts of Athens, putting them once more at risk of gender-based violence, as intimate spaces (showers and toilets, and so on) are not locked, and tents are often shared with strangers (Amnesty International, 2018).

Repoliticising Vulnerability

Temporary and humanitarian programmes do not really address what vulnerability is, and what produces it. To understand the vulnerability of migrant women, it may be useful to rely on the analysis of Robert Castel (1994). For Castel, vulnerability must be considered to be a consequence of two phenomena: first, the increase in long-term unemployment and the promotion of temporary employment; second, the weakening of primary social connections and the growing feeling of isolation. From the vulnerability zone it is easy for migrants to fall into the disaffiliation zone. Being disaffiliated means no longer having any social relations that may offer support, and no employment. In this state of extreme marginality, in Castel's analysis, individuals are considered by society to be useless. Returning to the situation of migrant women in Greece, this theory perfectly illustrates their precarity, the difficulty in finding employment, the succession of temporary jobs, and the need to rely on networks of solidarity to find a place to sleep. Moreover, this theory implies that vulnerability and inequality do not come under the umbrella of humanitarian aid which only takes action in the case of an emergency or crisis, and they cannot be solved by temporary solutions. The vulnerability that migrant women experience in Greece, which is deeply linked to precarity, must also be analysed in terms of the distinct power relations related to class, gender and race (Kergoat, 1992).

Repoliticising vulnerability by taking into account the socio-spatial con-ditions of vulnerability paves the way for a political criticism of the impact of migration policies (border control, camps and temporary programmes for vulnerable people) on women's lives in Greece. Vulnerability does not equate to passivity, or a lack of agency: On the contrary, the strategies to bypass spaces where they may suffer sexist and racist violence (by not taking the bus, for example), and the will to denounce the violence they suffered during pushbacks (by talking about it during the vulnerability assessment), attest to the fact that vulnerability is not, in itself, a lack of agency. But the precarity of their situation, linked to the risk of exploitation, the perpetual insecurity, the lack of a long-term solution of accommodation, makes it especially difficult to project themselves in the future. Renewing the concept of vulnerability, linked to the perpetuation of the gendered power dynamics of the Southern European Migration Model, also puts the political discourse around the migration crisis into perspective. If we consider the new power dynamics created by human-itarian government and anti-migrant policies, we cannot help but notice that, in the long term, they actually reproduce and reinforce the same precarity and gendered division of labour that were observed in the 1990s. An analysis of policies that focus on vulnerability highlights the existence of the paradox that forces migrant women to perform vulnerability in order to be transferred to social housing in Athens, to escape the vulnerability they experience in the camps. Furthermore, the goal of integrating migrant women fails to truly address their everyday exclusion, which is reinforced following their involve-ment in the aid programme as they often have no choice but to move from one place to another, relying on their networks, to accept domestic work where the risk of exploitation is high, or to return to the unsafe environment of the camps.

CONCLUSION

The growth of anti-migration laws, the extension of camps as a means of controlling borders, and the political discourse surrounding the so-called migration crisis, have led to the emergence of a new paradigm of humanitarian government. The need to filter and select those considered to be vulnerable and therefore deserving was driven, in part, by the need to expel those felt to be undeserving economic migrants. In this new paradigm, vulnerability policies classify who are considered in need of humanitarian assistance, and consequently rely on gender stereotypes of victimhood. To leave the difficult living conditions of the camps, women must embody powerlessness and adopt 'strategical essentialisation', where they are forced keep the narratives of their agency at bay. In this context, vulnerability is considered to be a form of weakness that must be handled urgently. This is the reason why the accom-modation scheme for vulnerable migrants has never been thought about in the long term. Yet, migrant women find themselves in a paradoxical situation: the risk of suffering gender-based violence in the camp is never considered to be a vulnerability, or as something that should grant them the status of 'vulnerable migrant'. When they are provided with accommodation, it is only temporary and most of them are at risk of homelessness. Often the only solutions for survival involve finding a job and relying on solidarity networks. However, here they encounter the same difficulties as migrant women from the 1990s: a gendered and racialised division of work which is poorly paid, often undeclared, and which carries a risk of violence and exploitation. However, unlike migrant women of the 1990s, most of them have no other choice but to return to live in the camps. Thus, these elements provide a new perspective on gendered vulnerability: a long-term precariousness reinforced by contextual intersectionality. Far from the discourse on the 'migration crisis', analysing the experiences of migrant women nowadays and comparing them to experiences outlined in the Southern European Migration Model requires an understanding of vulnerability as something that falls not within the competency of humanitarian aid, but of social policy.

NOTES

1. Articles 39(5)(d) and 58(1) of the IPA Act establish as 'vulnerable groups': children, unaccompanied minors, persons who have lost a close member of their family following the sinking of a boat, people with disabilities, the elderly, pregnant women, single parents with minor children, victims of trafficking, people with serious illness, people with cognitive disabilities, and victims of torture, rape, or other forms of psychological, physical or sexual violence (such as people with genital mutilation).
2. On 7 June 2021, a ministerial decision of the Ministry of Foreign Affairs and the Ministry of Immigration and Asylum determined a list of countries whose nationals can be returned to Turkey: Syria, Afghanistan, Pakistan, Bangladesh and Somalia.

REFERENCES

AIDA (2019). *Country Report: Greece*. Available at: https://asylumineurope.org/wp -content/uploads/2020/07/report-download_aida_gr_2019update.pdf.

Agier, M. (2013) Espaces et temps du gouvernement humanitaire. *Pouvoirs*, vol. 144, no. 1, 113-123.

Akoka, K. and Clochard, O. (2015). Régime de confinement et gestion des migrations sur l'île de Chypre. *L'Espace Politique*, 1–28, doi: https://doi.org/10.4000/espacepolitique.3381.

Amnesty International (2018). Women face daily dangers in Greek refugee camps. Accessed 27 June 2021, https://www.amnesty.org/en/latest/campaigns/2018/10/women-daily-dangers-refugee-camps-greece/.

Anthias, F. (2000). Metaphors of home: gendering new migrations to Southern Europe. In Anthias, F. and Lazaridis, G. (eds), *Gender and Migration in Southern Europe: Women on the Move*. London: Routledge, pp. 15–47.

Butler, J., Gambetti, Z. and Sabsay, L. (2016). *Vulnerability in Resistance*. Durham, NC, USA and London, UK: Duke University Press.

Carpenter, C. (2005). Women, children and other vulnerable groups: gender, strategic frames and the protection of civilians as a transnational issue. *International Studies Quarterly*, 49 (2): 295–334.

Castel, R. (1994). La dynamique des processus de marginalisation: de la vulnérabilité à la désaffiliation. *Cahiers de la recherche sociologique*, 22: 11–27, doi: https://doi.org/10.7202/1002206ar.

Dorlin, E. (2008). *Sexe, genre et sexualités*. Paris: Puf.

Fineman, M. (2008). The vulnerable subject: anchoring equality in the human condition. *Yale Journal of Law and Feminism*, 20: 1–24.

Freedman, J. (2018). The uses and abuses of 'vulnerability' in EU asylum and refugee protection: protecting women or reducing autonomy? *Papeles del CEIC*, 1 (papel 204): 1–15, doi: http://dx.doi.org/10.1387/pceic.19525.

Garrau, M. (2021). Agentivité ou autonomie? Pour une théorie critique de la vulnérabilité. *Genre, sexualité & société*, 25: 1–19, doi: https://doi.org/10.4000/gss.6794.

HRW (2019). Greece: camp conditions endanger women, girls. Accessed 17 June 2021, https://www.hrw.org/news/2019/12/04/greece-camp-conditions-endanger -women-girls.

Kergoat, D. (1992). Des rapports sociaux de sexe et de la division sexuelle du travail. *Cahiers du GEDISST (Groupe d'étude sur la division sociale et sexuelle du travail)*, 3: 23–26.

Keygnaert, I. and Guieu, A. (2015). What the eye does not see: a critical interpretive synthesis of European Union policies addressing sexual violence in vulnerable migrants. *Reproductive Health Matters*, 23 (46): 45–55, doi: https://doi.org/10.1016/j.rhm.2015.11.002.

King, R. (2000). Southern Europe in the changing global map of migration. In King, R., Lazaridis, G. and Tsardanidis, C. (eds), *Eldorado or Fortress: Migration in Southern Europe*. London: Palgrave Macmillan, pp. 1–27.

Kourachanis, N. (2020). Forms of housing and social policies for asylum seekers in Greece. In Larocca, G., Di Maria, R. and Frezza, G. (eds), *Media, Migrants and Human Rights*. Berne: Peter Lang, pp. 167–187.

Lazaridis, G. and Psimmenos, I. (2000). Migrant flows from Albania to Greece: economic, social and spatial exclusion. In King, R., Lazaridis, G. and Tsardanidis, C. (eds), *Eldorado or Fortress? Migration in Southern Europe*. London: Palgrave Macmillan, pp. 170–186.

Lieber, M. (2008). *Genre, violences et espaces publics. La vulnérabilité des femmes en question*. Paris: Presses de Science Po.

Low, M. (2006). The social construction of space and gender. *European Journal of Women's Studies*, 13 (2): 119–133, doi: https://doi.org/10.1177%2F1350506806062751.

Miranda, A. (2010). Les multiples situations migratoires féminines dans la Méditerranée. *NAQD*, 28 (1): 21–34, doi: https://doi.org/10.3917/naqd.028.0019#xd_co_f=NTc2MGY0NTUtNWM0ZS00MGIyLThkNDktZDM5ZThjNTE1YTJi~.

Miranda, A. (2020). Hiérarchies spatialisées: jeux de miroirs entre migrant.e.s et non migrant.e.s à Terzigno (Naples). In Micha, Irène and Vaiou, Dina (eds), *La ville autrement: Questions théoriques et outils méthodologiques*. Londres: ISTE éditions, pp. 35–53.

MIT (2021). Input by civil society to the 2021 EASO Asylum Report, https://euaa .europa.eu/sites/default/files/Mobile-Info-Team_Combined.pdf.

Papada, E. (2021). Engaging the geopolitics of asylum seeking: the care/control function of vulnerability assessments in the context of the EU–Turkey agreement. *Geopolitics*: 1–25, doi: https://doi.org/10.1080/14650045.2021.1884548.

Papatzani, E. (2020). The geography of the 'ESTIA' accommodation program for asylum seekers in Athens. *Athens Social Atlas*, https://www.athenssocialatlas.gr/ fr/article/la-geographie-du-programme-estia/.

Rafenberg, M. (2020). À Athènes, la détresse des réfugiés en voie d'expulsion de leurs appartements. *Le Monde*. Accessed 25 June 2021, https://www .lemonde.fr/international/article/2020/06/10/a-athenes-la-detresse-des-refugies-en -voie-d-expulsion-de-leurs-appartements_6042412_3210.html#:~:text=Gr%C3 %A8ce-,A%20Ath%C3%A8nes%2C%20la%20d%C3%A9tresse%20des%20r %C3%A9fugi%C3%A9s%20en%20voie%20d'expulsion,apr%C3%A8s%20avoir %20obtenu%20l'asile.

Rodier, C. (2008). Externalisation du contrôle des flux migratoires: comment et avec qui l'Europe repousse ses frontières. *Migrations Société*, 116: 105–122, doi: https://doi.org/10.3917/migra.116.0105#xd_co_f=NTc2MGY0NTUtNWM0ZS S00MGIyLThkNDktZDM5ZThjNTE1YTJi~.

Sözer, H. (2019). Categories that blind us, categories that bind them: the deployment of vulnerability notion for syrian refugees in Turkey. *Journal of Refugee Studies*, 34 (3): 1–29.

Spathopoulou, A., Carastathis, A. and Tsilimpounidi, M. (2020). 'Vulnerable refugees' and 'voluntary deportations': performing the hotspot, embodying its violence. *Geopolitics*, 27 (4): 1–28, doi: https://doi.org/10.1080/14650045.2020 .1772237.

Spivak, G. (1988). Can the subaltern speak? In Nelson, C. and Grossberg L. (eds), *Marxism and the Interpretation of Culture*. Urbana, IL: University of Illinois Press, pp. 271–330.

Tassin, L. (2019). L'approche Hotspots, une solution en trompe-l'œil. Compte-rendu d'enquête à Lesbos et Lampedusa. In Lendaro, A., Rodier, C. and Vertongen, Y. (eds), *La crise de l'accueil. Frontières, droits, résistances*. Paris: La Découverte, pp. 165–185.

Ticktin, M. (2011). The gendered human of humanitarianism: medicalising and policising sexual violence. *Gender and History*, 23 (2): 250–265, doi: https://doi.org/ 10.1111/j.1468-0424.2011.01637.x.

Tyner, J. (2011). *Space, Place, and Violence: Violence and the Embodied Geographies of Race, Sex, and Gender*. New York and London: Routledge.

UNHCR (2018). Refugee women and children face heightened risk of sexual violence amid tensions and overcrowding at reception facilities on Greek islands. Accessed 10 September 2020, https://www.unhcr.org/news/briefing/2018/2/ 5a7d67c4b/refugee-women-children-face-heightened-risk-sexual-violence-amid -tensions.html.

UNHCR (2019). Accommodation update. Accessed 12 January 2020, http://estia .unhcr.gr/en/greece-accommodation-update-december-2019/.

Vaiou, D. and Stratigaki, M. (2008). From 'settlement' to 'integration': informal practices and social services for women migrants in Athens. *European*

Urban and Regional Studies, 15 (2): 119–131, doi: http://dx.doi.org/10.1177/0969776407087545.

Conclusion to *Migration Patterns Across the Mediterranean*

Adelina Miranda and Antía Pérez-Caramés

The contributions presented in this book confirm that the history of migration from Southern European countries is complex and varied. By examining the current visibility of migrants in the Mediterranean space, the chapters contribute to questioning the importance of mobility in this 'moving space', as Braudel (1977) defined it. Without ever assuming a position that would essentialise the Mediterranean as a cultural entity, this book details the diverse nature of the history of migration in the region. The research presents a plurality of migratory situations demonstrating, on the one hand, the challenge of studying continuities as well as ruptures, and on the other hand, the heuristic interest in multiplying images of Mediterranean migrations. Thus, the book invites us to revisit the interpretative categories used, to move beyond a state vision, and to consider the articulations between global, national, regional and local levels. This concluding chapter, in line with the research presented, is based on the observation that migratory events in the Mediterranean area do not follow evolutionary and linear logics, but that they are created through the 'principle of coexistence'. This involves considering the entanglements around and beyond the Mediterranean of different historical, spatial and political scales. It also allows us to consider the fact that, as Natalia Ribas-Mateos and Jorge Malheiros point out in the Foreword to this book, the Mediterranean is not only considered to be the *plaque tournant* of migrations, but also has long been conceived of as the heart of civilisation. Therefore, we believe that the principle of coexistence can become an interpretative tool to create dialogue around the different perspectives used to study migrations in the Mediterranean.

REVISITING THE SOUTHERN EUROPEAN MIGRATION MODEL

The Mediterranean Migration Model has highlighted the importance of recent changes in migration, in particular in Spain, Italy, Greece and Portugal. Proposed to explain the migratory phenomenon in these countries due to their sharing certain historical, economic, demographic, socio-cultural and political characteristics, the Southern European Migration Model (SEMM) has resulted in a discourse of coherent migratory unity that neglects the divergences that exist. As the model spread, it lost its heuristic potential. Criticised above all for its lack of empirical solidity (Boucher and Gest, 2014) and its Eurocentric vision, and despite attempts to revise it (Peixoto et al., 2012; Pugliese, 2012), this model has revealed shortcomings in its ability to explain migratory changes in the region. In line with this critical perspective, the contributions of this book, while confirming that migration is a consubstantial feature of the Mediterranean, question 'the topic of contemporary mobilities' (Natalia Ribas-Mateos and Jorge Malheiros, Foreword to this book), restoring the different facets of the phenomenon and their evolution. Based on four focal points, this book expands on the homogeneous vision of migrations in the Mediterranean, allowing a better understanding of the contributions of the SEMM.

This book, first, highlights the importance of moving beyond a linear and evolutionary representation of migration. In this respect, it should be recalled that the SEMM evokes a migration phenomenon with a self-sustaining capacity by means of the movement of populations from southern to northern Mediterranean countries. However, as the contributions by Fabio Amato (Chapter 4), Michel Peraldi (Chapter 5) and Belén Fernández-Suárez and Alberto Capote Lama (Chapter 6) show, it is necessary to take into account the multiplicity of migratory flows both within each country and between European countries. Mediterranean migratory configurations are increasingly multipolar; in Italy, immigration is sustained by flows from Eastern European and Asian countries, which intermingle and overlap with flows from African countries (Fabio Amato, Chapter 4). Young, qualified Spanish women going to France and Germany are an example of the current reconfiguration of intra-European migration (Belén Fernández-Suárez and Alberto Capote Lama, Chapter 6). For countries of the Maghreb, as Michel Peraldi (Chapter 5) points out, while Europe remains the centre of migratory aspirations and the principal destination, new routes are opening up, at the same time as the Maghreb itself is becoming a migratory space. Moreover, if we look at the migratory phenomenon over the long term, we are faced with a constant reconfiguration of migratory flows which allows us to observe that mobility is not a condition that is added to or parallel to the sedentary world: in fact, the mobility/sedentarity tension runs through the Mediterranean space (Wolfgang Kaiser and Claudia Moatti, Chapter 1).

Second, in order to achieve an understanding of the issue of migration, this book invites us to consider the disposition of relations of domination in this geopolitical area. Wolfgang Kaiser and Claudia Moatti (Chapter 1) recall that the Mediterranean is a space of negotiation of 'relations between political communities', because these relations are 'not only of predation or domination, but also of reciprocity'. The historical perspective shows the Mediterranean as a reticular space that connects the three intra-continental migratory spaces (Maghreb/European group, Balkan group, and Near East group) through variable forms of control and management. Therefore, as Natalia Ribas-Mateos and Jorge Malheiros point out in the Foreword, in order to understand current migrations, it is necessary to take into account the system of domination that was set up in the 19th century. It appears, then, that colonisation and decolonisation have influenced and continue to influence migration on the shores of the Mediterranean, and that economic migration and postcolonial migration, in all their variations and combinations, have been superimposed, creating specific migratory hierarchies. Indeed, as Liauzu (2009, 233) recalls for France, migratory flows from the colonies were managed by the administration through a colonial logic: 'Separated, registered, and monitored by specialised services, this population is subject to close surveillance, which is much tighter and more powerful than that of foreigners coming from Europe during the same period'. Colonisation and migration continue to be treated as 'dissociated histories', whereas Mediterranean migration can be considered 'postcolonial' since it refers to the political, economic and cultural continuities and ruptures that still shape the relationship between colonising and colonised countries today. The arrival of migrants, particularly Africans, but also Latin Americans in the case of Spain and Portugal, has awakened Western consciousness to its colonial past and has conferred a different value on migration compared to that from Southern to Northern European countries, thus questioning its 'obliteration' from the historiography of migration. Today, it seems urgent to question the ways in which colonisation and decolonisation have a different impact on the history of countries belonging to the southern and eastern shores of the Mediterranean. As María-Jesús Cabezón-Fernández (Chapter 2) points out, migration in Spain expresses a process of otherness regarding the articulation of the cultural identity of the 'Other Moor'. This involves adopting a postcolonial perspective that considers continuities based on the prevalence of the cultural view and stereotypes of the Maghrebi population in Spain. Furthermore, as Mustapha El Miri (Chapter 3) points out, migratory mobility itself becomes a test for the forms of domination inherited from colonialism, and contributes to deconstructing them from the base. From the author's perspective it is not simply a matter of considering the continuities between migration, racism, discrimination and postcolonial categorisation of immigrants, but of returning to the basis of the construction of interpretative categories. We add that it is also a question of interrogating the renewed attention paid to the issue of migration in the political debate (McMahon, 2017), the reduced acceptance of migrants (Cea d'Ancona, 2016), and the rise of extreme right-wing parties and of a xenophobic discourse (Barberà, 2021; Fernández-Suárez, 2021).

Third, it should be emphasised that the SEMM was drawn up on the assumption that the countries of emigration in the northern Mediterranean would be transformed into countries of immigration. However, the contributions in this book confirm that the simultaneous presence of immigration and emigration in these countries represents a further increase in the complexity of migratory events, which calls for a rethinking of the place of representations of migratory events. Migration is interpreted and categorised from the perspective of a hierarchical evolutionary vision that conceals a certain notion of progress (Ribas-Mateos, 2017). As Natalia Ribas-Mateos and Jorge Malheiros point out in the Foreword, migrations are:

> structured by a hierarchy that still influences both commonsense and geoeconomic approaches. The division still prevails between the enhanced stereotypical images of the developed and disciplined countries of Northern Europe, and the undisciplined, unindustrious people of the less developed Southern European nation-states. These stereotypes have their roots in the transfer of the geopolitical and economic centre of the world to Northwest Europe after the 16th century, and were strengthened by the disciplinary culture of the industrial capitalism of the 19th century.

This foundation has a dual implication. On the one hand, the bipolar representation of the migratory phenomenon around the Mediterranean has an important function: it constitutes the basis of a vision of the hierarchy, referring to the values associated with the countries of immigration and emigration (Sayad, 1999). The figure of the immigrant is not a mirror image of that of the emigrant. The values, representations and judgements that accompany the two categories do not coincide, because the two figures embody the processes of subalternity and domination differently. On the other hand, the fact that Italy, Greece, Portugal and Spain have also become countries of immigration should not conceal (as we have already pointed out) the resumption of emigratory flows and the fact that their diasporas produce their own system of relations with their places of origin. Studies into 'old migration processes' demonstrate the creation of new social dynamics (putting into action processes of distancing from the figure of the migrant of the past) and political dynamics (with the implementation of policies of valorisation of diasporas on the part of countries of departure). The complexification of population movements is demonstrated by a map of migration around the Mediterranean, where the boundaries between migrant categories appear increasingly blurred and reversible, and the distinctions between 'new' and 'old' migration, irregular and political migration, pendular migration, stabilisation migration, return migration, and between internal, intra-regional and transnational migration, are constantly being questioned (Castles and Wihtol de Wenden, 2006).

Fourth, the variation of spatio-temporal scales should be considered to be an essential principle in the understanding of migration phenomena around and beyond the Mediterranean (Baby-Collin et al., 2021). The contributions in this book question the geographical and historical scales that act in/on migration events. The adoption of such a principle of analysis provides the theoretical and methodological basis for studying the variability and heterogeneity of migratory patterns in the Mediterranean. The contribution of Wolfgang Kaiser and Claudia Moatti (Chapter 1) shows that the historical scale allows us to understand how the importance of mobility in pre-contemporary societies is no longer in question. This scale is therefore necessary for a revision and broadening of what we mean by 'mobility', 'migration' and 'diaspora', and to grasp the articulation between three spatial scales: the Mediterranean, the urban, and the political scale, that of the states. Fabio Amato (Chapter 4) underlines how, by varying the geographical gaze between and within the countries included in the SEMM, a variety of localised situations emerge that question its heuristic capacity. Although this is a useful interpretative model, it must be acknowledged that if we are to go beyond in the interpretation of the migratory process by means of a macro vision that gives space to a more complex reading that takes into account race, gender, temporality, individual choice and above all interaction with place, then the Mediterranean Migration Model is a less useful common denominator.

These four focal points allow us to better understand how the evolution of the political and economic context in the Mediterranean area has influenced the SEMM. The new geopolitical delimitation put in place by the European Union, rather than highlighting the polymorphous character and valence of the borders of the Mediterranean, has produced a reconfiguration of the relationship between the countries of the South and those of the rest of Europe. The implementation of European migration policies has played a fundamental role in this process. They have transformed the Southern European countries into guardians of the European Union's borders, reinforcing the process highlighted by King (1998). In the 1990s, Southern European countries had virtually no migration legislation and applied 'soft' migration controls. Now, the migration policies of each state converge towards the same objective: to control, filter and select immigrants. The European Union's strong preoccupation with controlling its external borders has ended up producing criminalisation, exploitation, repression, and blockages of migrants in circulation (Schmoll et al., 2015). Moreover, since the Barcelona Conference in 1995, the European Union has been trying to become the privileged interlocutor in the Euro-Mediterranean region; the consequence of this being that we are now witnessing a convergence towards the same migration management in all the countries of the northern and southern Mediterranean, the Middle East and the Balkans. The discursive connection between migration and security that creates categories of migrants and of migration, is also produced and reproduced through border humanitarianism (Casaglia, 2021). The processes of securing borders, which have become stronger since the 2011 Arab Spring, produce a hardening of migration policies that increasingly extends beyond the countries of the Mediterranean basin so that, as Alice Latouche (Chapter 10) points out for Greece, and Kamel Doraï and Imad Amer (Chapter 9) for Lebanon, the humanitarian challenge posed by the 2015 refugee crisis has made it more difficult to exercise the right to asylum.

The global economic recession that began in 2008 has further complicated the economic context analysed by the SEMM, which had highlighted the importance of matching migration to a post-Fordist economic structure. The austerity response has determined greater control over policies regulating the arrival and settlement of immigrants, and at the same time has determined a resumption of emigration flows from Southern European countries. As Fernández-Suárez and Capote Lama point out in Chapter 6, the reactivation of Spanish emigration to other European countries is also due to the deterioration of the economic conditions of the population in the countries of Southern Europe (Finotelli and Ponzo, 2018).[1] However, as the SEMM has demonstrated, the social model of the welfare state on the one hand, and the demands for a flexible and cheap labour force on the other, continue to structure immigration. The combination of these two elements is at the origin of the demand in the two most important labour niches occupying the migrant population: agricultural work, and domestic and care work. Without denying the growing importance of migration linked to family reunification and asylum applications, migratory movements to countries such as Italy, Spain, Portugal and Greece are primarily driven by economic logic. As Francisco Checa y Olmos, Francesco Saverio Caruso and Alessandra Corrado (Chapter 7) point out, the industrialisation of the primary sector in recent years is dependent on migrant labour. This research confirms that informalisation, criminalisation and exploitation have become constitutive of agricultural capitalism. At the same time, in these places, we are witnessing the development of political struggles and resistance whose scope goes beyond the agricultural sector (Perrotta, 2017; Arab, 2018). The demands made by migrants exceed their specific situation because they invite changes in the components and limits of citizenship.

For his part, Maurizio Ambrosini (Chapter 8) considers how the demand of Italian families for *badanti* (carers) is a response to the inability of the Italian state to respond to social and demographic changes in the population. More generally, however, research into women's migration in the Mediterranean has made it possible to understand the place that the sphere of reproduction occupies in society (Anthias and Lazaridis, 2000; Pérez-Caramés, 2010). As a result, the study of migration challenges an essentialist vision of the family in the Mediterranean (Albera et al., 2001), which was built on the representation of the assignment of women to sedentary life.

COEXISTENCE OF MIGRATORY FORMS

As we have just pointed out, studying migration from Southern Europe requires a return to former categories, theories and scales.[2] The recomposition of discourse around the SEMM that we have outlined confirms that the use of the Mediterranean as a category continues to be controversial, and that it is difficult to identify a framework capable of reconfiguring the various scientific positions of the researchers who have studied and continue to study migrations in this region. Without seeking a common thread capable of bringing together the different positions, it seems important to recall the multiplicity of views that are brought to the articulation of migration and the Mediterranean. We believe that discussing the contributions of the SEMM together with other migration paradigms allows us to experiment with new approaches, tracks and research methodologies, and to better understand migration dynamics in the Mediterranean. Indeed, following the crisis of the 1970s and the imposition of a post-Fordist management of migration, we are witnessing the development of different interpretative perspectives that attempt to explain the dynamics of migration which no longer appear to be 'ordered' in the sense described by Sayad (1999): that is, they do not respond to the requirements of the large-scale Fordist industry. These explanatory levels can be considered to be articulated around three poles.

The first pole restores the depth of the migratory phenomenon between settlement and movement here and there (de Villanova et al., 1994; Charbit et al., 1997), pendularism (Miranda, 1996), and double presence (de Gourcy and Chachoua, 2018). The authors who value this articulation look at conti-nuities across generations and, even when they do not come from a historical perspective, note the importance of the migratory phenomenon over the long term, particularly in the study of family dynamics. The second pole highlights the importance of circulation. This perspective looks at connections and exchanges across migratory scales and stresses the need to analyse the articu-lation between sedentariness, immobility and mobility (Péraldi, 2002; Tarrius, 2002; Cortes and Faret, 2009; Mata-Codesal, 2015, 2017; Cortés Maisonave and Oso, 2017; Schewel, 2019; Antunes and Blažytė, 2021; Gruber, 2021). Research referring to this paradigm is articulated with field studies on the migratory journey, the migratory project and the migratory experience (Scioldo-Zurcher et al., 2019). The third pole situates the migratory dynamics of the Mediterranean in a broader context of globalisation, transnationalism and neoliberalism. This perspective raises fundamental issues and highlights the impact of the power of control and borderisation (Rigo, 2007; Mezzadra and Brett, 2014; Agier, 2018). Attention to border dynamics emphasises that borders concern not only identity, but also a time and place in which subjects enter into relationships in an interplay of conflicts, exclusions and the loss of rights.

Putting the studies presented in this book into perspective allows us to highlight the dialogue between these three interpretative poles and the research conducted under the umbrella of the SEMM. It is important to point out that most researchers working on migration in the Mediterranean do not question the relevance of this specific scale of investigation. Indeed, while the Mediterranean has become a category increasingly associated with migration, little critical reflection regarding this has occurred, and the contributions in this book underline the importance of grasping the complexity of migration around the Mediterranean. The contributions confirm an arrangement of migrations in a migratory space where the Mediterranean retains its specificity. Doraï and Amer's Chapter 9 emphasises the importance of not losing sight of this scale of analysis because, as they point out, 'The question of the migration policies of the host countries must therefore be analysed over time and placed in their regional and Euro-Mediterranean context'. These authors recall the existing links between a certain geopolitical (dis)order of the Mediterranean, and the implementation of European and state migration policies.

However, retaining the relevance of the Mediterranean scale leads to a significant question: how to approach the overlapping of various migratory configurations in time and space?

The plurality of migratory situations analysed by the contributors to this book opens three avenues of investigation. The first is that it is necessary to move beyond denial of the co-temporality of the different migratory flows. This proposal, inspired by the anthropologist Fabian (1991), considers that migrants and non-migrants are caught up in the same 'communicative inter-actions' and invites us to look at migration in the Mediterranean through the concept of coexistence. This allows, on the one hand, a move beyond the 'tax-onomic methods' associated with migrations and offers the basis for studying mobilities and sedentarities as stratified in time and space. On the other hand, the synchronic consideration of the different migratory phenomena questions the coherent and linear explanatory models. The simultaneity of migratory phenomena, which may appear to the researcher to be incompatible (as in the case of the coexistence of emigration and immigration), invites an account of how migration is integrated into sedentary life (Miranda, 2018). Natalia Ribas-Mateos and Jorge Malheiros recall in the Foreword that migratory flows give rise to chains, flows, interactions, negotiations, crossings and meetings, producing a social situation that differs from sedentary societies with their own specific rules and norms. Wolfgang Kaiser and Claudia Moatti (Chapter 1) demonstrate how mobility structures social life, of regional micro-mobilities and seasonal mobilities, of the phases of mobility in individual lives, of the sharing of roles within families, over several generations, in chains of migrations, or of the close links between geographical and social mobility. They also add that we are witnessing the creation of mixed identities but also in-between identities. Peraldi (Chapter 5) demonstrates how subjects have circulated in the past and continue to circulate in the present within networks, appropriating local spaces, especially urban ones, according to the opportunities offered by the formal and informal economy, using the information of those who have settled down, traversing different legal contexts. Finally, María-Jesús Cabezón-Fernández (Chapter 2) reminds us that the Mediterranean region is a web of cultures in contact, conflict and dialogue, and she finds in the caravanserai analysed by Ribas-Mateos the exemplary image of this situation.

The second line of investigation considers the importance of the sedimentation of different migratory configurations. In the Mediterranean, migrations are articulated by means of a stratification of forms of identification and alteration that interact with each other. This perspective requires moving beyond a substitutive vision according to which the 'new' migrants take the place of the 'old' ones who, in the meantime, have become integrated in the places of settlement. The chapters presented in this book show that the arrival of 'new' migratory flows does not automatically replace 'old' migratory flows, rather creating new mixes and differentiations. In countries with 'old' immigration, recent national and ethnic concentrations coexist with those that have been built up over time; where they meet is the origin of comparisons and evaluations between different migratory fields (Corti and Miranda, 2018). Kamel Doraï and Imad Amer (Chapter 9) highlight the fact that coexistence within the same population of migrants of different legal status is one of the features marking migration in the region studied. Hierarchical intersections arise from the superimposition and intermingling of emigration/immigration, internal/international migration, economic/political migration, transit migration and settled migration. Michel Peraldi (Chapter 5) demonstrates the differentiated treatment of migrants in the Maghreb and how their status plays a fundamental role in the structuring of their pathways, experiences and (non-)insertion. Chapter 6 by Belén Fernández-Suárez and Alberto Capote Lama, regarding Spanish women who emigrate, demonstrates the context of this more recent phenomenon of emigration to be very different from that of past waves of intra-European migration flows, both before and after the introduction of free movement. This is a reflection of the inequalities inherent within the European Union, with some countries performing the role of sending countries and others that of receiving.

The third line of investigation considers the links created between race and gender relations, colonialism, and migration policies. The colonial imaginary has accompanied and continues to accompany the political construction of migration and is at the basis of the symbolic as well as the economic elaboration of current mobilities. For Mustapha El Miri (Chapter 3), the study of the

links between colonial memory and migratory issues demonstrates the existence on the 'front line' of the historical processes of colonisation and decolonisation that participated significantly in the socio-political construction of
this racial and cultural classification/segmentation applied to colonised people.
The construction of racism can therefore be seen as a process of internalisation
of migratory hierarchical logic useful in the structuring of certain sectors
of activity. The comparison between migration regularisation campaigns in
Andalusia and Calabria (Francisco Checa y Olmos, Francesco Saverio Caruso
and Alessandra Corrado, Chapter 7) demonstrates the technological and organisational innovation, modernisation, and the crisis resulting from the neoliberal
restructuring of agri-food and the role played by migrations. The cumbersome
nature of progressively restrictive migration policies has inevitably led, in both
Spain and Italy, to systematic measures of mass regularisation to address the
hundreds of thousands of undocumented migrants produced. Alice Latouche
(Chapter 10) recalls the role played by gender relations in the implementation of migration policies that create hierarchies between national groups of
female migrants. An analysis of the experience of migrant women with regard
to gender-based violence has begun to be taken into account in European
migration policies as a specific source of vulnerability, thus acknowledging
the specific needs of gender-based and sexual violence survivors in terms of
protection and healthcare (Schmoll, 2020). Maurizio Ambrosini (Chapter 8)
points out that, in contrast to discourse about immigration in other aspects of
Italian society, migrant women working in the service of Italian families, and
while taking care of their frail seniors, are generally tolerated. Due to the irregular status of many of these migrants when they arrive, Italian families have
played a crucial role in campaigns aimed at the regularisation of unauthorised
migrants. Anti-immigration policies and internal demands for care services are
not easy to conciliate.

FOR FURTHER REFLECTION

By demonstrating the heterogeneity of population movements in the countries
of Southern Europe, the chapters presented in this book confirm the need to
reflect on migration in the Mediterranean. The Mediterranean scale is indeed
used at different levels as a device operating for political and economic
purposes in the redefinition of geopolitical balances at the global level. At
the same time, the contributions show that both the SEMM countries and the
Mediterranean are merely useful scales in grasping the evolution of migration
phenomena. Thus, the book invites us not only to move beyond a Eurocentric
and nationalist perspective of migration studies, but also to place the analysis
of migration phenomena at the heart of a critical analysis of social sciences,
in order to examine the historical, economic and cultural conditions that orient

thought and contribute to the construction of a geopolitics of knowledge within a globalised epistemic space. From this perspective, we believe that fostering dialogue between the different perspectives in the study of migration in the Mediterranean is an avenue to pursue. We propose three objects of study that might serve to feed this exchange. First, recalling that the Mediterranean is made up of connections in movement which link sedentarities (by considering the fact that sedentariness is not immobility) and migrations (by taking into account the fact that migration does not only imply movement), questions the propensity of geopolitical borders being increasingly associated with this geopolitical area, and broadens the debate to include relations which are established between internal borders in the continuity of external borders and vice versa. Second, a recognition that economic and postcolonial migrations, in all their variations and combinations, have been superimposed, creating specific migratory hierarchies that still operate today, suggests an analytical framework based on the different political, social, economic and legal scales to investigate accommodations and conflicts that occur between the different political, social, legal spheres and cultural representations. The third proposes to study migration by observing the way in which the processes of alteration are elaborated in a wider imaginary than the Mediterranean. We have noted that the representation of migratory phenomena in this area participates in the construction of a supranational European identity through a supposed opposition between a 'Christian West' and an 'Islamic East', which is now fixed around the figure of the 'Islamic' migrant, but it would also be necessary to revisit the postcolonial relations maintained by countries such as Spain and Portugal with Latin America.

NOTES

1. Furthermore, accessing the European Union does not prevent Italy and Spain from continuing to use extraordinary regularisation processes (Spencer and Triandafyllidou, 2020), even in times of pandemic.
2. Our position is inspired by the epistemological tradition of De Martino's (1977) 'critical ethnocentrism'. For this Italian anthropologist, the exercise of 'critical ethnocentrism' constitutes an awareness of the limits of the categories and intellectual tools used by the Western world to apprehend the historical possibilities of the human being.

REFERENCES

Agier, M. (2018). *L'étranger qui vient: repenser l'hospitalité*. Paris: Seuil.
Albera, D., Blok, A. and Bromberger, C. (eds) (2001). *L'anthropologie de la Méditerranée/ Anthropology of Mediterranean*. Aix-en-Provence: Maisonneuve & Larouse.

Anthias, F. and Lazaridis, G. (2000). *Gender and Migration in Southern Europe: Women on the Move*. New York: Routledge.

Antunes, C. and Blažytė, G. (2021). Mobility and displacement in and around the Mediterranean: an introduction. *Ler História*, 78: 9–15, doi: https://doi.org/10.4000/lerhistoria.7983.

Arab, C. (2018). *Dames de fraises, doigts de fée. Les invisibles de la migration saisonnière marocaine en Espagne*. Casablanca: Edition En toutes Lettres.

Baby-Collin, V., Mourlane, S. and Bouffier, S. (eds) (2021). *Atlas des migrations en Méditerranée*. Paris: Actes Sud.

Barberà, O. (ed.) (2021). *Facing the New Far Right in Southern Europe*. Bruselas: Coppieters Foundation, https://ideasforeurope.eu/activity/publication/facing-the-new-far-right-in-southern-europe/.

Boucher, A. and Gest, J. (2014). Migration studies at a crossroads: a critique of immigration regime typologies. *Migration Studies*, 3 (2): 182–198, doi: https://doi.org/10.1093/migration/mnu035.

Braudel, F. (ed.) (1977). *La Mediterranée. Les hommes et l'héritage*. Paris: Flammarion.

Casaglia, A. (2021). The regime of the Euro-African frontier between humanitarian reason and security imperative. In Laine Jussi, P., Moyo, I. and Changwe Nshimbi, C. (eds), *Expanding Boundaries, Borders, Mobilities and the Future of Europe–Africa Relations*. London: Routledge, pp. 85–99.

Castles, S. and Wihtol de Wenden, C. (2006). Framing international migration: from national models to transnational critique. In Vasta, E. and Vuddamalay, V. (eds), *International Migration and the Social Sciences*. London: Palgrave Macmillan, pp. 222–251.

Cea d'Ancona, M.A. (2016). Immigration as a threat: explaining the changing pattern of xenophobia in Spain. *Journal of International Migration and Integration*, 17: 569–591, doi: https://doi.org/10.1007/s12134-015-0415-3.

Charbit, Y., Hily, M.A. and Poinard, M. (1997). *Le va-et-vient identitaire: migrants portugais et villages d'origine*. Paris:Puf.

Cortes, G. and Faret, L. (eds) (2009). *Les circulations transnationales. Lire les turbulences migratoires contemporaines*. Paris: Armand Colin.

Cortés Maisonave, A. and Oso, L. (2017). Birds of a feather in a transnational flight: return, gender and mobility/immobility strategies between Ecuador and Spain. *Revista Española de Sociología*, 26 (3): 359–372, doi: https://doi.org/10.22325/fes/res.2017.28.

Corti, P. and Miranda, A. (2018). Éditorial: coexistence, imbrication et superposition des flux migratoires italiens. *Revue européenne des migrations internationales*, 34 (1): 21–28, doi: https://doi.org/10.4000/remi.9903#xd_co_f=NTc2MGY0NTUtNWM0ZS00MGIyLThkNDktZDM5ZThjNTE1YTJi~.

de Gourcy, C. and Chachoua, K. (eds) (2018). Mobilités et migrations en Méditerranée. Vers une anthropologie de l'absence? *Revue des mondes musulmans de la Méditerranée*, 144, doi: https://doi.org/10.4000/remmm.11538.

De Martino, E. (1977). *La fine del mondo. Contributo all'analisi delle apocalissi culturali*. Torino: Einaudi.

de Villanova, R., Leité, C. and Raposo, I. (1994). *Maisons de rêve au Portugal*. Paris: Editions Créaphis.

Fabian, J. (1991). *Time and the Work of Anthropology*. Chur: Harwood Academic Publishers.

Fernández-Suárez, B. (2021). Gender and immigration in VOX: the discourse of the radical right in Spain. *Migraciones*, 51: 241–268, doi: http://dx.doi.org/10.14422/mig.i51y2021.009.

Finotelli, C. and Ponzo, I. (2018). Integration in times of economic decline. Migrant inclusion in Southern European societies: trends and theoretical implications. *Journal of Ethnic and Migration Studies*, 44 (14): 2303–2319, doi: https://doi.org/10.1080/1369183X.2017.1345830.

Gruber, E. (2021). Staying and immobility: new concepts in population geography? A literature review. *Geographica Helvetica*, 76: 275–284.

King, R. (1998). The Mediterranean Europe's Rio Grande. In Anderson, M. and Bort, E. (eds), *The Frontiers of Europe*. London: Pinter, pp. 109–134.

Liauzu, C. (2009). *Colonisations, migrations, racismes. Histoires d'un passeur de civilisation*. Paris: Syllepse.

Mata-Codesal, D. (2015). Ways of staying put in Ecuador: social and embodied experiences of mobility–immobility interactions. *Journal of Ethnic and Migration Studies*, 41 (14): 2274–2290, doi: https://doi.org/10.1080/1369183X.2015.1053850.

Mata-Codesal, D. (2017). Gendered (im)mobility: rooted women and waiting Penelopes. *Crossings: Journal of Migration and Culture*, 8 (2): 151–162, doi: https://doi.org/10.1386/cjmc.8.2.151_1.

McMahon, S. (2017). The politics of immigration during an economic crisis: analysing political debate on immigration in Southern Europe. *Journal of Ethnic and Migration Studies*, 44 (14): 2415–2434, doi: https://doi.org/10.1080/1369183X.2017.1346042.

Mezzadra, S. and Brett, V. (2014). *Confini e frontiere. La moltiplicazione del lavoro nel mondo globale*. Bologna: Il Mulino.

Miranda, A. (1996). *Migrants et non-migrants d'une communauté italienne*. Paris: L'Harmattan.

Miranda, A. (2018). Déconstruire les paradigmes migratoires à travers les études sur les émigrations et les immigrations des femmes en Italie. *Revue européenne des migrations internationals*, 34(1): 173–194.

Peixoto, J., Arango, J., Bonifaci, C., Finotelli, C., Sabino, C., Strozza, S. and Triandafyllidou, A. (2012). Immigrants, markets and policies in Southern Europe. In Okólski, M. (ed.), *European Immigrations: Trends, Structures and Policy Implications*. Amsterdam: Amsterdam University Press, pp. 107–148.

Péraldi, M. (ed.) (2002). *La fin des Norias? Réseaux migrants dans les économies marchandes de la Méditerranée*. Aix-en-Provence: Maisonneuve & Larose, Maison méditerranéenne des sciences de l'homme.

Pérez-Caramés, A. (2010). Configuraciones del trabajo de cuidados en el entorno familiar: de la toma de decisión a la gestión del cuidado. *Alternativas*, 17: 121–140, doi: https://doi.org/10.14198/ALTERN2010.17.7.

Perrotta, M. (2017). Nuovi contadini e nuovi braccianti: i movimenti dei lavoratori della terra in Italia tra mutualismo e resistenza. *Parolechiave*, 2: 125–140, doi: https://www.rivisteweb.it/doi/10.7377/89832.

Pugliese, E. (2012). Il modello mediterraneo dell'immigrazione: il contesto, lo spazio, il modello e i tempi, le caratteristiche, la stabilità. In Miranda, A. and Signorelli, A. (eds), *Pensare e ripensare le migrazioni*. Palermo: Sellerio, pp. 35–44.

Ribas-Mateos, N. (2017). *The Mediterranean in the Age of Globalization*. London: Routledge.

Rigo, E. (2007). *Europa di confine. Trasformazioni della cittadinanza nell'Unione allargata*. Roma: Meltemi.

Sayad, A. (1999). *La double absence. Des illusions de l'émigré aux souffrances de l'immigré*. Paris: Seuil.

Schewel, K. (2019). Understanding immobility: moving beyond the mobility bias in migration studies. *International Migration Review*, 54 (2): 328–355, doi: https://doi .org/10.1177%2F0197918319831952.

Schmoll, C. (2020). *Les damnées de la* mer*: Femmes et frontières en Méditerranée*. Paris: La Découverte.

Schmoll, C., Thiollet, H. and Wihtol de Wenden, C. (2015). *Migrations en Méditerranée. Permanences et mutations à l'heure des révolutions et des crises*. Paris: CNRS.

Scioldo-Zurcher, Y., Hily, M.-A. and Ma Mung, E. (eds) (2019), *Étudier les migrations internationals*. Tours: PUFR.

Spencer, S. and Triandafyllidou, A. (2020). *Migrants with Irregular Status in Europe*. London and New York: Springer.

Tarrius, A. (2002). *La mondialisation par le bas. Les nouveaux nomades de l'économie souterraine*. Paris: Balland.

Index